Jerusalem

Wiley Blackwell Brief Histories of Religion Series

This series offers brief, accessible, and lively accounts of key topics within theology and religion. Each volume presents both academic and general readers with a selected history of topics which have had a profound effect on religious and cultural life. The word "history" is, therefore, understood in its broadest cultural and social sense. The volumes are based on serious scholarship but they are written engagingly and in terms readily understood by general readers.

Other topics in the series:

Published

Jerusalem

A Brief History

Michael Zank

WILEY Blackwell

This edition first published 2018
© 2018 Michael Zank

The right of Michael Zank to be identified as the author of this work has been asserted in accordance with law.

Registered Office(s)
John Wiley & Sons, Inc., 111 River Street, Hoboken, NJ 07030, USA
John Wiley & Sons Ltd, The Atrium, Southern Gate, Chichester, West Sussex, PO19 8SQ, UK

Editorial Office
The Atrium, Southern Gate, Chichester, West Sussex, PO19 8SQ, UK

For details of our global editorial offices, customer services, and more information about Wiley products visit us at www.wiley.com.

Wiley also publishes its books in a variety of electronic formats and by print-on-demand. Some content that appears in standard print versions of this book may not be available in other formats.

Library of Congress Cataloging-in-Publication Data

Names: Zank, Michael, author.
Title: Jerusalem : a brief history / by Michael Zank.
Description: Hoboken, New Jersey : Wiley, [2018] | Series: Wiley Blackwell brief histories
   of religion | Includes bibliographical references and index. |
Identifiers: LCCN 2018014790 (print) | LCCN 2018021809 (ebook) |
   ISBN 9781118533291 (pdf) | ISBN 9781118533321 (epub) |
   ISBN 9781405179713 (cloth) | ISBN 9781405179720 (pbk.)
Subjects: LCSH: Jerusalem–History.
Classification: LCC DS109.9 (ebook) | LCC DS109.9 .W55 2018 (print) | DDC 956.94/42–dc23
LC record available at https://lccn.loc.gov/2018014790

Cover Image: © Norman B. Leventhal Map Center at the Boston Public Library
Cover Design: Wiley

Set in 10.5/13pt Minion by SPi Global, Pondicherry, India
Printed in Singapore by C.O.S. Printers Pte Ltd

10 9 8 7 6 5 4 3 2 1

Contents

About this Book

Cities fascinate us. They move us to travel and make pilgrimage. They give us the terms for citizenship, civilization, politics, and civic-mindedness. Cities combine the utterly unique and particular with the ideal of the city as such. Each city is a draft of the City of God.

Jerusalem is a remarkable city. It is very ancient (about 4,000 years) and, unlike many other ancient Near Eastern cities, it has been continuously inhabited for virtually this entire duration. Most ancient cities were either abandoned or new, more convenient and greater ones, were established nearby. Cities rebuilt in this fashion were usually strategically located. They served as border fortifications, port cities, or administrative capitals in places begging for settlement and favorable to social, economic, or political aggregation.

The first Jerusalem, nestled on the watershed in the central highlands of the southern Levant between the Jordan Valley and the Mediterranean, was neither conveniently located nor served as border or port city. Commerce, trade, and industry passed it by and its population was sparse, especially as compared to the urban centers of Egypt and Mesopotamia. What made the city stand out over time was the extraordinary reputation it acquired as a sacred place whose fates were perceived as evidence of divine special providence. Out of the ashes of ancient Jerusalem arose a myth that was disseminated to the ends of the earth: through psalms, hymns, and prophecies, represented in word and image, and more recently through mass media and the Internet.

Beginning with the Bible, many books have been written about Jerusalem. Perhaps we should not be writing any more books about the Holy City. If it had been up to the great fourth-century Christian scholar and translator St. Jerome, no one would write about the earthly Jerusalem at all, nor pay any special attention to it, because no one should think that one is closer to God in one place than in others. In fact, much like his great prophetic predecessors in the Bible who chided Jerusalem, he considered it not a holy city but an unholy city, a city lacking in holiness, because it lacked in justice. From this ancient critical perspective, the holiness of Jerusalem is very much in question.

The study of Jerusalem forces us to think about Judaism, Christianity, and Islam as related phenomena, as a family of religions, with Jerusalem as part of their common inheritance. Jewish, Christian, and Muslim identity formation is implicated in what secular humanists refer to as "religious violence," a violence vacillating between martyrdom and genocide.[1] In Jerusalem, the "kingdom of god on earth" appears in the paradoxical form of rocky outcroppings and caves, signs of absence, that are surrounded by magnificent shrines that commemorate and anticipate divine presence. What kind of city is holy to a god who is both present and absent, hidden and manifest? What kind of religions are these that are jostling over the right to represent an absent god?

In this holy city there is always a temptation to force the end. The ancient Jews produced an unsurpassed world heritage by giving voice to human yearning for the presence of God in His place, a demotic love-poetry in praise of Zion and its God that inspires hope and faith in many millions of people across the globe.[2] But the Jewish attachment to this place is also forever associated with violence suffered and inflicted, Israelite conquest and extirpation, commanded in the laws of Deuteronomy, and the lament over the destruction of Jerusalem and its central symbol, the temple of Solomon. Over the course of the past 1,700 years, Christians and Muslims produced beautiful art and architecture and established profound civilizations, but their drive for empire, especially where frustrated, also gave rise to intra- and inter-communal recrimination, mutual contempt, and perennial resentment that periodically erupts into violence. The history of Jerusalem is thus a story of divinely sanctioned conquest, rule, loss, and the desire for retrieval and rectification.

From a modern perspective, too, perhaps it would be better if there were no more books on Jerusalem. In fact, the very religious conflict that flares up at the holy places on regular occasions might be avoided if everyone turned off their cameras. Perhaps Israelis and Palestinians could relax a bit if we all turned off our devices, ignored our news feeds, and allowed the city to breathe.[3]

Perhaps there shouldn't be holy places. But judging by the evidence of folklorists and ethnographers, shrine religion has been around for as long as human civilization.[4] People always saw and revered invisible powers, depicted in many forms and invoked by many names, "on every hill and under every leafy tree," as the Bible says about the Israelites. What Jews, Christians, and Muslims condemn as "paganism" used to be the norm. Ancient Israelite religion was no different. Archaeology tells us that YHWH, the god of the Israelites, wasn't always alone but had a female partner. Jerusalem's original god, after whom the city was named, was the Evening Star, twin-brother of the Morning Star. Those were the days when not even God was a monotheist. Jerusalem's career as the holy city *par excellence* commenced when one of its kings decided to banish the worship of all other gods and restricted the worship of YHWH, the nation's ancestral deity, to the royal shrine in Jerusalem. Thus arises the notion of YHWH as a "jealous" god who demands exclusive veneration. To "appear before the LORD," as all male Israelites were henceforth commanded, one had to go up to Jerusalem. In those days, veneration of YHWH in Jerusalem alone meant bringing or sending one's gifts to only one shrine, i.e. to pay one's taxes to the king and thereby strengthen the royal center of the state. That act made Jerusalem the "Rome" of ancient Israel: *omnes vias hierosolymam ducunt*, the place to which all roads lead. Later, when that city was nevertheless destroyed, something else happened that made Jerusalem and the god who resided in Jerusalem more consequential. Israelite prophets, lawyers, and scribes began to think of the god of Israel as different (Hebrew: *qadosh*), discovering the notion of an all-powerful creator of the universe, the only god there is, inventing the very God Almighty that, to this day, inspires Jews, Christians, and Muslims and holds them in thrall. It was, as philosopher and psychologist Karl Jaspers put it, an "axial age" breakthrough whose consequences are still with us and that, for better or worse, continues to shape our idea of what it means to be human.[5] There are important social, political, and historical consequences to biblical monotheism. If God is different, then the people he chooses are different. They are obliged to live and act differently, separate and distinguish themselves from others by dress, conduct, or both. We will have an opportunity to consider the secessionist, sectarian, and utopian apocalyptic implications of monotheism. God, capital 'G,' enables us to suffer and die for God as martyrs and he makes us kill for God, because he wants it (*deus lo vult*, as the Frankish Crusaders used to say in their medieval Latin when they waded in the blood of God's enemies and theirs, "up to their stirrups").[6] Compared to this God and the forces he unleashed in the souls of believers and in the world of holy war propaganda, the old shrine religions of the peasants were downright harmless. If it weren't for those kings who condemned the shrines, the Elijahs who wreaked havoc on the priests of Ba'al on Mount Carmel, the prophets who declared there is no God but God, perhaps no one would write books on Jerusalem today.

Before you put aside this book as the work of a cynic, let me quickly assert that I believe that religion can also be a force for good. Even Sigmund Freud – archcritic of religion and Jewish godfather of psychoanalysis – thought religion may be necessary for us to behave in civilized ways, even though he considered the Jewish and Christian religions "illusions" aimed at repressing the violent and libidinous urges that have characterized primate behavior since time immemorial.[7] The history of Jerusalem teaches us that many of the great emperors and caliphs who cast themselves as the representatives of God on earth not only did well by Jerusalem materially but also maintained law and order for extended periods of time. Some of them, especially the Muslim ones, were master-negotiators of the ethno-religious differences prevalent in late antique and medieval *Al-Quds*, the Holy City, and beyond. Jerusalem's history is not all blood and gore, war and conflict. Even today, there are many wonderful people among the Jews, Christians, and Muslims who call Jerusalem home, who want nothing more than peace and are deeply invested in whatever it takes to make peace and get along with one another. They are part of a global move away from exclusivist narratives and toward ecumenism, dialogue, and conciliation between creeds and nations. In Israel, there are the courageous Rabbis for Human Rights who protect Arab farmers and their fields from aggressive hyper-nationalist-religious settlers.[8] There is an Israel Interfaith Association[9] that brings together Christian, Muslim, and Jewish clerics to discuss matters of common concern. More recently, a Jerusalem music center was transformed into a temporary common prayer space for all three of the Abrahamic religions, making the point that religion does not need to divide but can bring people together.[10] Our religions are complicated things. The social and political functions of religion and the religious behavior of individuals and communities change over time. Christian missionary institutions founded by imperial regimes have turned into places of service to the community. On the other hand, Israel's commitment, in its declaration of independence, to equal rights of access to holy places nowadays serves Jewish extremists as a legal basis to argue for a radical revision of the *status quo* at the holy places. Islamic notions of a greater and lesser *jihad* are widely exploited to seduce disoriented youths to commit suicide attacks as acts of martyrdom. Jerusalem, largely temperate in mood and climate, sometimes seems overwhelmed by too much religion and too many sacred places.[11] For a visitor who spends time living and studying in the city, the plethora of nations and communities attached to Jerusalem for religious and other reasons make this metropolis[12] a fascinating place, and it has been this way for a very long time. Jerusalem's beauty and holiness strike some people, who come from afar, so strongly that they have visions or lose their minds in a condition known as the "Jerusalem syndrome." Jerusalemites live a great variety of ordinary and extraordinary lives and the city valiantly wrestles with the complex social, economic, and political challenges that arise from its peculiar character.

This book is my prayer for the well-being of Jerusalem. It is dedicated to my Jerusalemite friends, companions over the years during which I was privileged to visit, live, study, work, eat, drink, love, pray, walk, and drive around the hills and neighborhoods, take in different sights and perspectives, listen to different viewpoints, and think about how to tell the story of this holy city, its history, its communities, its charms, challenges, and meanings.

Though a history, this book does not strictly proceed in chronological order. I start with modern Jerusalem and I end with it. In the second part, I tell the story of Jerusalem's emergence as a holy city in three different ways, focusing each time on another aspect of the biblical past. In the third part, I consider the transformation of Jerusalem from a formerly Jewish temple city, condemned to oblivion by its Roman destroyers, into an imperially sponsored Christian theme park, and the afterlife of that same city under later Byzantine and Muslim rulers. I also consider the age of the Latin Kingdom of Jerusalem, which strikes me as important for its architectural and ideological legacies. The medieval rhetoric of *jihad* that concerns us so much today used to be balanced out by protracted cultural exchanges between Frankish knights and Saracen commanders that took place at the same time.[13] In the last part, I bring the story of Jerusalem back to the present, looking at the development of the modern city under the Ottomans and the British, the history of division and reunification, and the ongoing jostling over access to, and sovereignty over, Jerusalem's contested holy places. In short, this book is about the idea of Jerusalem as a holy city, the emergence of that idea from an ancient political theology, its adoption and dissemination through the rhetoric of cult restoration and royal/imperial patronage, and its transformation in an age of acutely modern (though biblically inflected) competing colonial and national projects.

Notes

1. See Juergensmeyer (2000), Sloterdijk (2009).
2. On the cultural history of the dissemination of Christianity see Brown (2013).
3. Cf. Meron Benvenisti in Misselwitz and Rieniets (2006), 43: "The less you discuss Jerusalem, the better the chances that there will be a solution."
4. On the persistence of shrine religion see Frankfurter (1998), Christian (1981), Margry (2008).
5. See Bellah and Joas (2012), Zank (2012).
6. *Gesta Francorum*. See Krey (1958 [1921]), 256–257. For an echo of Crusader rhetoric in Arab sources see Littmann (1904), 195.
7. See Freud (1975 [1927]).
8. Information at http://rhr.org.il/eng/(accessed December 5, 2017).
9. See http://www.lee-achim.de/html/i-faith/english/index2.htm (accessed December 5, 2017).
10. See Tarnopolsky (2016). On inter-religious dialogue in Israel see Kronish (2015).
11. See e.g. Pullan et al. (2013).
12. On the modern metropolis as a subject of sociological interest see Kasinitz (1995), Mieg (2011).
13. The complexities of medieval Jerusalem are beautifully documented and considered in Boehm and Holcomb (2016), a catalogue and volume of essays produced in connection with an exhibition on "Jerusalem 1000–1400," curated by these authors, at the Metropolitan Museum of Art, New York. For a review of the exhibition see Zank (2016a).

Acknowledgments

I have been teaching Jerusalem since 1999. I inherited the course from my colleague, biblical scholar and Samaritologist James Purvis. Jim's collection of images, documentaries, and bibliography gave me a solid start. In its early iterations I relied on the magisterial work of F. E. Peters, Bernard Wasserstein, and Karen Armstrong.[1] Later I used Kamil Asali's edited volume, *Jerusalem in History*.[2] A few years into teaching the subject, my then-colleague Peter Hawkins brought me to the attention of Blackwell publisher Rebekka Harkin and encouraged me to make a pitch for a brief history of Jerusalem. I did so without anticipating that writing a brief history was going to require as much time as writing a long one, or more.

This volume is based on a review of research in many areas of specialization that bear on one or another aspect of the story of the Holy City, including Ancient Near Eastern studies, classical, medieval, and modern European and Middle Eastern history, archaeology, the history of art and architecture, biblical studies, church history and the history of Christian doctrine, Jewish and Islamic studies, Roman, Persian, Arab, and Ottoman history, and Israel and Palestine studies. I read not just for information but also for approach. This led me to consult theories of religion, rhetoric (propaganda and persuasion), sociology, political theory, and urban studies. In the end, what remains central in my thinking about Jerusalem is how image and reality of the city are shaped by the interplay between biblical heritage and justifications of rule, presence, and ownership.

A brief history cannot be comprehensive. I pay relatively little attention to the Solomonic temple, which by some accounts is central to the status of the Holy City.[3] In making choices of what to include and how to tell the story, I tried to focus on the city qua such and its function in political narratives of divinely sanctioned rule. I aimed to offer a fresh view of the history of Jerusalem as an object of faith and desire, a city shaped by interpretations of the biblical heritage in light of a shifting rhetoric of power and powerlessness. Given the long history and the great variance in these conceptions of Jerusalem across the epochs, given also the variety of bodies of scholarship and the differences between the primary languages entailed in their study, I needed to allow for some degree of fragmentation and discontinuity in terminology and style of exposition. The brevity of the book forced me here and there to opt for telling vignettes in place of lengthy disquisitions. The reference section lists only the works cited, which are carefully selected from the material I reviewed. These must suffice as suggestions for further reading.

My family and friends showed much patience with me on this journey, which took me longer than it took the Greeks to vanquish Troy. In the meantime, several other single-authored volumes on Jerusalem appeared in print, most notably James Carroll's *cri de-coeur*[4] and Simon Sebag Montefiore's stylish "biography" of the Holy City.[5] Readers interested in what I think or learned from my antecedents and contemporaries are referred to the footnotes, as well as to the bibliographic and online resources mentioned in this book. I learned a lot more than I can mention, let alone discuss, from these and other scholars who have written on all or part of Jerusalem's history and present.

Special thanks to my friend Tomás Kalmar as well as to Nancy Evans (Wheaton College), Nahum Karlinsky (Ben-Gurion University), and Boston University colleagues Deeana Klepper, Pnina Lahav, and Adam Seligman who commented on various drafts of this book, as did the fellows of the Boston University Center for the Humanities and its directors, James Winn and Susan Mizruchi, and the members of a works-in-progress group convened by Susannah Heschel. Lord Stone of Blackheath kindly included me in a 2016 gathering of experts at the House of Lords in London where I had the opportunity to discuss Jerusalem issues with members of the "Two States, One Homeland" initiative. Jerusalemites who generously shared insights with me include Avner Haramati, Anat Hoffman, Rami Nasrallah, Sari Nusseibeh, Osnat Post, Gilad Sher, Khalil Shikaki, Mustafa Abu Sway, and Naomi Tsur. I enjoyed the help of undergraduate researchers Mano Sakayan, Emily Levin, and Danielle Liberman. Mr. Saman Abazari helped to compile the reference section.

When in Jerusalem, my friends Barhum and Nahla Azar, Ofrit and Itzik Kimchi, Michael and Daniele Krupp, and Nirit and Georg Roessler hosted and sustained me time and again. Thanks to the staff of the Boston Public Library Leventhal Map Collection and the St. Louis Public Library who kindly provided access to their special collections. The work could not have been done without access to Harvard's Widener Library and Boston University's Mugar and School of Theology libraries.

This book would not be the same without the original drawings by Miriam Shenitzer. The lyrical quality of her lines renders Jerusalem's monumental architecture ephemeral while giving due to the piety of presence of those who hold the city dear.

Special thanks to Kelly Sandefer and Jonathan Wyss of Beehive Mapping in Watertown, Massachusetts, for drawing the maps for this publication.

I would have liked to share this book with some of my teachers who have passed away, foremost among them Bishop Krister Stendahl, Rabbi Marvin Fox, and Professor Rolf Rendtorff. Krister Stendahl introduced me to the "Judaism and Christianity" seminar at the Hartmann Institute in Jerusalem and, along with Dr. Fox and the very kind William A. Johnson, mentored me at Brandeis University as a student of Near Eastern and Judaic Studies. Prior to that, in Heidelberg, I studied under Rolf Rendtorff, who bridged the worlds of Protestant Old Testament scholarship, Israeli biblical studies, and rabbinic literature. May their memory be for a blessing.

Notes

1. I discuss the work of Karen Armstrong and describe what I learned from teaching this course in Zank (2008).
2. Asali (2000 [1990]).
3. See e.g. Lundquist (2007).
4. Carroll (2011).
5. Montefiore (2011).

Maps

Map 1　Jerusalem in its regional context. Source: Author and Beehive Mapping.

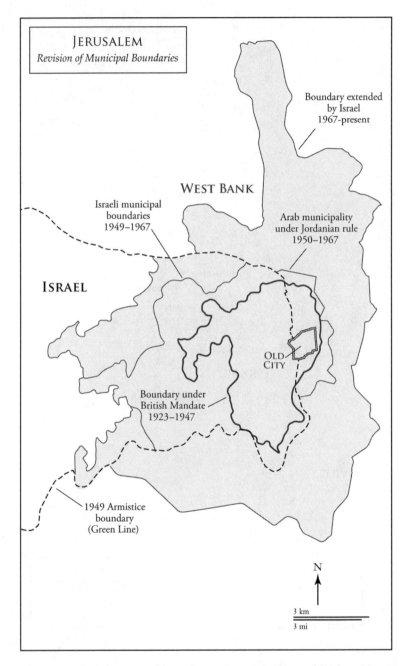

Map 2 Revisions of municipal boundaries. Source: Author and Beehive Mapping.

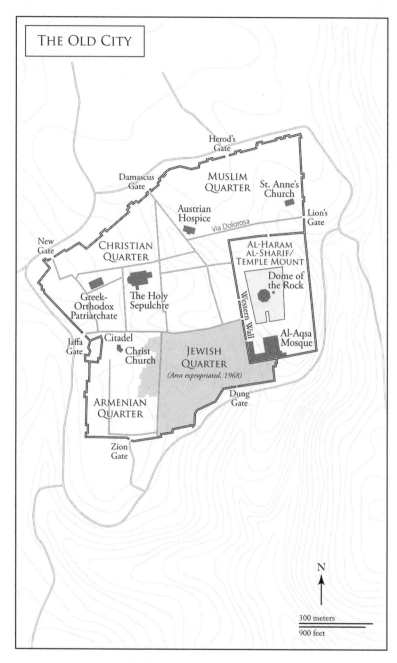

Map 3   The Old City. Source: Author and Beehive Mapping.

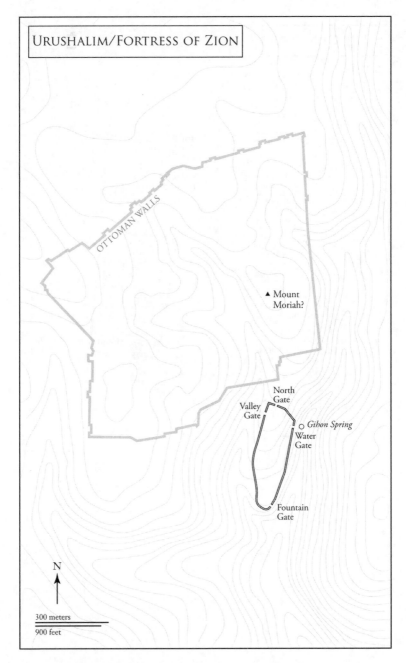

Map 4 Urushalim/Fortress of Zion (late Bronze and early Iron Age). Source: Author and Beehive Mapping.

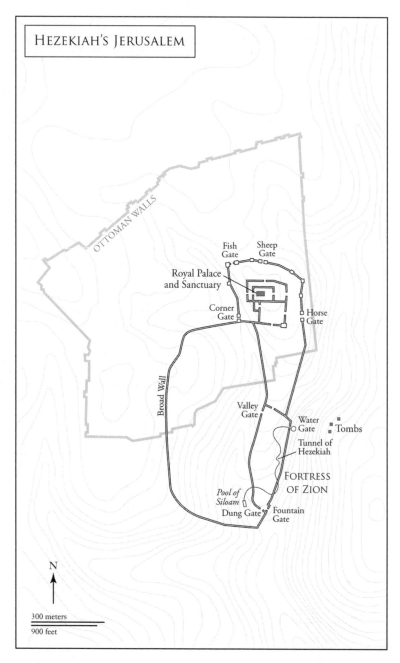

Map 5 Hezekiah's Jerusalem (late eighth to early sixth century BCE). Source: Author and Beehive Mapping.

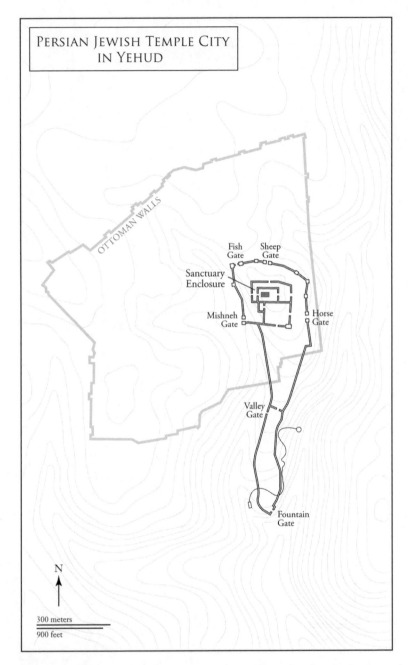

Map 6   Persian Jewish temple city in *Yehud* (early fifth to late fourth century BCE).
Source: Author and Beehive Mapping.

Map 7   Seleucid/Hasmonean *Yerushalem* (early second to mid-first century BCE).
Source: Author and Beehive Mapping.

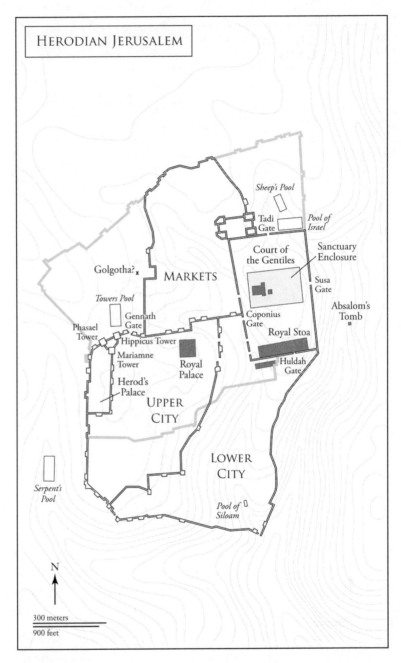

HERODIAN JERUSALEM

Sheep's Pool

Tadi
Gate

Pool of
Israel

Court of
the Gentiles

Sanctuary
Enclosure

Golgotha? ×

MARKETS

Susa
Gate

Towers Pool

Gennath
Gate

Coponius
Gate

Absalom's
Tomb

Phasael
Tower

Hippicus Tower

Royal Stoa

Mariamne
Tower

Royal
Palace

Huldah
Gate

Herod's
Palace

UPPER
CITY

LOWER
CITY

Serpent's
Pool

Pool of
Siloam

N

300 meters

900 feet

Map 8   Herodian Jerusalem (late first century BCE to late first century CE). Source:
Author and Beehive Mapping.

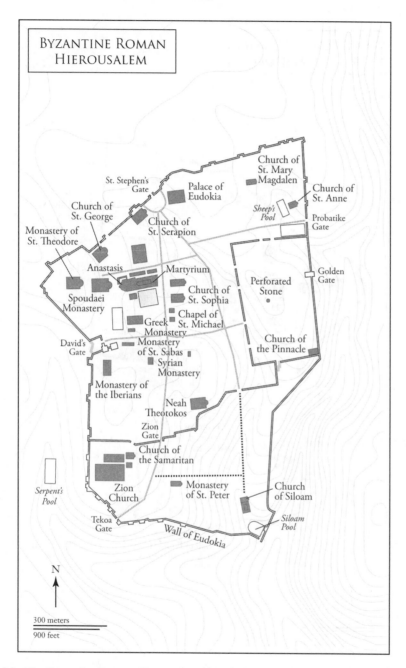

Map 9 Byzantine Roman *Hierousalem* (fourth to early seventh century). Source: Author and Beehive Mapping.

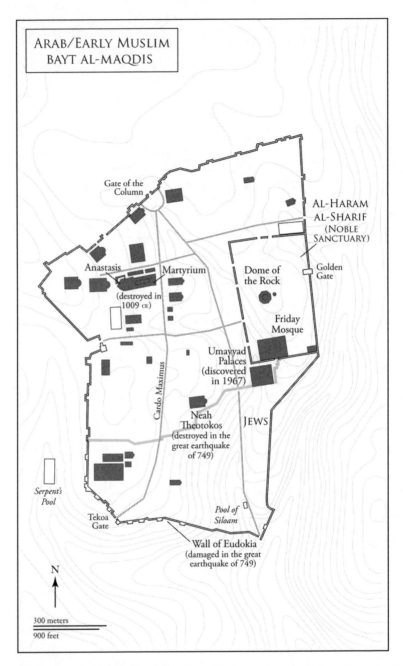

Map 10 Arab/early Muslim *bayt al-maqdis* (seventh to late eleventh century).
Source: Author and Beehive Mapping.

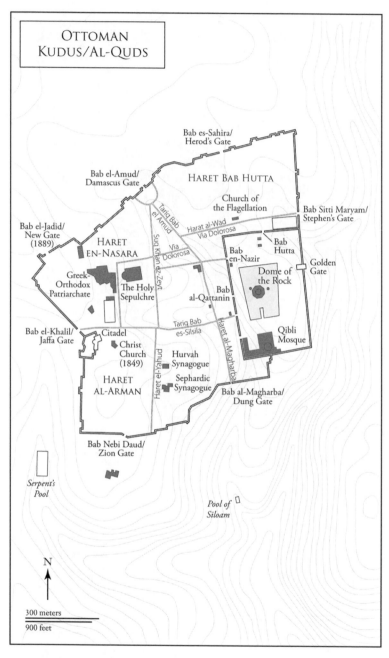

Map 11 Ottoman *Kudus/Al-Quds* (sixteenth to nineteenth century). Source: Author and Beehive Mapping.

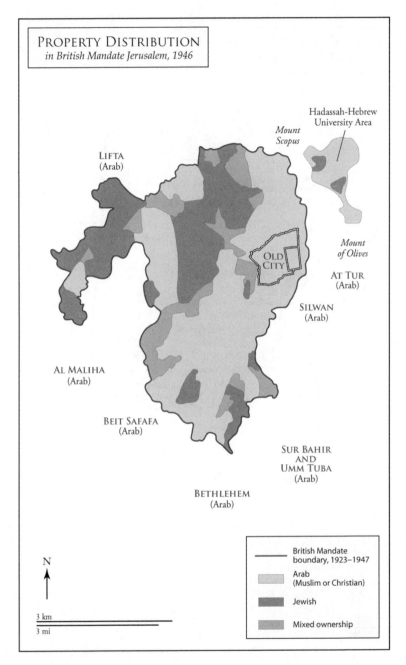

Map 12 Property distribution in British Mandate Jerusalem (1946). Source: Author and Beehive Mapping.

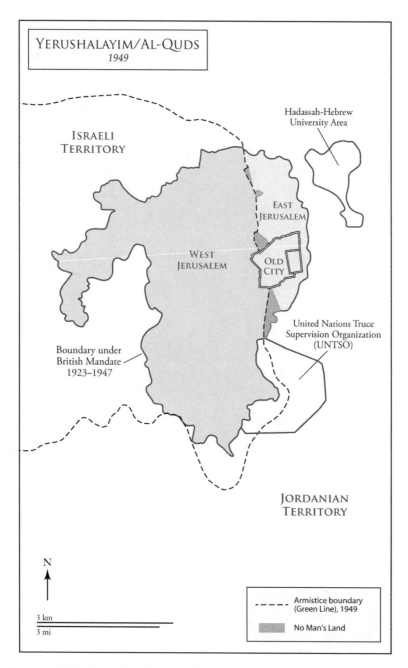

Map 13 Divided city: *Yerushalayim/Al-Quds* (1949). Source: Author and Beehive Mapping.

Part I

Introducing Jerusalem

1

Location, Recent History, Demography

Location

Jerusalem is a city with shops and businesses, hotels and restaurants, sports arenas, police stations, schools, hospitals, and everything else we might expect of a modern city, including effective governance, equitable urban planning, efficient trash collection, and proper law enforcement. This modern city is located in a dramatic landscape and enjoys an appealingly mild climate. It boasts traditional holy places, world-class museums, and modern sites of memory. It is a center of higher education and government, a national capital, and a popular magnet of religious pilgrimage and cultural tourism.

Jerusalem is located at 31.47 degrees latitude and 35.13 degrees longitude and nestled on the watershed of the central highlands of the southern Levant, in the Judean mountains. It is not mere fancy that Jewish, Christian, and Islamic lore refers to Jerusalem as the "navel of the earth." The place from which they believe the world was born connects the old continents of Africa, Asia, and Europe. The Holy Land, a crossroads of water and land routes that facilitated a millennial exchange of goods and ideas between the early high urban civilizations of Egypt, Mesopotamia, and the Mediterranean basin.

At an elevation of about 700 meters above sea level, the original city was surrounded by higher peaks and hence invisible from afar. Protected by

Jerusalem: A Brief History, First Edition. Michael Zank.
© 2018 Michael Zank. Published 2018 by John Wiley & Sons Ltd.

natural glacis and fortifications, its perennial source of fresh water, the Gihon spring, accessible from within the walls, the city was thought of as impenetrable. The major ancient seaports and the King's Highway were miles away. A city on the hill for a nation dwelling apart.

Jerusalem enjoys the advantages of the proximity of the Mediterranean to the west, the dry climate of the desert to the east, and reliable rainfalls in the winter due to its relative altitude. The summer is the dry season with an average of zero millimeters of precipitation. The relative humidity is highest in January (65%), which is the peak of the rainy season with an average of 128 millimeters of precipitation.[1] Jerusalem is never as humid as the cities of the coastal plain and never as hot as it is in the desert to the east. When snow falls in Jerusalem it is a major event, as one can see from postcards sold to celebrate the unusual spectacle. It is, and always has been, a great place to visit or retire in.

Jerusalem's dwellings and other structures used to be built so as to collect rainwater in cisterns, as well as to keep residents cool during the heat. The interiors of older houses boast shaded courtyards, lush with bougainvillea, that are invisible from the outside and accessible only through gates that could be closed overnight. In Roman times, when the city was retrofitted by King Herod and his successors to accommodate large numbers of international pilgrims offering vast quantities of animal sacrifices, a great amount of water was needed to keep the city clean. One still finds huge cisterns, now defunct, and the remains of ancient pools, aqueducts, and drainage systems built at various times to provide for the needs of the erstwhile temple city and its populations. UN climate specialists have been advocating for a revival of these cheap and efficient rainwater-fed systems across the Middle East.

The Mount of Olives to the east of Jerusalem overlooks the Judean Desert with a gradual drop to the Dead Sea (422 meters or 1,385 feet below sea level). Since late antiquity, these hills have been dotted with secluded monasteries and dominated by migrating Bedouin and their herds of sheep and goats. If one follows the natural path of the Kidron Valley one can walk to Jericho, one of the oldest cities in the world, near an oasis in the *Wadi Araba/ha-Arava*, an arid rift valley forged by the Jordan River, which now – diverted in the Galilee for the purpose of irrigation – is a mere trickle. If one continues along the western shores of the Dead Sea in the direction of the Gulf of Aqaba/Eilat (preferably in an air-conditioned bus or car) one passes the oasis of Ein Gedi, once famous for its date palms and coveted by Queen Cleopatra. Nearby are the ruins of Qumran, where an ancient sectarian library was found hidden in caves, and Masada, a mountain palace hewn out of the rock by the famously paranoid King Herod. This virtually inaccessible fortress served as the last bastion for the most fanatical among the ancient Jewish resistance fighters commanded by Eleazar ben Yair whose story of foolish heroism was immortalized by Josephus Flavius.[2] Everything in and around Jerusalem breathes history.

To the west, a highway winding through the reforested Judean mountains leads to the plains along the Mediterranean coast. On the way to Tel Aviv one passes al-Qastel, the former Crusader castle Beauverium, destroyed in 1191 by Sultan al-Adil shortly after the fall of Jerusalem to the Ayyubids. It was at this strategically located outlook that, in April 1948, Abd al-Qadr al-Husayni, commander of the Palestinian forces in charge of the roads to Jerusalem and himself a prominent Jerusalemite, lost his life to Jewish paramilitary snipers during a reconnaissance mission in the run-up to the end of the British Mandate.[3]

Just a stone's throw to the south of Jerusalem is Bethlehem with its famous Church of the Nativity that, in a diplomatic victory for the Palestinian National Authority's bid for international recognition of Palestinian statehood, was adopted by the United Nations Educational, Scientific and Cultural Organization (UNESCO) as a protected World Heritage site. If one continues on Route 60 in a southwesterly direction for another 20 km one reaches Hebron, also known as *el-Halil*, the city of Abraham, whom Muslims revere as the first "monotheist" (*hanifa*), Jews regard as the first Jew, and Christians consider the father of all believers. Hebron served as the capital of the first Judean monarchy, before King David conquered Jerusalem, and is the site of another great Herodian structure, the Tomb of the Patriarchs, built over the biblical Cave of Machpelah. Further south, on the cusp of the colorfully rugged Negev Desert one reaches ancient Nabatean Arad and, eventually, the Sinai Peninsula, an austere liminal space between African Egypt and the Western Asian Levant.

A mere 16 km north of Jerusalem is Ramallah, administrative center of the Palestinian National Authority (PNA)[4] in the West Bank, which is one of the two regions of Palestine (the other being Gaza) that the Oslo Accords of 1993 and 1994 between Israel and the Palestine Liberation Organization (PLO) assigned to a future Palestinian state. Jerusalem's place in any future settlement of the Israeli–Palestinian conflict is complicated by the fact that the West Bank is no longer simply Arab territory and that Jerusalem and its surroundings have significantly changed since June 1967. Jerusalem is no longer a frontier city at the end of a narrow corridor surrounded on three sides by Arab territory. Instead, it increasingly resembles the territorial and symbolic center of the "greater Israel" first envisaged by Revisionist Zionists in the 1920s and actively pursued by Israeli governments since 1977, when the electorate first replaced the socialist parties that had dominated the country for the first 30 years of its existence with a coalition of nationalist and religious parties.

Jerusalem is nearly equidistant between Tel Aviv (64 km) – hub of Israel's secular "fun" culture, nerve center of its globalized high-tech economy, and a gem of 1920s *Bauhaus* architecture – and Amman (71 km), about the distance from Boston, Massachusetts, to Providence, Rhode Island (see Map 1). Amman is the capital of the Hashemite Kingdom of Jordan, released into independence in 1946 by the British and sustained by American and Saudi aid. Though the Hashemite Kingdom lost Jerusalem and the West Bank in June 1967, king and country remain vitally interested and involved in the fate of the Holy City.

The distance from Jerusalem to Damascus in the northeast is a mere 209 km, closer than Boston is to Augusta, the capital of Maine. From Jerusalem to Cairo it is about 418 km about the distance from Boston to Philadelphia, Pennsylvania. The city's relative proximity to the most important regional power centers explains why Jerusalem was rarely independent and commonly subject to changes due to shifts affecting the entire region, a ping pong ball in the political and military games played by the rulers of the more populous and strategically better located centers of Egypt, Syria, and Mesopotamia in their millennial struggle for hegemony over the Levant. Today, as the seat of government of the only (officially unacknowledged) nuclear power in the Middle East, Jerusalem maintains security partnerships across a volatile region from which it was virtually cut off until 1977 when Egyptian president Anwar al-Sadat made his famous visit to Jerusalem, breaking Israel's isolation.

Recent History

We will look at Jerusalem's modern emergence in more detail in Part IV. The following provides a quick overview. For exactly four centuries, from 1517 until 1917, Jerusalem was part of the Ottoman Turkish Empire that at its greatest expanse bordered on Austria, Hungary, Russia, and Iran and controlled land and sea trade across North Africa and the Eastern Mediterranean. In late 1917, when the Great War was at a stalemate in the

European theatre, a Franco-British contingent commanded by General Allenby took the city from the Ottomans, a rare public relations opportunity that London celebrated with church bells ringing as a "last crusade" and a "Christmas present to the English nation." To enlist Arab support, the British and the French stoked Arab ambitions of independence but the actual post-war reorganization of territories was a different matter. Under British rule, Jerusalem served as the capital of Palestine, a League of Nations mandate to be readied for eventual release into independence. The territorial boundaries of Western Palestine or Cis-Jordan resembled those of biblical Israel, a landscape familiar to Christian Zionists in England, the United States, and elsewhere who promoted a return of the Jews to their ancient homeland. In November 1917, His Majesty's government expressed sympathy for, and in 1920 the League of Nations confirmed, the project of establishing a "Jewish homeland in Palestine." The arrival of waves of Jewish immigrants in the 1920s and 1930s led to tensions between Jews and Arabs, culminating in the Arab rebellion of 1936–1939. In November 1947, half a year before the expiration of the British Mandate, the UN General Assembly voted to partition Palestine. The map accompanying the UN partition plan assigned the majority of territory west of the Jordan to a future Arab state, based on the Arab demographic majority of Palestine. Jerusalem was to be kept united under an international regime. This plan was never implemented. Jewish and Arab militias ratcheted up the violence, and prepared for war. The British cracked down on the militias while managing their own departure. On May 14, 1948, Israel declared independence. The next day, the armies of Egypt, Jordan, Lebanon, Syria, and Iraq invaded the country. A UN-brokered ceasefire and the tacit support of the Soviet Union allowed Israel to rearm. At the end of the war, Israel had consolidated its territory, held on to a fiercely embattled West Jerusalem, and over half a million Arabs had fled the areas held by Israel. Jordan took the West Bank, Syria held on to the strategic Golan Heights, and Egypt was in control of the Gaza Strip.[5] Jerusalem was divided between Israel and Jordan. In December 1949, Israel's Prime Minister David Ben-Gurion declared Jerusalem the capital of Israel and began moving government offices to areas in western Jerusalem under Israeli control. This decision was made in defiance of the UN Partition Resolution and placed Jerusalem in limbo. Member states of the UN who wished to establish diplomatic relations with Israel were not supposed to recognize Israel's claim to Jerusalem. Most of those countries, including the United States, have therefore kept their embassies in Tel Aviv. The Hashemite Kingdom also defied the international community, but their measures did not elicit the same diplomatic response. After the Arab notables of East Jerusalem and the West Bank placed their political fortunes under the auspices of King Abdullah I, East Jerusalem became the provincial center of the West Bank.[6] The seat of government remained in Amman. Jordan saw itself as the temporary caretaker of Palestinian national interests in all of Palestine, including territories now under Israeli control. The Kingdom eventually yielded this claim to the PLO, but even now the Hashemites continue to serve as guardians of the Christian and Muslim holy places of Jerusalem.

In June 1967, in a short but consequential preemptive war against the combined armies of Egypt, Jordan, and Syria, the Israel Defense Forces (IDF) captured the Sinai Peninsula, the Golan Heights, and the West Bank. Arab East Jerusalem, including the Old City and its holy places, were now in Israeli hands and placed under civilian administration. Some military and religious leaders, for whom the conquest of Jerusalem's Old City seemed like the beginning of the messianic age, wanted Israel to declare full sovereignty over the Temple Mount, the Islamic Noble Sanctuary (*al-Haram al-Sharif*). Instead, the government – fearing repercussions beyond the diplomatic gestures of displeasure it was suffering – ordered the IDF to withdraw the Israeli flag that had been hoisted on the Dome of the Rock in the enthusiasm of the moment. In his speech to the UN, Israeli Foreign Minister Abba Eban contrasted Israel's policies with those of the Jordanians, who, when East Jerusalem was under their control, had allowed for the ancient Jewish cemetery on the Mount of Olives to be defiled and prevented Jews from visiting their holy places. He assured the international community, that Israel was to guarantee access to the holy places and freedom of religious worship. The administration of the Muslim holy places remained under the auspices of the Jerusalem Islamic Endowment (*a-waqf*). The municipal administration of long-term mayor Teddy Kollek, now extended to Arab East Jerusalem, promoted Israeli–Arab coexistence, while national governments, beginning with Golda Meir, supported the building of Jewish neighborhoods in East Jerusalem, so as to keep the city united and unified under Israeli rule.[7] In 1980, following the Camp David agreement between Israel and Egypt, the Israeli Knesset passed the so-called Jerusalem Basic Law, declaring Jerusalem the eternally undivided capital of Israel.[8] A negotiated redivision of Jerusalem between Israel and the Palestinians, who claim East Jerusalem as the capital of their future state, was briefly on the table during the 2000 Camp David negotiations brokered by US President Bill Clinton, but recent opinion polls show that the majority of Israelis as well as the majority of Palestinians oppose a redivision of Jerusalem. Both sides desire to keep the city whole, though each under their own sovereign rule. Jerusalem's future remains one of the final status issues to be resolved between Israel and the Palestinians as part of the two-states solution envisaged by the Oslo Agreements, the Wye River Agreement, the George W. Bush administration Roadmap for Peace, the Geneva Accords, and many other preliminary bilateral and multilateral peace plans.[9]

Demography

One of the most striking features of modern Jerusalem is the dramatic growth of its population from no more than 45,000 or perhaps 60,000 inhabitants in 1900 to about 815,000 in 2012. There are several reasons for this growth. One is the high rate of fertility, especially among the ultra-orthodox Jews and Muslim Arabs. More significant still are the waves of immigration to Jerusalem during the British Mandate and under Israeli administrations. Another reason for this growth is the revision of Jerusalem's municipal boundaries (see Map 2). From the sixteenth until the middle of the nineteenth century, the city's area was defined by the Ottoman walls that now enclose the Old City, an area of 1,000 dunams or 1 km². Land purchase and establishment of religious, charitable, and residential compounds outside of the Old City walls began in the 1860s, following the Crimean War.[10] The territory under the jurisdiction of the municipality has since been expanded several times, first in 1931, following a decade of neighborhood development under British administration, then again in 1949 when Israelis and Jordanians redrew the boundaries of the part of the city under their respective jurisdiction (Jordanian East Jerusalem: 6 km² or 6,000 dunams; Israeli West Jerusalem: 38.1 km² or 38,100 dunams). In 1967, Israel extended the boundaries to an area of 108 km² or 108,000 dunams and, in 1990s, brought the city to its current size of 126.3 km² or 126,300 dunams.

The municipality founded by the Ottomans and revised by British, Jordanian, and Israeli administrations represents modern means of governance and administration that rely on abstract boundaries and definitions of territory rather than on physical barriers. Over the past decade, Israel saw itself compelled to revert to the pre-modern means of defining who is in and who is out by establishing a physical barrier, the so-called Separation Fence, between Jewish and Arab centers of population that, in certain areas, crisscross the municipal boundaries established by prior Israeli legislation.

Equally as striking as the growth in Jerusalem's population is the shift in the ratio between the city's constituent communities. Over the past two centuries, the Christian community experienced significant ups and downs, growing from about 3,500 residents in the early 1830s (total number of residents: 20,000) to about 30,000 shortly before the end of the British Mandate, including expatriates (total number of residents in 1945: 157,080). Around 1900, Christians began to outnumber Muslims, something not seen since the time of the Crusades. Over the past 70 years, while the overall population grew, the number of Christians steeply declined, dropping to 14,500 in 1995, or from 19% of the population in 1946 to a mere 2% in 1995. The main reason for the decline of Jerusalem's Christian population is the departure of the British administration and the *Nakba* or flight and expulsion of Arab residents of West Jerusalem at the time of Israel's War of Independence.[11]

Until the early 1800s, Jews were the minority in Jerusalem, ranking behind Christians and Muslims. Although nineteenth-century estimates for the city's population are not very reliable, some sources indicate that the Jewish community began to overtake the Muslim population in the 1860s. Some foreign (as opposed to Ottoman) estimates for the 1880s show more Jewish residents than the combined number of Muslims and Christians. The general condition for this rapid growth, including the increase in the Christian population, was Ottoman reform (*Tanzimat*), which granted equal rights to religious minorities, provided increased safety, and encouraged foreign immigration, investment, and infrastructure development. Overall, the Jewish community grew from less than one quarter of the population in 1806 (perhaps 2,000 out of 8,774) to almost three quarters of the population in 1967, while the total number of inhabitants grew by more than a factor of 10 just over the past century.[12]

With a municipal territory of 126 km^2 Jerusalem is the largest city in Israel, more than twice the size of Tel Aviv (51 km^2) or Haifa (58 km^2). With its more than 800,000 inhabitants and growing, Jerusalem is also the most populous city in Israel. Large average family size among Haredi Jews and Muslim Arabs and the development of foreign-owned, high-end but underutilized apartments has led to serious shortages in affordable housing and high population density. In comparison, the city of Boston, Massachusetts, which also suffers from lack of affordable housing, nevertheless provides twice the acreage for about the same number of residents.

The first master plan for the development of the city approved by the Israeli cabinet after June 1967 designated most of the newly added areas surrounding the built-up city center as green space. Attention to rebuilding was initially focused almost entirely on the Jewish Quarter of the Old City. Political concerns with the threat of a redivision of the city, however, persuaded the Labor-led government coalition under Prime Minister Golda Meir in the early 1970s that the areas surrounding the city center should be used to establish a ring of new Jewish neighborhoods, to ensure the city would remain united and that the Jewish community was to constitute a decisive demographic majority. In the 1980s, Prime Minister Menachem Begin (Likud) initiated the building of a second ring of settlements around Jerusalem, outside its municipal jurisdiction, which led to an erosion of government funding for the city and a negative migration since housing in the new settlements was cheaper and hence particularly attractive to those sections of the Jewish population that were living with high unemployment, below-average wages, and high rates of fertility, especially among the ultra-orthodox Haredim.

Far from achieving the goal of establishing a stable rate of growth of the Jewish demographic majority, the initiatives of the national government inadvertently led to a significant increase in the Arab population of the city after 1967 and to a growth of the ratio of Arab and other residents relative to the Jewish population. The objective of creating and maintaining an integrated and unified Jerusalem had largely failed (see Figure 1). This failure was openly acknowledged by the Israeli government under Ehud Barak in 2000, the first Israeli government willing to reach an agreement with the Palestinians on a redivision of Jerusalem and a sharing of sovereignty over the Old City and its holy places. Subsequent governments abandoned the rhetoric of redivision and have since pursued renewed Jewish settlement building within and around the city.

On the Palestinian side, the struggle for presence, housing, and maintaining the Arab character of East Jerusalem has fostered the development of both violent and non-violent means of resistance to Israeli civilian governance and political control. The majority of Arab residents of the city have boycotted the municipal elections since 1967, so as not to confer legitimacy on the Israeli annexation. Even though the Arab residents of Jerusalem have the right to apply for Israeli citizenship, only a few have availed themselves of this opportunity and those who do, I was told by an Arab architect and city planner, mainly use it as a way of obtaining a green card for emigration to the United States.

As Moshe Amirav points out in his book, *The Jerusalem Syndrome*, in the 2003 municipal elections a mere 20% of the city's eligible voters changed

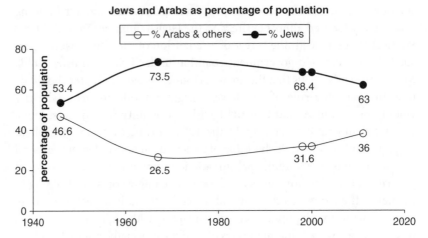

Figure 1   Demographic proportion Jews to Arabs, 1946–2012.

the majority in the city council and upset the hitherto secular system of governance by electing an ultra-orthodox Jew, Uri Lupolianski, as the city's mayor. Given their demographic strength, Jerusalem's Arabs could decide to abandon their boycott and return an Arab to the mayor's office. Since the 1990s, Palestinian activists, most prominently among them Faisal Husseini (1940–2001), called for "steadfast attachment" (*sumud*)[13] to Jerusalem as a form of peaceful resistance to policies aimed at pressuring the Arab population to abandon the city.[14] Among these policies (as tracked by human rights organizations such as B'tselem[15]) are the revoking of Arab residency permits, neglecting housing and infrastructure in the Arab neighborhoods, keeping the process of obtaining building permits costly and cumbersome, and bulldozing of illegal housing. While temporarily eclipsed by the Al-Aqsa Intifada (2000–2005) and disrupted by occasional spikes in violence, such as occurred in the wake of the collapse of the American-brokered peace talks of 2014, peaceful resistance and civil disobedience have created a culture of non-violent political action that appeals to moderates and enhances civil institutions that will be essential for Palestinian society to maintain itself alongside Israel.

In the following two chapters, we will complete our brief look at some of the basic aspects of the urban space that is modern Jerusalem by considering the "cities within" the city (Chapter 2) and the constituent communities that inhabit the city without always living together (Chapter 3).

Notes

1. Source: http://www.jerusalem.climatemps.com/precipitation.php (accessed November 21, 2017).
2. Cf. Klawans (2013).
3. On the Husayni (or Husseini) family's place in Palestinian society see Pappe (2002).
4. See http://www.mofa.pna.ps/en/,https://www.britannica.com/topic/Palestinian-Authority, and http://palestine.dk/palestine/government/(accessed November 21, 2017).
5. Trans-Jordan, originally part of the British Mandate for Palestine, was exempted from Jewish homeland building in 1922, following the first violent clashes between Arabs and Jews, to accommodate the ambitions of the Hashemite Amir Abdullah. The territory was released into independence in 1946, effectively making good on the British wartime promise of creating an Arab state in Palestine.
6. See Katz (2005).
7. On Israeli policies and policy goals for Jerusalem since 1967 see Amirav (2009). An excellent introduction to Jerusalem since 1967 is Dumper (1997).
8. See Zank (2016a).
9. See Ben-Ami (2006), 240–284, Molinaro (2009), Klein (2003), Lapidoth and Hirsch (1994), Hirsch, Housen-Couriel, Lapidoth (1995).
10. See Chapter 14.
11. On Jerusalem's communities see more in Chapter 3.
12. For demographic facts and figures see Ben-Arieh (1984), 267–179, Kark and Oren-Nordheim (2001), 28–29, Schmelz (1987), Dellapergola (2001), Tamari (1999).
13. On *sumud* and other terms Palestinians use to describe forms of popular resistance see Qumsiyeh (2011), 11.
14. On Faisal Husseini's role in Palestinian politics see Musallam (1996), 51–67.
15. See http://www.btselem.org/topic/jerusalem (accessed November 21, 2017).

2

Cities Within

If Jerusalem is the "heart" of Israel/Palestine, the Old City is the "heart" of Jerusalem, its pre-modern symbolic and religious core toward which everything else converges. In architectural terms, the Old City of Jerusalem is for the most part a medieval to early modern city, with remnants of late antique city planning, hydraulic engineering, and monumental architecture, resting on ancient foundations buried underground. The walls that make the Old City the jewel it is were established in the sixteenth century by Ottoman Sultan Suleïman "the Lawgiver" (aka "the Magnificent"), whose given name is an unmistakable homage to biblical King Solomon. To a Dominican friar by the name of Felix Fabri, who visited the city half a century earlier, Jerusalem appeared as a "village with monumental buildings."[1] Suleïman restored the city to its ancient grandeur. On his mind was more than the city's safety, which had been perfectly maintained without walls throughout two and a half centuries of Mamluk rule. Rebuilding the walls of Jerusalem on their ancient foundations was a symbolic act on the part of the first Ottoman ruler to receive the title of caliph. It constituted a gift to the Holy City from Constantinople under Muslim rule, a work reflecting the piety and benevolence of their builder.[2]

Under the Ottomans, *Kudus/Al-Quds* retained its character as a "Muslim city," a technical term in urban history that denotes a particular form of social, economic, and administrative organization.[3] This type of city

Jerusalem: A Brief History, First Edition. Michael Zank.

included the protection of ethno-religious nationalities (*millet*), including Jews, Samaritans, Armenians, Syriac Christians, Latins (Roman Catholics), Greeks, and others who paid the traditional poll tax (*jizya*) levied on the heads of families that belonged to one or another of these "corporations." Each nation was internally governed by their own civil laws and represented by a religious or lay leader who collected the poll tax and kept records. Jurisdiction went with the family and was not determined by the place of residence. Muslims were exempted from this taxation and enjoyed other rights denied non-Muslims, such as riding on horseback or wearing green, the color of the Prophet, though court records show that these laws were not consistently enforced.[4] The nineteenth-century emancipation of non-Muslims was meant to strengthen Ottoman citizenship and trans-ethnic solidarity, but corporate identities tended to persist.[5] The mosaic pattern of distinct ethno-religious communities continued to characterize Jerusalem neighborhoods even after the demise of the Ottomans. In contrast to the typical Ottoman-period Muslim city, which was both hierarchical and pluralistic (Turkish officials on top, Arab Muslims as the privileged population, other inhabitants divided by religious nationality with semi-autonomous institutions), the villages surrounding the city were always based on kinship and clan solidarity, creating a stark contrast between city and hinterland. As a major pilgrimage city, Jerusalem boasted hospices where pilgrims from across the Christian world were able to lodge safely by affiliating with one of the recognized "nations," some of which even enjoyed foreign protection through a system of capitulations.[6] Institutions of hospitality proliferated in the nineteenth century and many of them still exist today. Now one of the most luxurious spots in the Old City, located in the Muslim Quarter near the *Via Dolorosa*, is the Austrian Hospice, where Kaiser Wilhelm II and Kaiserin Augusta Victoria lodged during their historic visit to Jerusalem in 1898. Communities that enjoyed the protection of foreign consuls were, much like their *corps diplomatique*, granted a kind of exterritorial immunity.

While many languages can be heard on the streets of Jerusalem, the dominant local idiom in the Old City and elsewhere in East Jerusalem is Palestinian Arabic, one of the many dialects of the Arabic language spoken across North Africa and the Middle East. Arabic is the language of the Qur'an and represents a cultural and religious heritage widely disseminated and carefully maintained since the late seventh century, when Umayyad Caliph Abd al-Malik made Arabic the administrative language of Syria, displacing Greek, which had dominated the Middle East for a millennium and remains the language of the Greek Orthodox Community. Despite a near millennium of Turkic dominance, the Turanian languages never became the local vernacular, and the *millet* system allowed for the various ethno-religious communities of the region to keep their languages alive. Jerusalem's official languages today are Hebrew, English, and Arabic.

The city enclosed by the Ottoman walls shows remnants of twelfth-century Frankish-Romanesque architecture[7] (see Map 3). The façade of the main entrance to the Church of the Holy Sepulchre and much else in the amorphous conglomerate of chapels that enshrine Golgotha, the tomb of Christ, the tomb of Adam, and other holy places, are of Frankish vintage (see Figure 2). The original buildings, Emperor Constantine's *Martyrium* and *Anastasis*, a large basilica and an open rotunda that had faced one another across an open courtyard, were dismantled in 1009 by the flamboyant Fatimid Caliph Al-Hakim, who took offense at the annual Christian

Figure 2   Window above the Frankish main entrance to the Church of the Holy Sepulchre with its immovable ladder. Illustration by Miriam Shenitzer.

ritual of the "Holy Fire." The Frankish rebuilding of Christendom's holiest place ignored the floor plan and orientation of its antecedent. The remains of an archway, part of the original entrance to Constantine's basilica, are still visible inside a bakery located near the stairway that now leads to the back entrance to the Church, via its roof. The Holy Sepulchre was the center of medieval Christian life in Jerusalem. The nearby modern Lutheran Church of the Redeemer was built on the remnants of an erstwhile Crusader church and hospital, across from the erstwhile Frankish market known as "Muristan." A major religious feature for Christian pilgrims to Jerusalem is the *Via Dolorosa*, a pilgrimage way that starts at the Lion's Gate in the east, leads past the western edge of the *al-Haram al-Sharif* (the Noble Sanctuary), turns a corner near the Austrian Hospice, goes uphill through the *suq*, and enters the Holy Sepulchre through the back. If one pays attention on the way, or if one simply drifts about the Old City and walks around the quietly dignified *Haram* area, one notices the repetition of red and yellow angular striped ornamentation as well as of a certain honeycomb pattern found in archways. These are the hallmarks of Mamluk architecture, built between 1250 and the early 1500s. Private sponsors, as well as Egyptian rulers of that period, created endowments to support the pious and the poor. They added schools, soup kitchens, and public fountains (*sabil*), as well as private residences.[8]

Though the layout of the streets and the location of major buildings and gates of the Old City are based on a Byzantine grid, the current street level is elevated by several feet above the Roman street level. Places where the earlier Roman and Byzantine architecture is on display are the restored section of the *Cardo maximus*, the main thoroughfare of the Byzantine city, the excavated gates below the current *Bab el-Amud* (Damascus Gate), and parts of the archaeological park around the Western Wall and *al-Haram al-Sharif*.

Until 1967, when Israeli archaeologists began to excavate sections of Jerusalem's pre-Islamic past, only a few truly ancient monuments were visible through the ages. The most striking remnant of Roman-age Jerusalem – from a time when the city was a Jewish temple city and center of a Jewish commonwealth – is the temple platform on the eastern edge of the Old City. To be precise, only the lower ranks of giant blocks of the retaining wall, most of which are hidden by construction established on the ruins of ancient Jerusalem, and the subterranean support arches of the platform, known – falsely – as Solomon's stables, are of Herodian vintage (first century BCE). Almost everything else generations of visitors encountered over the centuries in their perennial quest to see and touch the places

where God walked the earth, or a prophet descended to heaven, were mere
simulacra of sacred history, buildings erected or recreated to commemorate
particular moments of the city's sacred past in one or another putative location. One of the ironies of this holy city is, that the tenuousness of these
sacred locations is belied by the solidity of the artifice of representation.

Within the Old City, the only area that has seen considerable reconstruction over the past 50 years is the Jewish Quarter and the area adjacent to the
Western Wall[9] (see Figure 3). Karaite and Rabbanite Jewish communities
have been present in Jerusalem for more than a millennium. In early
Muslim times, Jews resided south of the erstwhile temple area, in formerly
Byzantine neighborhoods ravaged during the Persian invasion. Later we
find Jewish neighborhoods north and west of the Noble Sanctuary.

Figure 3   Western Wall/*Al-Buraq*, a contested space of contemplation. Illustration
by Miriam Shenitzer.

Settlement patterns changed with the growing influx of new immigrants in the second half of the nineteenth century. Traditional Jewish life in the Old City ended with Israel's War of Independence, when Jews were forced to evacuate. The lyrics to Naomi Shemer's nostalgic "Jerusalem of Gold," first performed in May 1967, express the sentiment that Jerusalem's Old City was abandoned and forlorn as long as Jews were not allowed to live there. Following the conquest of June 1967, Israel expelled the residents of what was to become the new Jewish Quarter, conducted demolitions and emergency excavations that yielded impressive historical information about the biblical city and later periods, and rebuilt the entire area as an exclusively Jewish neighborhood. One of the first measures taken after the city came under Israeli control was the creation of the Western Wall plaza. Until then, the Wailing or Western Wall (Hebrew: *ha-qotel ha-ma'aravi*; Arabic: *Al-Buraq*[10]) was accessible only by way of a narrow alley that bordered on a Moroccan (*Magharbi*) settlement established as far back as Ayyubid times, in the early thirteenth century CE. After the Six Day War had ended, the Israeli military brought in bulldozers, evicted the residents of the Magharba quarter and razed it to the ground in order to establish the large plaza for Jewish worship and Israeli state and military ceremonies that is now the focal point of Jewish national-religious pride. Removing the Moroccan quarter (*Haret el-Magharba*) linked the Western Wall/Temple Mount area directly to the Jewish Quarter, creating a solid Jewish enclave in the predominantly Arab Old City.

Aside from these changes and the introduction of a modern system of waste management, the Old City's architecture and lifestyle still display the same cultural mix, the variety of dress, smells, tastes, and wares that accrued to Al-Quds and similar Muslim cities across the Middle East for centuries, with the added ingredients of modern merchandize and the lingering unease between Jews and Arabs going about their business as best they can while trying to ignore what Israelis call "the situation" (*ha-matzav*). Narrow alleys, rows of shops, vendors (mostly young and male) displaying their goods and enticing pilgrims and tourists in every language spoken on earth to stop and partake of their offerings: Hebron glass, Armenian tiles, ancient coins and antiques with and without certificates of authentication, cheap Indian clothes and Moroccan carpets, vast bags of spices in every earthen color, sweets dripping with honey, the display of grotesque chunks of goat and lamb, fragrant coffee and cardamom seeds, jewelry, daggers, dumbeks, waterpipes, headscarves, printed T-shirts, and mounds of incense. Pushcarts pulled by donkeys and piled high with supplies or driven by boys noisily jostling (*Yalla! Yalla!*) through throngs of an international mix of visitors and locals, Hasidic Jews in fur hats, black gabardine, and white knee socks, modestly elegant urban Arab ladies shopping, Bedouin matrons offering dates, bundles of mint, or figs; in the ubiquitous tea house, *shesh besh*-playing idle middle-aged businessmen; Israeli men or women with Uzis slung over their shoulders rushing through the David Souk herding American Jewish kids on Birthright Israel sponsored trips[11] to the Western Wall and back. The view from the ramparts affords a glance at rowdy schoolyards with uniformed children, small orchards, and quiet living quarters near safely enclosed medieval churches, mosques, and synagogues: a densely packed, complex living organism of a medieval city inhabited by a dizzying array of nations.

The Old City is the core of Arab East Jerusalem. Under Jordanian rule, East Jerusalem was the most significant urban center of the West Bank and it retained this character during the first three decades of Israeli rule. One can get a measure of the modern Arab city by passing into the neighborhood through Herod's Gate, where one finds the Arab central bus station, near the Protestant Garden Tomb first identified by General Gordon, around the corner from the German Schmidt-Schule. The area, which extends north to Sheikh Jarrah and east to Wadi el-Joz, remains the commercial center of Arab East Jerusalem and includes important historical and cultural institutions, such as the Rockefeller Museum and the American Colony Hotel. In recent years, property ownership in Arab East Jerusalem has been legally contested by Jewish organizations eager to reclaim property lost during the War of Independence. In some heart-rending cases, Arab refugees from West Jerusalem who had taken residence in abandoned Jewish properties were evicted once again because they were unable to show title.

West Jerusalem, expanded and claimed by Israel as its capital since late 1949, is the home of Israel's parliament, the Knesset (inaugurated in 1966), the Israel Museum, the National and University Library, and the Hebrew University on Mount Scopus, which, during the years of partition, remained an Israeli enclave. During partition, the Jerusalem Zoo was moved from East Jerusalem to the west, as was Hadassah Hospital, now one of the most advanced medical centers in the world, and with the notable exception of the ministry of defense, which remains in Tel Aviv, all government ministries were moved to West Jerusalem. Cut off from the ethnically diverse multi-religious Old City and from Jerusalem's Arabs, West Jerusalem developed a profile of its own. The substance of West Jerusalem's pre-1949

housing that gave the Jewish part of the city its distinctive character consisted of a variety of residential neighborhoods that were developed in waves,
each with their distinctive purpose and style, including the international
style of the 1920s and 1930s and the more pedestrian *mamlakhti* ("Statist")
style of the 1950s and 1960s. During a 1968 visit American architect Louis
Kahn disparaged the latter as an expression of the "religion of Solel Boneh,"
a functionalism indifferent toward the spiritual needs of actual human
beings that he blamed on the socialist corporation, which had held a
monopoly on public works since the early days of the British Mandate.[12]
Among the oldest settlements, now integrated into the Jewish city, were the
quaint stone houses and lush gardens of the late nineteenth-century
German and Greek settlements along Emek Refaim Street, the stylish 1920s
and 1930s apartments of Rehavia, the formerly Arab villas of Talbiya, and
the lower-middle-class housing developments Shaarei Hesed, Nahalat
Shiv'ah, and Kerem Avraham. The new national institutions were placed in
and around a valley west of the city's commercial center, the traditional
Mahaneh Yehudah, in an area that, only a century earlier, was remote
enough from Jerusalem (i.e. the Old City) that it only featured a Greek
monastery built like a fortress. Further to the west, new residential neighborhoods were added, such as Kiryat Hayovel, many of them consisting of
affordable but unattractive apartment buildings that absorbed some of the
half million Jews expelled from Arab countries in the early 1950s in retaliation for Israel's refusal to allow Palestinian refugees trapped in UN Relief
and Works Agency-monitored camps across the region to return to their
homes in what was now the State of Israel.

Since 1967, Israeli national, regional, and municipal planning has aimed
to remake Jerusalem as a single coherent, well-managed, economically
viable, and internationally recognized city of predominantly Jewish and
Israeli character that is attractive to pilgrims, tourists, business, and
investment. Under Teddy Kollek, who served as the city's mayor from 1965
until 1993, these goals were pursued with the assumption that they could be
achieved while fostering Jewish–Arab coexistence. When the first Intifada
broke out in December 1987, the Israeli government tried to keep Arab
Jerusalem separate from the uprising against Israeli occupation in Gaza
and the West Bank. The Israelis had harbored the illusion that Jerusalem's
Arabs, who enjoyed Israeli civilian administration rather than military
rule, would eventually integrate themselves into Israeli society and, as had
many Israeli Arabs in places like Haifa or the towns of the Galilean
"Triangle," learn to see themselves as Israelis. Instead, East Jerusalem ever

more openly displayed its loyalty to the PLO, widely considered as the only legitimate representative of the Palestinian people while then still officially shunned by Israel as a terrorist organization. In the mid-1990s, the focal point of this controversy was the Orient House where Faisal Husseini served as the unofficial representative of the PLO in Jerusalem. Ehud Barak's meeting with Yasser Arafat during the 2000 Camp David peace negotiations brokered by US President Bill Clinton was the first time that an Israeli prime minister entertained the idea of a redivision of Jerusalem and thus acknowledged that Israel's policies of unification had largely failed. As Israeli scholar Menachem Klein argued in evaluating Jerusalem, 40 years after unification, the city remained a "frontier city," on the boundaries between the Jewish state of Israel and Arab Palestine.[13] Ten years later, this may no longer be the most accurate description of the place of Jerusalem within Israel/Palestine, which now seems more like a complex and fluid binational space on its way to a one-state reality.

Notes

1. See *Palestine Pilgrims' Text Society*, vols 7/8 and 9/10. The erudite Swiss-born friar visited Jerusalem in 1480 and 1483.
2. On the architectural history of Ottoman Jerusalem see Auld and Hillenbrand (2000).
3. The term "Muslim city" was coined by French colonial theorists in the 1950s. It is contested in urban studies as an "Orientalist" concept and has been criticized for imposing a value judgment on the post-classical cities of the Middle East. It is also a misnomer in that it suggests that a Middle Eastern type of urban settlement applies to all "Muslim" civilizations from Al-Andalus to India and Central Asia. I am using it here as originally intended, namely as an urban settlement typical for the formerly Greco-Roman cities of the Levant. For one among many studies of the transformation of the typical Middle Eastern city from Greco-Roman antiquity to Byzantine-Arab late antiquity (with an ample bibliography) see Liebeschuetz (2001).
4. On social historical sources and approaches in the study of medieval and early modern Jerusalem see Cohen (1982), Little (1980), Lufti (1985), and Müller (2008).
5. See Parolin (2009), 74, Qafisheh (2008), 26–37. The Law of Ottoman Nationality of January 19, 1869, comprehensively regulated citizenship and naturalization, including by intermarriage. For an exception to this law, see Kern (2011). On Ottoman citizenship since 1908 see Campos (2011).

6. For the system of Ottoman capitulations in the eighteenth century see Boogert (2005). Grants of consular protection of non-Muslim interests, which proliferated in Jerusalem in the second half of the nineteenth century. See the list compiled by Schölch in Asali (2000 [1990]).
7. See Weiss (2004), Boas (1999).
8. On the architecture of Mamluk Jerusalem see Burgoyne (1987), Rabbat (2010).
9. On the urban renewal and rebuilding of the Jewish Quarter see Ricca (2007).
10. See Barakat (2007).
11. Cf. Kelner (2010).
12. See Sakr (2015).
13. See Klein (2008).

3

Communities and Meanings

Jerusalem is old and new, east and west. But it is more than one city also in other ways. It is a city built on immigrants and native populations, communities that are unequal for historical, political, religious, and ethno-cultural reasons. Other cities are similarly divided along ethnic, economic, and religious lines. In Jerusalem, certain minorities go as far as rejecting the authority of the national regime and resent the municipal administration. Some vote, some opt out *en bloc*. It is a city where some communities live in close proximity to one another without really living together.

Palestinians refer to Jerusalem as *Al-Quds al-Sharif*, or *Al-Quds* for short. For them, Al-Quds is the capital of Palestine, a landscape deeply grounded in history and a state as yet unrealized. Jerusalem's Arabs were shocked when Israel took over their city and they are troubled by the city's ongoing transformation. Even a friendly gesture, such as Teddy Kollek's surrounding the walls of the Old City with greenery and palm trees, can be perceived as a misstep. "Why palm trees?" they ask. "Did he think this was Gaza?" The extensive excavation and manicured display of remains representing the city's ancient Jewish past is also seen as problematic in that it seems to efface Arab and Palestinian history. The tourist's view seems distracted from the Arab city that is right in front of their eyes and directed toward what is not there: a biblical Jewish city. Even the name Al-Quds has been effaced in official Israeli communication. The Arabic name used on road

Jerusalem: A Brief History, First Edition. Michael Zank.
© 2018 Michael Zank. Published 2018 by John Wiley & Sons Ltd.

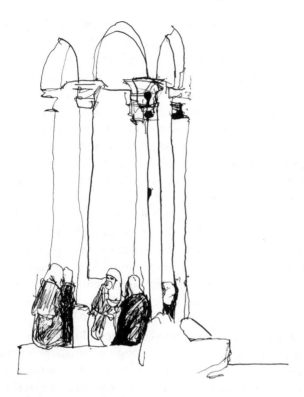

Figure 4 Muslim women under the dome of *Al Khidr* (St. George) on *al-Haram al-Sharif*. Illustration by Miriam Shenitzer.

signs and elsewhere is not Al-Quds but *ursalim*, an Arabized version of the biblical name of the city underscoring the city's antiquity and Jewishness.

Muslims traditionally revere Jerusalem as the City of the Holy House (*madinat bayt al-maqdis*), a reference to the primordial temple and site of future resurrection and last judgment. The established Islamic view of Jerusalem's holiness, forged over the decades that marked the transition from conquest to rule, foregrounds the tradition of a mystical Night Journey (*al-isra*) of Prophet Muhammad to a Distant Sanctuary (*al-masjid al-aqsa*)[1] (see Figure 4). Originally referring to heaven, this "place" became identified with Jerusalem's Noble Sanctuary (*al-Haram al-Sharif*). It is from here that Muhammad is said to have ascended to heaven (*al-miraj*) where he was introduced to the earlier prophets, including Moses and Jesus, and received instruction from the Almighty Himself, before returning to Mecca. Palestinian Muslims share a sense of responsibility as the guardians of the two noble sanctuaries (*al-haramayn al-sharifayn*), the *Masjid al-Aqsa* in Jerusalem and the Tomb of the Patriarchs in Hebron, both incidentally Herodian structures. These as well as many other smaller holy places across the countryside were often traditionally venerated by both Muslims and Jews. For Jerusalem's Muslims, Palestinian national identity, Arab history, and religious heritage are virtually indistinguishable. They all flow together in a heroic imperative of attachment. The rhetoric of Palestinian protest against Israeli measures and all violent and non-violent resistance against "the occupation" comes back to the demand for a return to the *status quo ante*, though Palestinians differ on what "*ante*" they have in mind: before 1967, before 1948, or before 1917.

Not all Arabs are Muslims and not all Muslims are Arabs. The local laity of Palestinian Christians is ethno-linguistically Arab and, though shrinking in numbers, strongly engaged in Palestinian politics. Palestinian Christians participate in every type of economic, cultural, and political activity. Many are vocal in the struggle for secular Palestinian statehood because their future, if it is to be in Palestine rather than in the growing Arab Christian diaspora, depends on keeping their bond with the Sunni Muslim majority on the neutral ground of non-sectarian citizenship. Palestinian Christians and the moderate Muslim majority among the Palestinians have much at stake in resisting the Islamist radicalization of the younger generation. Muslim fundamentalists see little room for Christians or secular Muslims in a restored caliphate.

Not all of Jerusalem's Christians are Arabs. Consider the Armenians, for example. Jerusalem's Old City boasts an Armenian Quarter, a residential fortress within the Ottoman walls centered on the Armenian Orthodox church of St. James, a twelfth-century basilica dedicated to two major saints by the same name: the son of Zebedee and the brother of Jesus who served as the first bishop of Jerusalem. When did an Armenian community become part of Jerusalem's patchwork? Armenia was once a powerful kingdom on the northern border between Rome and Persia with dreams of empire of its own. During the reign of a Hasmonean queen by the fitting name of Salome Alexandra (r. 76–67 BCE), Judah was nearly conquered by Mithridates, one of Armenia's strongmen. At the time, the Armenian elite was devoted to Persian gods such as Ormuzd and Mithras. In 301 CE, Armenia officially converted to the Judaic redeemer cult of Christ that was soon also adopted by the Romans. In the early Middle Ages, the Armenians of Edessa (Urfa) were allied and intermarried with the Frankish knights who established the Latin Kingdom of Jerusalem. After the fall of Jerusalem

(1187), the *franj* (a generic term for western European or Latin Christians) were allowed to maintain charitable institutions in the city and the Armenians remained a constituent part of its population, a nationality (*millah*) taxed but tolerated by Mamluks and Ottomans. Like the Greeks, the Armenians served as middlemen in Ottoman foreign trade. During the Great War, the Turks forced Armenians out of Turkey in what was to be the first among many twentieth-century acts of ethnic cleansing. Survivors of deathly marches through the Syrian Desert took refuge in Jerusalem's by then no longer Turkish-ruled Armenian Quarter, swelling its ranks and making Jerusalem the center of an Armenian revival. Since 1989, engagement of the sizable Armenian diaspora has shifted toward rebuilding the former Soviet Republic of Armenia while attention to Jerusalem has declined. Still, to Armenians across the globe, Jerusalem remains a beloved symbol of heaven that is glorified in hymns even when it is somewhat neglected in reality.[2]

The Armenians are but one of several major and many minor Christian nations, communities, sects, and movements who have made Jerusalem their second home. Christianity, still the world's largest religion, is profoundly divided by language, creed, and nationality, and yet Jerusalem is holy to all. This is not to deny an ancient and persistent Christian ambivalence toward this and any holy city, an ambivalence nourished by the Bible itself. Ancient Christian tradition associates Jerusalem with a grotesque number of imprisoned, tortured and killed prophets. But rather than rendering Jerusalem odious, the blood of its martyrs sanctified it beyond measure. Christians resolved the ambiguity of the city's holiness by mapping it onto a history of salvation. Jewish Jerusalem, city of Christ's death, was tainted; hence the rightness of its destruction by the Romans. But the death of Christ also sanctified Jerusalem for the Christians. Hence hundreds of thousands of Christians visit Jerusalem every year in search of the lingering presence of Christ's passion, death, resurrection, and his assumption into heaven, and they traditionally believe that this is where he will return to judge the living and the dead. To this day, two sections of the Old City (an area of one km²) are nominally Christian, the Armenian Quarter and the Christian Quarter. The holiest place of Christendom and center of the Christian Quarter, the Church of the Holy Sepulchre, is shared by six different communities (Greek, Armenian, Syriac, Ethiopic Orthodox, Roman Catholic, and Egyptian Coptic) in an uneasy *status quo* established by the Ottomans in the middle of the nineteenth century and carefully policed by British, Jordanian, and Israeli regimes ever since.

In late antiquity, the city was a bastion of Greek Orthodoxy, a religious cult fostered by Emperor Constantine that became the official religion of the Roman Empire under Byzantine Emperor Theodosius I (d. 395). Under Muslim rule the population gradually became more diverse but Jerusalem's Arabized Greek Orthodox laity remains a major demographic and cultural factor, even though it has declined in numbers since the end of the British Mandate. Following Greek independence from the Ottomans (1821), the Greek Church acquired land in and around the city and became the largest landowner in Jerusalem. Selling property to Jews is shunned, forcing today's Jewish developers and settlers to use middlemen to conduct sensitive real estate deals in East Jerusalem. There have been several scandals that have deepened long-standing divisions between the Arab laity and Greek expatriate leadership. Similar tensions between local community and direction from afar has beset the Armenian community as well. In 1987, the Vatican broke with the pervasive tradition of expatriate leadership when Pope John Paul II appointed the first Palestinian Arab, Michel Sabbah, as Latin Patriarch and Archbishop of Jerusalem, a significant gesture at an important juncture that went beyond strengthening the Christian segment within the Palestinian community. Indigenous Palestinian Christians wish to remain present in Palestine and participate in the building of a just and equitable civil society that respects the rights of all Palestinians.[3]

Jews and Arabs are not the only populations living in close proximity without living together. In Jewish Jerusalem, which in many ways reflects the secular character of Israeli society – it is the capital of a state founded on the modern principle of religious freedom; it is the seat of a parliament (the Knesset) that represents every community; there is no gender separation on the buses or the gleamingly new light-rail system; some bars and other places of entertainment remain open on the Sabbath; there is an annual gay pride parade – some neighborhoods are controlled by strict religious law and custom. Take Meah Shearim, for example. This exterritorial neighborhood was one of the first intentional communities established outside the walled nineteenth-century city of Jerusalem. The founding collective of 100 shareholders (hence the name, "A Hundred Gates") desired to withdraw from the increasingly densely populated and distracting environment of the Old City. Meah Shearim's ultra-orthodox (*haredi*) community is internally divided into many sects and movements that like to hate one another, but the majority of residents agree that any needless contact with modern society is to be avoided. The Haredim tend to respond aggressively when their standards of behavior are ignored and remain aloof from the modern

Jewish city that grew up around them. As part of the historic "old *yishuv*" or pre-Zionist Jewish presence in the Land of Israel, they fear Heaven more than the agents of the modern Jewish state. Paradoxically, their anti-modern stance attracts many tourists who view the area as a kind of living museum of life in the *shtetlakh* (Jewish villages) of Eastern Europe, destroyed in the *Shoah* but magically preserved in the modern Middle East. To avoid conflict, the residents have posted signs at the entrances to the neighborhood to discourage visitors and admonish the undeterred to dress in keeping with the community's standards of modesty (*tsni'ut*). In some areas handrails divide walkways to allow men and women to walk separately, so as to avoid the accidental transfer of menstrual impurity. If you were so foolish as to drive your car through Meah Shearim on Shabbat, your vehicle might be stoned. But then, why would you? As a Jerusalemite you know which parts to avoid at certain times, and you know how to behave if you can't avoid them. One simply knows this is a world where the rules of an ordinary secular civil society do not obtain. It is also an area where the laws of the state of Israel are routinely ignored. To some, the state does not exist and where it intrudes on their turf, must be resisted. Certain groups, like Neturei Karta ("Guardians of the Holy City"), would prefer to live under Palestinian sovereignty. Ignoring the authority of the state comes at a price. Those who fail to apply for identity cards or register the births of their children forgo financial aid for their large families. In contrast to the majority of Arab Jerusalemites, many Haredi Jews vote in municipal and national elections giving clout to a slew of ultra-orthodox parties that, as long as their demands are met, give an edge to national-religious coalitions in the Knesset. The rapid natural growth of the ultra-orthodox community means that more neighborhoods are becoming Jewishly "religionized."[4] Urban planning in Jerusalem is only gradually beginning to meet the challenge of accommodating the needs of this internally diverse and growing segment of the city's Jewish population.[5]

For many Jews, modern Jerusalem, united under sovereign Jewish statehood, is like the awakening from a nightmare that lasted nearly 2,000 years. Even those who might be skeptical of ultimate redemption within the confines of mundane history believe something profound changed when Israel captured the Old City and returned to its most sacred places. Jewish sovereignty and presence at the Western Wall still moves Jews from across the world to tears of joy when they first arrive. (The same is true for many Christian pilgrims to the Holy Sepulchre.) The significance of Jerusalem in collective Jewish imagination cannot be overestimated. For Jews, Jerusalem has the power of a fundamental religious and national creed. Yet the meanings attached to Jerusalem and its holy places are complex and contested across the spectrum of Jewish political factions and religious movements in Israel and the diaspora. More simply put, now that the Jews have control of Jerusalem, they radically disagree on what to do with it.

In Jewish tradition, Jerusalem is *miqdash melekh*, royal sanctuary and location of first and second temple, the token of divine kingship and of the priestly calling of Israel, to be rebuilt by King Messiah at the end of days. Messianic hopes fueled by Ottoman rule brought Jews from within and without the far-flung boundaries of the empire back to Jerusalem in several waves. Early political Zionists, including Theodor Herzl, envisaged a modernist "new Jerusalem" alongside the old, while cultural Zionists like Martin Buber saw it as the epicenter of a spiritual renewal of Judaism across the diaspora. Since the near miraculous victory of June 1967, which followed upon a period when Jewish Israelis and Jews across the globe acutely feared a second Holocaust, Jewish resolve to hold on to united Jerusalem has become a fundamental creed. National-religious Jews see holding on to Jerusalem ("complete and united") as essential to Jewish statehood. They believe that Jerusalem is to be settled, controlled, built up, and held on to forever by collective Jewish action and, if necessary, by force. Among the ultra-orthodox Haredim are those, most vociferous among them the Neturei Karta, mentioned above, who reject Zionism and national self-redemption as a blasphemous rebellion against the divine decree of exile that can only be reversed by a divine decree of redemption.[6] Others, most notably those inspired by Rav Avraham Isaac Kook, the first Ashkenazic chief rabbi under the British Mandate, regard the modern Zionist enterprise and the establishment of the State of Israel as the "beginning of the sprouting of our redemption" (*reshit ts'mikhat ge'ulatenu*).[7] There is a widely shared religious sentiment that the victory of June 1967 was an act of divine providence (a biblical "war of YHWH") and that to trade "land for peace" is a cardinal sin. Some particularly inspired groups and organizations including the Temple Institute and Yeshivat Ateret Kohanim, located in the Muslim Quarter, are preparing for the inauguration of the Third Temple by weaving *kosher* garments for the priests and teaching members of the clans of *kohanim* and *leviim* the laws of sacrifice (see Figure 5). Under Minister of Culture and Sports Miri Regev (Bayit Yehudi), the Israeli government introduced knowledge about the temple and fostering appreciation for the messianic prospect of establishing a temple on the Temple Mount into the public school curriculum. Privately funded glossy websites projecting the past and

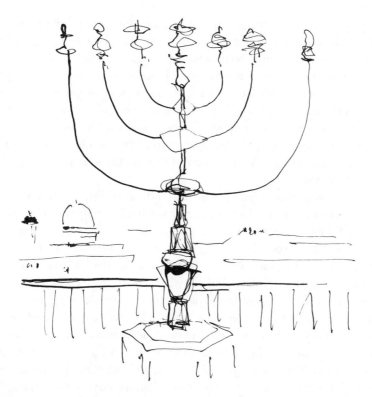

Figure 5   A golden Menorah, placed across from the Temple Mount anticipating the Third Temple. Illustration by Miriam Shenitzer.

future temple onto the Herodian platform currently occupied by Muslim buildings promote the messianic prerogative as an innocuous matter of information and pious imagination. Critics of this policy are wary that initiatives of this sort undermine the peace process and contribute to the mainstreaming of a fringe movement[8] by giving succor to radical "*meshikh-istim*" or "messianists" who would risk cataclysm to force the end.[9]

On a more mundane level, many Israelis either encounter the city on secular or religious school trips, or they simply live there, or they commute to their places of employment in one of the city's major industries of tourism, government, and education. Secular Israelis may be proud of the city as a national treasure or loathe it for the heavy financial and security burdens it imposes on the rest of the country. Not everyone appreciates the holy places or feels comfortable venturing into the unfamiliar territory of Arab East Jerusalem. There is a demographically significant secular Jewish flight from Jerusalem of young people who seek opportunity elsewhere. Setting aside economic factors, such as the high cost of living and the preference of Israel's high-tech industry for safer and less costly locations, many of those who turn their backs on Jerusalem are disheartened by the political stalemate, alienated by the mushrooming of garish hotels and apartment buildings designed to accommodate high-holiday tourism from abroad, or simply wish to escape the psychological pressures of the constantly simmering and periodically erupting inter-ethnic conflict. Israelis either love Jerusalem with a passion or they loathe it, but rarely are they indifferent toward it.

Jewish Jerusalemites include the descendants of former Ottoman subjects of Sephardic and Ashkenazi extraction, pious immigrants from South Arabia, Ethiopia, Central Asia, India, and the Caucasus, great-grandchildren of refugees from Czarist pogroms, and families whose elders were among the Zionist pioneers from Russia, Poland, the Ukraine, Romania, Germany, Austria, Hungary, and elsewhere in Europe. Their family trees include Zionists who built their colonies under late Ottoman and British rule, Jews who fled Nazi Germany and neighboring countries before and during World War II, and survivors of the concentration camps who sought refuge in the nascent Jewish state. There are Jews who can trace their origins to Syria, Iraq, Iran, Egypt, Morocco, and other North African and Middle Eastern countries, hailing from millennial communities destroyed or dismantled by the mass migrations of the decade following Israel's War of Independence. Recent waves of immigrants include hundreds of thousands of Russians who came to Israel following the collapse of the Soviet Union and, in the past decades, also ever more American Jews eager to support Israel, and French Jews fleeing a resurgence of anti-Semitism among France's Muslims of North African descent. Each of these groups represents cultures and civilizations in their own right, each of them has a story of weal and woe to pass down to their descendants, each one came with the hope for a better life in the land of Israel, and many of them experienced difficulties and disappointments that hardened into new grudges and resentments. This rich tapestry of migrations from across a wide range of cultures of origin explains to some degree why so many Jews and Israelis cling to this place as they do. For them, Jerusalem is their ancient homeland and, by divine, natural, and political-historical right, their one inalienable property on earth. The often difficult experience of imperfect absorption and renewed prejudice in a new place also explains some of the lingering alienation between some of these communities. It took the Jews of North African and Middle Eastern descent, collectively known as the *edah mizrahit*, until the late 1970s to find their political voice. In the 1977 elections, the *panterim sh'khorim* ("Black Panthers"), as the younger generation of North-African Jews called themselves, helped to unseat the Labor coalition that had ruled and shaped Israel since its founding and heaved Likud to power, creating what is now often referred to as the "second republic."

We will return to this modern city-in-flux, its immediate past and its present, in Part IV of this book. First, our task is to describe how this complex plurality of attachments came about. What predisposed a minor, thinly populated, and remote center of an ancient Near Eastern nation to attain such eminence and significance across time and space? What (and who) shaped the imagination of Muslims, Christians, and Jews so as to persuade them to look at Jerusalem with such longing? How did Jerusalem become the Holy City of Jews, Christians, and Muslims? To answer this deceptively simple question, we need to think about religion and the sacred as configured in the biblical tradition and modulated by its adopters. This, along with a bit of world history, is the task of parts II and III of this book.

Notes

1. Qur'an Sura 17.
2. On the Armenian Quarter of Jerusalem see Azarya (1984).
3. See Raheb (2014).
4. The word may not be good English, but I've liked it ever since I heard Moshe Zimmermann use it in a lecture.
5. See the study by Friedland and Hecht (2000). Jerusalem's former acting city engineer Osnat Post kindly introduced me to this and other complications faced by Jerusalem's municipal planners.
6. On Neturei Karta see Inbari (2016).
7. On Kook see Mirsky (2014).
8. See Klein (2010).
9. On Christian and Jewish movements to hasten the "end of days" see Gorenberg (2000). On movements to build the Third Temple see Inbari (2009). On the *makhteret* or Jewish underground and past attempts to blow up the Dome of the Rock see Sprinzak (1991) and (1999). On right-wing Jewish terrorism in Israel also see Pedahzur and Perliger (2009).

Part II
Biblical City

4

"Holy City": A Clarification of Terms

Jerusalem was not always a holy city, at least not more so, or in a more eminent sense, than other ancient cities. Jerusalem's extraordinary reputation is connected to the rise of Israel's national deity, YHWH, to the status of Almighty God. Name and conception of this deity spread to the ends of the earth, and with it the fame of Jerusalem. The cosmic significance Jerusalem achieves in late antique and medieval times rests on the transformation of ancient Jerusalem into "biblical" Jerusalem, the holy city of a holy book from Almighty God with a message of ultimate importance that came to sanction, and contest, Christian and Muslim imperial rule.

Jerusalem requires us to think about changes in religion. It requires us to think about the curious emergence, among the ancient Jews, of a rhetoric of exclusivity and covenant that positioned itself against a widely shared rhetoric of "mutual translatability" of cultic and religious practices. The Egyptologist Jan Assmann called this the "Mosaic distinction." This emphasis on difference did not stop with the Jews. What Israelite prophets condemned as forbidden idol worship, Christians repressed as paganism and Muslims subdued with the sword; Rome, Baghdad, and Istanbul claimed Jerusalem using scriptures inherited from the Jews in support of their own claims to divinely sanctioned rule. It is the Jerusalem of scripture that has forever invested the imagination of these communities with the utopian ideal of divine kingship realized on earth.[1]

Jerusalem: A Brief History, First Edition. Michael Zank.
© 2018 Michael Zank. Published 2018 by John Wiley & Sons Ltd.

We will look at the transformation of Jerusalem from an ordinary holy city of the ancient southern Levant into the Holy City of Jews, Christians, and Muslims in parts II and III of this book. The present chapter serves to clarify some of our terms. What do we mean by Judaism, Christianity, and Islam, by "religion," and by "holy" or "sacred"?

Conventional wisdom refers to Judaism, Christianity, and Islam as "Abrahamic"[2] religions. There are good reasons why they are classed together in this way. They are historically related and morphologically comparable, which is not to say that they are basically the same. Because of their global dissemination they are thought of as "world religions." Because of their common origin and shared typology they are also considered "western" religions, in contrast to the "eastern" religions of South and East Asia.

Neither Judaism, nor Christianity, nor Islam is internally homogeneous. Jews, Christians, and Muslims are divided by languages, beliefs, and practices. A Moroccan Jew shares language, culture, cuisine, and customs with her fellow Moroccans, just as, unbeknownst to himself, an American Jew may be more like an American Protestant in tastes and prejudice than he wants to admit. What then is the function of calling oneself a Jew, a Christian, or a Muslim? It may be helpful to think of these class names not as expressions of a shared culture but as declarations of solidarity. Solidarity with a co-religionist is an obligation, an article of faith. The co-religionist is a member of our "tribe" or nation. In other words, religions *are* tribes or nations, or they frequently act as such.[3]

Tribes or nations indicate our need for outer limits of solidarity. The naming of a common religious identity represents a strategy of boundary maintenance, whether such a boundary is one of belief, descent, or practice. Like the membership in an exclusive club, it indicates who is in and who is out. Conditions of membership may change. "I am a Jew," means different things in different times and contexts. For the apostle Paul, for example, to be a Jew meant "not Greek." Paul was not the first to think in terms of this particular binary but inherited and used it to make a point about the new identity of one who believes in Christ. What he meant to say was that the distinction between Jew and Greek no longer mattered, indirectly attesting to its importance to other Jews (and Greeks). The distinction was understood and shared by his readers, who would have seen it as an incommensurable difference, a radical either/or. To claim it no longer mattered was shocking news. The first mention of this binary appears in the Second Book of Maccabees, a work in praise of Judaism written no more then two centuries before Paul. Here the term Judaism is used to distinguish a certain way of life, based on loyal devotion to the paternal laws of Jerusalem, from a life characterized as Hellenistic. The difference was not necessarily a matter of belief but it entailed a difference in practice and material culture. Hellenists among the Jews drank imported wine, using amphorae adorned with scenes from Greek mythology, and poured libations to the gods. Those embracing *ioudaismos* were discouraged from doing so, or proudly shunned such "foreign" ways.[4] The Jews were not the only ones who constructed a distinctive identity using dietary laws. The Brahmins of India as well used food restrictions as a means to create and maintain exclusivity. The message of Second Maccabees was to export the exclusive way of life associated with the paternal laws of the Jews to Alexandria where Jews lived among Greeks and Egyptians.

For reasons of their own, Christians and Muslims adopted Jewish traditions without converting to Judaism. Put differently, they developed Jewish and other traditions in ways that no longer presupposed the Jewish people as the outer limit of solidarity. Among the Jewish traditions Christians adopted, as did the earliest followers of the Arabian prophet, was their orientation of prayer toward Jerusalem. They all believed the Jewish prophetic tradition and its emphasis on Jerusalem's centrality to be true and divine. Throughout the ages, biblical psalms of ascent to God's holy temple in Jerusalem played an outsized role in the fortification of Jerusalem in the hearts and minds of Christians. This proximity and commonality resulted in a confusion of identities that required a struggle of separation. The fallout from this struggle is present in the anti-Jewish rhetoric of Christians and Muslims. Christianity and Islam were therefore constructed in processes of differentiation that also affected what became the Judaisms of the Christian and Islamic worlds. The relative, contextual, and political criteria by which our "tribes" are distinguished are nevertheless frequently phrased as essential statements of identity, difference, and excellence. Boundaries must be maintained, and so they are. Since most believers never visit the sacred convocations of others they have learned to despise, it largely escapes them how similar they often are.

While the terms Judaism, Christianity, and Islam suggest differences that we need to call into question, the term "religion" we apply to these and other cultural formations suggests a sameness that we may also call into question. Religion is a term of art, meant to describe a human phenomenon or cluster of human behaviors. Late nineteenth- to mid-twentieth-century western theorists of religion tended to emphasize the common religion in all religions, be it the feeling or attachment of the individual to what he or she considers divine[5] or be it the *mysterium tremendum/fascinosum* of "the holy" as such.[6] This modern usage of the term foregrounds subjective beliefs and experiences at the expense of social norms of behavior, the materiality of practice, and the social stratification entailed in maintaining public religious order. Judaism, Christianity, and Islam refer to collective social, political, cultural, and civilizational behaviors. They constitute a plurality of internally differentiated universes of symbolic forms, practices, and vocabularies that form and regulate particular communities. Religions guide us in how to eat, pray, and love. But traditionally they also furnish societies with civil and criminal laws, govern public and private affairs, determine their customs, and guide their thought and behavior. In this sense, religion is not just personal but public, not just spiritual but social and comprehensive.

Jews, Christians, and Muslims think of this comprehensive order as revealed by a transcendent but personal deity through special (angelic and prophetic) individuals and attested by saints and martyrs. It is something experienced in ritual prayer and mystical devotion, and reinforced by "religious virtuosos," the learned or charismatic priests, rabbis, imams, theologians, and lawyers that are specialists in their respective tradition. What these traditions call "true" religion comprises and reconciles within itself (in principle and over time) the natural, the social-political, and the personal-individual. The messianic end of these religions is divine rule on earth, a state of justice, collective and personal happiness, natural equilibrium, and perfection. The symbol of this state is paradise, or the Garden of Eden; an image derived from the royal pleasure gardens of the ancient Near East. Jews, Christians, and Muslims locate the hidden gates of paradise in Jerusalem. The Holy City provides the proscenium for the final drama of history as envisaged in Jewish, Christian, and Islamic apocalyptic imagination. It is part of the shared inventory of these universes of symbolic forms.

What predisposes a city to become part of such a shared inventory of symbolic forms? The ancient Near Eastern city was a conduit of order in a world threatened by forces of natural chaos. Cities were places where a widely revered deity took residence. Wherever a god took residence, there was order and divine blessing. Ancient Semitic mythologies narrated the origin of the gods (theogony) as the result of a war by which the forces of primordial chaos were vanquished (theomachy) and the tenuous order of the habitable world became possible. For a god like Marduk to reside in a place conferred on it the honor of serving as one of the palaces built by the gods in honor of this vanquisher of the watery chaos of old. Many Babylonian cities were named in his honor. Cities were temples, palaces of the gods, the economy that sustained the priest-kings of those cities guaranteed the continued blessing of the tutelary deity, and human labor fed the gods.

In contrast, biblical tradition and its adopters speak of God as creating heaven and earth "without opposition".[7] Here the forces of chaos are active on the historical rather than the natural plane. The apocalyptic trend within these traditions revives the old chaos-dragon myth in moralized and historicized form, placing it at the end of "this age." The place of this final battle is Armageddon (a biblical reference to the Bronze-Age Canaanite city of Megiddo), the place of final judgment: the valley of Jehoshaphat, located just outside the ancient walls of Jerusalem.

The shift of the great battle from the beginning to the end of time changes the subject of the drama. It is no longer a battle between the gods of chaos and the gods of order but a battle between good and evil people and regimes. The focus is now on the chosen few, the sacred remnant, the *ecclesia*, the *umma*. The heroes are not dying and resurrecting gods but dying and resurrecting nations, saints, and martyrs. I like to think of this shift as a kind of "demotization" of ancient mythology, a shift from aristocratic to demotic or popular agents. Biblical religion and its adopters, i.e. "biblicate" societies, emphasize "chosen people" rather than divine or semi-divine individuals, though representative heroism remains important and it returns with a vengeance when Judaism is admixed with Hellenism. The shift in perspective from the natural chaos of ancient mythology to a final battle between good and evil also changes the semantics of the Holy City. Instead of a place of immutable order, it becomes a *lieu memoire* of divine judgment and a symbol of hope for future redemption. Jerusalemite symbols of sacred pasts and communal longings are many. They include ruins, sacred relics, rocks, and empty tombs.

Some linguistic remarks on "holy" and related terms may be helpful as well. Like its German cognate *heil*, the English term "holy" evokes a state of wholeness, health, completeness, peace, and well-being. The most fitting Hebrew equivalent of holy in this sense is *shalom* (Arabic: *salaam*). The Hebrew word *kadosh* that is often translated as "holy" (as in "you shall be holy, for I YHWH your god am holy" Leviticus 19:2) literally refers to difference or separation. The verse just mentioned should therefore be rendered "you will be different/separate/other, because I am different/separate/other"). In other words, it signals the very struggle for self-differentiation we described above as the primary impulse of the ancient Judaic heritage adopted and adapted by Christians and Muslims as well. In the Bible, YHWH is unlike all other gods, he is unique among the gods, an unconventional god, a "living" god, whose very name indicates one whose existence may be apparent but whose being cannot be defined once and for all (see Exodus 3:14). The people of this god should be different, distinguished, special. The word *kadosh* itself does not suggest by what quality or virtue these people ought to distinguish themselves.

"Holy" is commonly used as a synonym for "sacred." But the latter derives from a Latin word that invokes *sacrificium* or sacrifice, which refers to an act of binding and a curse. The two ideas may be combined as cause and effect: only through the vicarious sacrifice, death, and the cursing of the victim can a state of holiness be achieved. This, in a nutshell, is the classical Christian doctrine of atonement. But it also applies to some of the sacrifices performed at the ancient temple in Jerusalem, which, in this regard, hardly differed from other sanctuaries in the ancient world.

Jerusalem is associated with the sacred with its elements of binding and cursing – as in the binding of Isaac on Mount Moriah that Jewish tradition locates at the Temple Mount in Jerusalem – and with the holy in the sense of wholeness or completeness. Its original name (*urushalim*) is a homage to a Canaanite god whose name *shalem* suggests temporal closure, completeness, and hence contentedness, an apt name for a remote mountain fortress. Jerusalem was not exclusively devoted to this deity. Several pre-Israelite kings of Jerusalem brought their own chief goddess, the Hurrian Hebat ("mother of all living"), to Salem's Founding. The induction of YHWH's ark and the building of a permanent house for the Israelite deity "YHW/ YHWH" (Yahu or Yahweh) under the Davidids did not fundamentally alter the city's character. As described in the Bible, the acquisition of a preexisting Jebusite "threshing floor" as the final "resting place" for the Ark of the Covenant, as narrated in the biblical books of Samuel, Kings, and Chronicles, brought symbolic closure to the Israelite history of exodus, wandering, and conquest. Solomon's throne name pays homage to the ancient Jerusalemite deity *shalem*. In narrative terms, Solomon's reign represents the closure of an eminent past. It also precipitates the dramatic decline that was to follow this high-water mark of Israelite history. To understand this, we need the third term, *kadosh*, which is central to the biblical idea of God. Hailed and condemned at the same time, Solomon's construction of a permanent house for YHWH renders YHWH like other gods who take residence on earth. Solomon in his unsurpassed wisdom becomes the unwitting symbol of the limits of human wisdom. This, too, is part of the mystique of Jerusalem.

As we shall see in the following chapters, Jerusalem's character – not as holy or sacred, but different – comes to the fore in revolutionary changes in the city's constitution that occurred centuries later when the very cults introduced or tolerated by Solomon and his successors were banished, sacred places desecrated, ritual practices outlawed, and altars destroyed, all in a situation when Jerusalem accrued new political significance as the central city of a neo-Israelite empire, in the context of a series of rebellions against the Assyrian Empire (late eighth century BCE and late seventh century BCE). This primordial moment of iconoclasm was enshrined in sacred history but its lessons were not immediately learned. The historical moment receded but it was not forgotten. Preserved in biblical literature, its memory exerted transformative force in the imagination of later generations.

For much of the second Jewish commonwealth (516/5 BCE–70 CE) Jerusalem functioned as a temple city where ritual sacrifices were offered that maintained a system of cultic purity on which depended the sustained presence of "the God who lives in Jerusalem," the conveyance of his blessings on the land and its resources, and the protection of its residents from famine, poverty, illness, and war. The sacred (in the above stated sense) was here harnessed to the maintenance of a nation and its way of life, which already then extended beyond the borders of the land itself. That geographic extension of blessing conveyed from Jerusalem to Jewish colonies abroad was the condition for the spreading of the fame of Jerusalem's deity to new boundaries and nations, the veneration of the "God of Israel" among god-fearing non-Jews. This system of temple devotion, which welcomed the gifts of non-Jews, was free of apocalyptic urgency. In terms of its phenomenology and practice, it was Solomonic in character and cognate with the sacred urban centers of the surrounding civilizations. The efficacy of the sacrifices and the pleasure of the deity with the ruling elite were called into question by dissenting Jews of late Hasmonean and early Roman times. It is among these sectarians that the biblical accounts of saintly kings and martyred prophets resonated and inspired their defiance of the powerful kings and empires of their own time. In the manner of modern Salafists, these Jewish rigorists yearned for a return to the putatively pure and saintly beginnings of the nation preserved in sacred literature.

It is a curious fact of history, one that defies any simple explanation, that this complex Judaic heritage of defiance, dissent, and difference became the founding ideology of entire nations and empires. This process, which was neither simple nor straightforward, came with attraction and repulsion, affirmation and negation, adoption and rejection, appropriation and reinterpretation of various parts of that heritage. Jerusalem's role in the history of early Christianity is ambivalent. As long as it represented the Jews' rejection of Jesus with the presaged destruction of the temple at the hand of the Romans as the just divine punishment for that rejection, Jerusalem was to many Christians more of a reminder of divine justice than a token of divine mercy. This changed in the fourth century CE, when Roman Emperor Constantine ordered a grand redesign of the city, restoring the city's name and biblical holiness/wholeness and making it a central place in the symbolic landscape of the *oikumene*, the inhabited world ruled by the Vicar of Christ *pantocrator* on earth. Three centuries later, the pride of Christendom was wounded, when Jerusalem fell to the Arabs.

Islam did not appear as a "new religion." Instead, the prophet's voice echoed a tradition reaching back to Adam. Emerging in a world riven by Roman and Persian imperial competition, Islam began as a movement of unification across the carefully policed boundaries of doctrine that separated Chalcedonians from non-Chalcedonians, Christians from Jews, Gnostics from Parsees. Over the course of the first centuries of conquest and rule, Islam solidified into the ideal of a unified *umma*, a newly formed post-tribal community of believers. Early Muslim sources attest that Muslims paid homage to Jerusalem as the direction of prayer, affirming the common ritual orientation of Jews and Christians. The new realm extended from North Africa to Persia and eventually grew to become one of the largest continuous land-based empires the world had ever seen, reaching from Spain to Central Asia. Syria-Palestine, the Christian and Jewish Holy Land, was the symbolic and geographic center of early Muslim power. The predominant populations were fiercely and diversely Christian, though internally much divided in regional and doctrinal terms. Under these circumstances, the Umayyads adopted and developed Jerusalem's long-neglected temple area and rebuilt it, to affirm the continuity of their dispensation with the biblical past, a restoration of the city's original holiness and wholeness. Architectural form, placement within the symbolic geography of the Holy City, experimentation with new images on coins, and other means of dissemination coalesced into a message that affirmed that Umayyad caliphs ruled not just as the legitimate commanders of the faithful (*amir al-mu'minin*) but also as the representatives of Allah on earth (*khalifat Allah*) and protectors of every "people of the book" (*ahl al-kitab*).

Judaism, Christianity, and Islam are eminently political religions. They are systems of identity formation and boundary policing that come with narratives of superiority, anteriority, authority, and other aspects of situating themselves vis-à-vis their proximate others. Jerusalem is a key symbol in this kaleidoscope of political group narratives. It anchors their respective aspirations in space. Jerusalem is a place where cultic practice, liturgical prayer, scripture and interpretation, visual art and architecture, the spoken word, and other means of dissemination contribute to a visualization of a political ideal, the rule of God on earth, which is either seen as triumphantly present or as tragically absent. Jerusalem, with its role in sacred history, is the place where Jews, Christians, and Muslims – each in their own way – vie for presence and/or dominance because they remember and venerate it as the place of divine presence in the past and where they anticipate God's return in the end of days.

Every sacred place is associated with divine presence. What sets the Jerusalem of scripture and of our "biblicate" civilizations apart from other ancient temple cities is its role in the religio-political imagination of Jews, Christians, and Muslims. This is not an abstract theoretical or distant historical observation. Jerusalem's ability to cast the spell of religious meaning onto the political sphere is in full evidence today. Without Jerusalem, the conflict between Israelis and Palestinians could be conceived as no more than a political or territorial conflict among others. With Jerusalem in the mix, this is not so. In Jerusalem and the "Holy Land" the religious and the political constantly interpenetrate and permeate one another. It will be all the more useful therefore, in this history, not to separate the religious from the secular and political, especially where traditional sources draw no such distinction. In ancient times religious and political spheres were not separate. Every city was a cultic unit, every elite a priesthood. Over the centuries and millennia, elites and forms of political organization changed but, until the modern era, the religious and the political were always to some extent intermingled, at least when it came to the world of rule and governance. Though the secular approach to law and politics has solid antecedents in Greek and Roman sources, with the rise of Christianity, and later with Islam, this approach was eclipsed, subdued, and integrated into a framework of divinely sanctioned, providential rule in the name of the one true God. As much as Jews became accustomed to life without political sovereignty, the framework of collective existence was the notion of exile (*galut*), giving Jewish life the character of a fundamentally tragic absence of redemption in the sense of national self-determination as in the days of old, a mood between nostalgia for return and enthusiasm for creating the right conditions for a coming of messiah ("speedily in our days").[8] Zionism – initially a secular political movement created at a time when

Europeans felt confident that demographic problems could be solved by means of large-scale social engineering – has meanwhile been usurped by a religious settler movement aiming to redeem the "complete land of Israel" (*erets yisrael ha-sh'lemah*). Similarly, the landscape of Palestinian nationalism, once dominated by a staunchly secular post-colonialist liberation movement, is now divided between an increasingly popular camp of Islamists and a shrinking secular *Fatah*, widely perceived as a corrupt and ineffectual American-Israeli puppet. That's where things stand today. Here as elsewhere around the globe, the European Enlightenment model of privatizing religion and secularizing politics has given way to a new wave of religious politics and political religions. History shows that the combination of religion and politics was not always inevitably poisonous and a recipe for conflict. When separation between religion and state was not an option, religiously sanctioned rule could serve as a rational way of organizing thriving and diverse civilizations. In other words, religion should not be an excuse for exclusivity and intolerance.

History provides no perfect model for emulation. The future is always different from the past. But historiography might help to defang some of the poison created by today's claims to represent the authentic voice of the past. Our new fundamentalists, those who fabricate "usable pasts" or rely on the authority of poorly understood religious traditions, will perhaps pay little attention to a work of secular and critical historiography. But the many people of good will who are now, and always will be, in the majority may take some solace from a sanguine approach to the religion and politics attached to this (un-)holy city.

Notes

1. Cf. Zank (2014).
2. Cf. Hughes (2012).
3. Classics of the social study of religion are Karl Marx, Émile Durkheim, and Max Weber. Also see the work of Marcel Mauss, Claude Lévi-Strauss, Ernest Gellner, Michel Foucault, Clifford Geertz, and Peter Berger. See Fenn (2009), Furseth (2006).
4. See Berlin (2005).
5. See Schleiermacher (1996 [1799]).
6. See Otto (1923 [1917]).
7. Levenson (1994).
8. From the conclusion of the Ashkenazic version of the daily *Amidah* prayer.

5

The Making of a Memorable Place

Cities did not exist from the beginning; they are latecomers in the development of human evolution. Historical time – in contrast to prehistoric times – coincides with the history of urbanization. Nineteenth-century historians looked to Greek and Roman cities to explain the origin of the city as an extension of the religious and economic life of kinship groups.[1] This somewhat romantic view of the origin of cities, of their rituals of founding and covenant, and of the sacerdotal rites entrusted to an aristocratic-civic leadership, sharply contrasts with the complex realities of the cities of ancient Egypt, Mesopotamia, and Asia Minor that came into view with the archaeological and epigraphic finds of the later nineteenth and early twentieth centuries. Gilgamesh, the great hero of a saga of Old Babylonian vintage diligently copied for ages, was violent, impulsive, and a slayer of the sacred bull of the gods, a rebel who only cared for his own immortality and, in the end, not only lost his best friend but had to resign himself to the fate of all humans. Gilgamesh represents the power, craftiness, and lust for life of an urban creature. His sly tale of self-wrought elevation and comeuppance resembles the wisdom of the Hebrew Bible, where the first builder of a city is an agriculturist who slays his peaceful pastoralist brother, and the megalomania of the urban landscape of Babylon is the reason that humans lose their primordial common language. In a nod to biblical anti-urbanism, the urban historian Lewis Mumford argued that cities are not just a break in

Jerusalem: A Brief History, First Edition. Michael Zank.
© 2018 Michael Zank. Published 2018 by John Wiley & Sons Ltd.

terms of human development, but the forces that led to the creation of cities continue to pose a fundamental threat to human life as well as to the ecological balance of the earth.[2]

Biblical wisdom was forged at the gates of Israelite and Judahite towns, where elders sat in judgment, literally on the fence between city and non-city. One of the Semitic words for city, *medina*, refers to the city as the seat of judgment (*din*). From an urban high priestly perspective, the non-city appeared as a place of exposure, a desert where Azazel ruled, a vengeful demon assuaged by a goat sent annually, like the virgins sacrificed to the Cretan Minotaur. But from the perspective of the village, sunk into undignified dependence on the House of Omri, the House of David, and similar urban elites whose *corvée* they were forced to work before tending to their own olive groves, vines, and fig trees, the city looked like a precarious dabbling in the ways of the Egyptians and the Canaanites. To wit, the oracles of Amos, a dresser of Sycamore trees from Tekoa who condemned the Israelite cult center at Bethel, and those of another Judahite villager, Micah of Moresheth, who spoke against the two capitals of Israel and Judah, Samaria and Jerusalem.

Jerusalem's fame is woven from a tale of rise, decline, destruction, and restoration. When first one and then the other royal center of Israel fell to greater, more voracious powers commissioned by divine justice, the wisdom of the elders, the erstwhile oracles of doom now enshrined in artful poetry and carefully tended by prophetic schools and priestly scribes, turned into a new bedrock of writing upon which a new city was to be built, one so beautiful and just, so full of instruction and wisdom and guided by peace and judgment, that it was to be a model to the nations, a place where many would flock and worship the God of Israel, creator of heaven and earth.

The biblical scriptures pivot around the relationship between YHWH, a god of enigmatic origin and being ("I Am Who I Am") who is elevated beyond all ordinary gods, and a people, the children of Israel, who were brought out of Egypt, the land of slavery, to inherit a land promised to their forefathers. Land matters more than city, even as Torah and biblical historiography abound with references to a place YHWH was to choose from among all of the tribes, "for his name to reside."[3] This center is not named in the Torah, where several contenders for this dignity appear by name, especially Shekhem, Bethel, and Mount Gerizim, places associated with the northern Israelites rather than with the southern Judahites, while Jerusalem is not explicitly mentioned at all.[4] Long after Jerusalem's sacredness was well established in Jewish and Christian imagination, Islam's sacred scripture, the Qur'an, is similarly coy about locating its "distant sanctuary" in any particular earthly location. But this coyness, equally puzzling in Torah and Qur'an, far from diminishes the city's holiness in the eyes of the believers.

The opposite is the case: just as the Holy One's name must not be uttered, the city of the God for whom silence is praise is rendered sacrosanct by hints and ruses. To refrain from expressly naming the Holy City allows for the divine choice of any place in this transient world to remain a divine prerogative; and, in any case, to associate the maker of heaven and earth with any place on earth remains a paradox and a theological conundrum.

In the Jewish scriptures land matters more than city, and what matters most of all are people, law, and the divine lawgiver and landowner who gives the land to whom he pleases. Built into this story is an echo of the dispossession of earlier masters of the land, those Amorites, Hittites, Hurrians, and Canaanites (a vague, generic term for a region, not a particular nation) who had built the cities "inherited" by the Israelites. According to the biblical narrative, these nations were driven out so that Israel could live in houses they had not built, and reap the fruit of vineyards they had not planted. According to this narrative, the Canaanite nations were expelled by the divine landowner because their sins had become too much. The land had vomited them out. This is stated as a warning example to the Israelites (Leviticus 24). The Israelite takeover of Canaan is couched in the language of cultic purification ("you must put them to the ban"). Lest one jump to conclusions about Israel's genocidal past, the point of the story seems, to me at least, to be that what ought to have happened by divine right (the driving out of the Canaanites) was not in fact accomplished. The Jewish scriptures themselves give an indication of the idealized nature of Israel's conquest. According to the Book of Judges, the indigenous people were never driven out with the requisite ruthlessness, which accounts for the fact that Israel was infected by their disease of "*idolitis*," the worship of false gods.[5] This explains why Israelite hold on the land turned out to be as tenuous as that of their predecessors. The Hexateuch (Torah plus Joshua) asserts that the divine side of the bargain had been upheld with the conquest under Joshua, but Judges proceeds on the assumption that the Israelites had a hard time fighting for the cities, which were still in the hand of their adversaries, that they were not as united in their struggle as they should have been, that their leaders were neither devoted to "worshiping YHWH alone" nor obedient to the laws of Moses, and that they therefore required frequent divine intervention, so they themselves would not perish or submit to corruption. YHWH had to empower individual "judges" with his fighting spirit. Those were "the bad days when there was no king in Israel."

The biblical historians suggest that the Israelites were latecomers in Canaan, that the land used to be cultivated by others before it was inherited by the sons of Jacob, who went on to establish kingship among themselves "like other nations." Though successful for a while, the seats of power ruled by Israelite and Judahite kings, high up in the central highlands of the southern Levant, were eventually destroyed, a loss that biblical historiographers blame on the sins of kings who did what was evil in the eyes of YHWH: a tale of woeful nostalgia for the good old days of David and Solomon, Hezekiah and Josiah, the few good apples in a rotten bunch.

In the Torah, this is prefaced by a patriarchal story that commences the tale of Israelite origins not with the exodus from Egypt but with the wanderings of *Avram*, meaning the exalted father, and his wife Sarai ("my princess"), who hailed from the city of "Ur of the Chaldeans" and entered Canaan via Haran in Northern Mesopotamia. *Ur kashdim* links the story of Abraham to the neo-Babylonians who destroyed Jerusalem in 586 BCE and exiled much of the city's elite. This tale, which now introduces the patriarchal saga located *in* the land, speaks the language of the exiled community of a time when these stories mattered most, the Persian age when Jews were encouraged to migrate and rebuild Jerusalem. Israelite history, as narrated in Genesis, thus begins (again) with the encouragement to leave a city they called home, and put down roots in a land promised by YHWH.

Key Dates (1800 BCE–70 CE)

c. 1800	Jerusalem mentioned in Egyptian magical texts
c. 1350	Jerusalem mentioned in Amarna correspondence
c. 1200	Decline of Canaanite city states
c. 930	Rise of Israelite kingdom (the "House of Omri")
722/1	Assyrians destroy Samaria; Jerusalem grows
701	Sennacherib's siege of Jerusalem; destruction averted
640	Assyrian empire collapses
622	Josiah's acts of centralization
586	Nebuchadnezzar of Babylon destroys Jerusalem
539	Cyrus of Persia enters Babylon
516	Jerusalem rededicated ("Second Temple period")
332	Alexander conquers Egypt (Hellenistic age)
300	Jerusalem under Ptolemaic rule
198	Jerusalem under Seleucid rule
168/7	Maccabean revolt against Antiochus IV
129–63	Period of independence (Hasmonean rule)
63 BCE–66 CE	Indirect Roman rule
66–70	Jewish uprising against Roman rule
70	Jerusalem destroyed by Titus Flavius the younger

The biblical historians accurately report that Jerusalem, too, belonged to others before it became the City of David. The Bible refers to the pre-Davidic rulers of the city as "Jebusites," a nation not mentioned in any ancient sources and most likely a ruse (literally: "those he has trampled," without naming who did the trampling).[6] In archaeological terms a Bronze Age city (roughly equivalent to the Mycenaean age in Greek archaeology), *urushalim* rose to significance around 1800 BCE when it is first mentioned in Egyptian execration texts, bowls or figurines inscribed with spells and smashed in apotropaic rites of magic.[7] Around the middle of the second millennium, Egyptian-dominated Canaan – famed for the purple dye produced in Tyre, lucrative for its corn, olive, and wine production, and coveted as a hub of land and sea trade – was conquered by the Hittites, who destroyed the Hurrian kingdom of Mitanni and competed with an Egypt mired in the self-absorbed reforms of Amenophis IV, better known as Akhenaten, a man whose acts of reformation were considered so sacrilegious that he was blotted out of Egyptian king lists. A fourteenth-century BCE Jerusalemite king of Jerusalem appears in the diplomatic correspondence with the Egyptian court at Akhet Aten (Tel el-Amarna).[8] The theophoric part of Abdi-Heba's name identifies him as a Hurrian devotee of *Hebat*, the "mother of all living" and possibly model of the biblical Eve who shares her name and epithet.[9]

In his fawning letters, the Hurrian king of Jerusalem seeks help against the *hapiru*, bands of "lawless" people harassing those among the city-state rulers who remained loyal to their Egyptian suzerain. Among the rebels were some of these cities' kings who had defected and joined the rebels. Canaanite city-states included fortresses like Megiddo that dominated the fertile plains of the littoral, and port cities, including Tyre and Sidon. This political and economic system eventually succumbed to the combined woes of foreign invasions (the sea-faring people, later settled as the "Philistines"), social upheaval (the *hapiru*), climate change (desertification), and Egyptian inaction. When Israel made its first appearance on the scene (on the Merneptah Stele, c. 1209 BCE) as having been "utterly destroyed, its seed is no more," the Bronze Age was coming to an end, cities were in ruins, and international commerce had ground to a halt. Out of the ashes arose new entities, forging new tribal identities and solidarities out of the common experience of destruction, flight, and survival, among them the common memory of *hapiru* origins. Israel had indeed escaped Egyptian slavery.[10]

Iron Age or later biblical historiographers remembered the collapse of the Canaanite system as a summary "driving out" of the nations that had held sway over the region before the Israelite conquest. Among these nations were the Amorites or Amurru, a Semitic people from Babylonia who had introduced Akkadian language and cuneiform writing into the world of international diplomacy; the Hurrians (the biblical Horites), who had their kingdom in Mitanni (roughly: modern Kurdistan) and were famed for their archery; and the Anatolian-based Hittites, who had wrested the Levant from Egyptian control. All of these are remembered as driven out before the Hebrews (=*hapiru*?), a band of escaped slaves, who settled on both sides of the Jordan, though mostly in the central highlands of the southern Levant, the Promised Land, the Land of Israel.

According to 2 Samuel 5, the Jebusite city's unlikely conquest was the feat of David, a Judahite warrior from Bethlehem who, after ruling the Judahites from Hebron, rose to kingship over all of the Israelite tribes. The biblical story of the origin of kingship in Israel, broadly narrated in the Books of Samuel, sanctions the consolidation of Israelite power in the hands of a Judahite dynasty. The original literary model for this rags-to-riches story, familiar to readers of the Bible from the biography of Moses, is the life of Sargon of Agade, founder of the Akkadian Empire. David's story is modeled on recognizable tropes of ancient storytelling.

Despite the dreaded change in constitution from charismatic leadership to dynastic rule ("a king like other nations," 1 Samuel 8) and despite enduring skepticism against human kings (Judges 9), David's kingship is prophesied to last "forever" (2 Samuel 7). The conquest of "Jebus" or the "Fortress of Zion," as the place is called in that context, is accomplished either by stealth or by force, or in fact peacefully, since the Jebusites are said to have continued to reside with the Judahites "to this day" (see Map 4). This friendly relationship between the Davidids and an antecedent elite is further underscored when David purchases the future grounds of the temple from "Arauna (Ornan) the Jebusite" (2 Samuel 24:16ff, 1 Chronicles 21). The only other time someone buys rather than conquers sacred ground is Abraham's purchase of the burial ground for Sarah in Hebron. These stories are adduced even today in disputes between Jews and Muslims over the right to "own" the Temple Mount and the Tombs of the Patriarchs, known to Muslims as the "two noble sanctuaries" of Palestine.

It is important to note that the story of the rise of the House of David is embedded in a prophetic narrative that looks at the rise and fall of the northern kingdom of Israel from a southern Judahite perspective. This narrative was forged in the wake of the destruction of Israel by the neo-Assyrian King Sargon II, who put an end to a Syro-Israelite uprising against Assyrian suzerainty that culminated in the obliteration of Samaria in 722/1 BCE.

Judah refused to join the anti-Assyrian coalition between Samaria and Damascus that precipitated Assyrian action, and it may have been Jerusalem's King Ahaz's call for Assyrian help against his northern cousins that provided Sargon with a *casus belli*. Sargon destroyed first Damascus and then Samaria, the royal center of the Israelites, exiled the rebels and their families, and integrated the vanquished territories into the Assyrian provincial administration.

Jerusalem not only survived unscathed but her gamble paid off. Hitherto in the shadow of her more powerful and ambitious northern rival, Samaria, the city was now free of regional competition and in possession of every advantage of friendly relations with the empire. Allied with Assyria but free of its most oppressive taxes, Jerusalem became a haven for Israelite refugees. In the aftermath of the destruction of Samaria, Jerusalem's population swelled to more than 10 times its prior size[11] (see Map 5). Judahite King Hezekiah, emboldened by a weakening of Assyria at a moment of dynastic transition, made himself the head of an anti-Assyrian coalition aimed at shaking off the Assyrian yoke altogether. He fortified the city[12] and also provided more than 40 other cities with fortifications and provisions in the case of a siege. In 701 BCE, the Assyrian Sennacherib neutralized Hezekiah by laying siege to Jerusalem and destroyed dozens of outlying fortified cities that crumbled under the onslaught. In his victory stele, Sennacherib boasts to have caught Hezekiah the Judahite "like a bird in a cage."[13] According to the detailed and dramatic account in the book of Kings (2 Kings 18–19), Jerusalem is saved by a miracle. The siege is lifted because of a pestilence that breaks out among the Assyrian troops. Assyrian and biblical sources affirm that Judah paid tribute and hence acknowledged Assyrian suzerainty. But the important fact was that Jerusalem had survived: temporarily diminished in power, but with its walls, population, and the House of David intact. This "miracle of 701," as I like to call it, cemented the reputation of Jerusalem as the place "YHWH chose for his name to reside." An empire responsible for the destruction of Israel-Samaria, a force of hitherto unknown speed, strength, and ruthlessness, left Jerusalem alone, a visceral attestation to the power of YHWH and his resolve to act on behalf of "Mount Zion, the city of the great king" (Psalm 48:2).

In the event, this Zion, pride of a neo-Israelite kingdom ruled by the House of David, also fell and was destroyed, a fact that helped to create a more complicated view of Jerusalem and its status among those who called her the city "YHWH chose for his name to reside."[14] In the war of words between kings and prophets contemporary to the Babylonian threat to

Jerusalem's cherished independence, Ezekiel – a Jerusalemite priest in exile – calls Jerusalem a foundling of Amorite and Hittite parentage, an ingrate, and a whore (Ezekiel 16). Much of biblical literature, written or edited in the wake of Jerusalem's destruction in 586 BCE at the hands of neo-Babylonian King Nebuchadnezzar II (r. 605–562 BCE), pivots around the drama of the rise, destruction, and re-founding of the city.

Jerusalem was founded anew in 516/5 BCE, following the Persian conquest of Babylon. The founder of the Achaemenid Persian Empire, Cyrus II of Anshan (d. 530), is gratefully remembered in the Bible. A late exilic prophet of the school of Isaiah calls Cyrus YHWH's "anointed."[15] Under Persian rule (539–332 BCE), Jerusalem was revived and resettled as a walled temple city[16] serving as the administrative center of *Yehud*, a sub-province of the satrapy of *avar-nahara* or Trans-Euphratene (see Map 6). The absence of kingship indicates that the city did not then regain its former independence. In the late fourth century BCE, the Macedonians commanded by Alexander "the Great" (356–323 BCE) conquered the Jewish temple city. For about a century, Jerusalem was dominated by the Egyptian successors (*diadochoi*) of Alexander, the Ptolemies, then it was captured by the Syrian Seleucids (198 BCE), a regime change that caused a crisis in Jerusalem mentioned in the Book of Daniel and amply described in First and Second Maccabees, written by historians on behalf of the family that emerged as the new Jewish rulers, the Hasmoneans. Hasmonean rule came to an end when the Romans under Pompey and his successors reorganized Syria and Egypt (63 BCE). Roman rule brought about Jerusalem's redevelopment under their Idumean client and "king of the Jews," Herod "the Great" (r. 40–4 BCE), remembered in the New Testament for his "murder of the babes" of Bethlehem. The last age of Jewish independence ended in a major rebellion against the Roman hegemon during which the Herodian temple was destroyed (70 CE). The last three centuries of Jerusalem's ancient Jewish history – from 200 BCE, when the Seleucids took the southern Levant, until 70 CE, when Titus destroyed Jerusalem – saw a proliferation of religio-political movements ("sects" or "parties") and abundant literary production, though most books produced at this stage were later rejected by the Jewish sages who reconstituted Jewish life in post-destruction Roman Palestine. Christians, on the other hand, retained much of this second string of literature and integrated it into their "Old Testament" or, in the case of the Protestant Bible, placed it into a secondary canon, referred to as the Apocrypha or "Hidden Books." To them, it was the story of their origins out of the "remains of the Jews."[17]

The idea of the city's fate as determined by divine *fiat* and as a measure of the degree to which Israel complied with the laws of YHWH emerged from the historical experience of a people who established two kingdoms among other, similar and related, local powers in Iron Age Canaan, that eventually succumbed to the much greater and more ruthless forces wielded by the Assyrian and neo-Babylonian empires. Biblical literature preserved memories of a *hapiru* past, reaching back to the Bronze Age, and it embedded the rise and fall of the kingdoms between laws issued in the desert (the precarious space beyond the fertile hills and plains of Canaan) and prophetic oracles aimed at reminding kings and commoners of the true owner of the land, the real king and judge, and his standards of righteousness and justice as the condition of tenure in a land flowing with milk and honey.

Even with the aid of archaeology and ancient history, biblical literature contains puzzles, riddles, and contradictions. Scripture speaks in many voices, and different readers draw different lessons and conclusions from this ancient body of text. More than just a matter of scholarly debates, these unresolved paradoxes confer a mystique on Jerusalem that has kept that holy city alive in Jewish, Christian, and Muslim imagination across the globe.

We have now briefly scanned the city's ancient history, its entry into the purview of Israelites and Judahites, the national hopes and aspirations the Jews attached to the city after the demise of Samaria-Israel, and the growth of Jerusalem as a neo-Israelite capital under Hezekiah and his successors. Law and prophecy added contingencies and provisions to ownership and permanence, which turned the fate of Jerusalem into a spectacle or a morality tale of sorts, leaving a city – believed by its rulers to have been rendered impervious to foreign invasions and protected by YHWH as his chosen city – open to humiliation. As the "good book" says, "Pride goes before destruction" (Proverbs 16:18).

***

What more is there to ancient Jerusalem? How come that, of all the memorable places of the ancient world, its Babylons, Thebes, and Ninevehs, this one is still known, revered, coveted, visited, embattled, and smothered by the attention of its local, regional, and global admirers?

The fate of ancient Jerusalem, though far from singular in many respects, still moves us because it is remembered. It is remembered because it was enshrined in a complex body of ancient literary works canonized in "the

Bible." The production and preservation of this literature is remarkable. That it survived where much other ancient literature did not, and that it is known beyond the confines of a circle of learned Jewish readers, is even more curious. This literature survived in part because it was adopted and adapted by people of non-Jewish extraction who considered themselves Israelites or Children of Abraham in an extended sense. By creating a kind of fan-fiction, these strong readers inscribed themselves into the text.[18] This process of reading and writing was boosted, enhanced, and regularized by powerful political empires that saw Jewish biblical literature, provided it was interpreted "correctly," as an attestation of their right to rule, a justification of divinely sanctioned government. With the revolutionary spread of the Bible as an instrument of rule came the transformation of Jerusalem into a site attesting to the truth of the biblical dispensation. Jerusalem acquired imperial relevance as evidence of divine providence in the realm of imperial history and governance.

Jerusalem's singular fame has to do with institutions of memory. The Jewish and Christian versions of the biblical canon preserve the memory of Jerusalem. Muslim tradition preserves the memory of *bayt al-maqdis,* the "holy house." The history of art preserves the memory of Jerusalem. Relics carried its memory abroad, and churches and synagogues were oriented toward Jerusalem, as were early Muslim prayers. Christians and Muslims who ruled Jerusalem for most of the past 1,300 years, and Jews who resided there, made Jerusalem a place that houses many different institutions of memory: schools, monasteries, madrasas, mosques, shrines, synagogues, houses of study (*batey midrash*), churches, and assorted memory "stations" for pilgrims to remember the *storia sacra* in the very place where it unfolded. Jerusalem became a memorial unto itself and was preserved as such not just by the Jews, who lamented the destruction of the first and second temple and prayed for it to be rebuilt, but even by the Romans, who destroyed Jewish Jerusalem.

As we are trying to describe why and in what sense Jerusalem became holy and why it has remained so for Jews, Christians, and Muslims, and before we turn to the age of the "biblicate" empires of Christendom and Islam, we need to take a closer look at biblical memory itself. Jerusalem's holiness is not just a theological notion but also something political, or a combination of the theological, the cultic, and the political. Later we will see how this biblical heritage was reconfigured at different times and by different historical agents, and how major shifts in the approach to scripture changed the image of, and attitude toward, Jerusalem. As scripture was allegorized or literalized, so was the Holy City.

There is a political dimension to biblical literature, which has been thoroughly and repeatedly exploited by what we might call "biblicate" civilizations, those theological-political formations that are based on these sacred scriptures. This political dimension is not just a matter of myth and ritual but of history, and it divides into a plurality of forces that interact with one another, or vie for the right to act on behalf of the Holy City. There is an *aristocratic* force that those in power can invoke to justify their claim to rule in the name of God or Allah, be they princes, high priests, emperors, caliphs, or popes. There is what we might call the *demotic* force that invigorates the fight against infidels as a meritorious act on behalf of one's religion, but also, and more profoundly, helps the individual at the end of the food chain of power to overcome the fear of violent death and embrace martyrdom or kill in the name of God. And there is the *eschatological* dimension, a pull toward the *dénouement* of history, that undermines all temporal constellations and thus infuses the theo-political world with revolutionary or utopian ultimacy. All three of these forces are configured in and through scripture or can be justified, as well as questioned, through recourse to this body of revealed literature. Jerusalem plays a significant role in biblical narrative, poetry, and prophecy, it is subject to biblical laws, it carries heightened historic meaning through its role as an indicator of divine pleasure and displeasure with the conduct of its rulers and inhabitants, and it receives its complex and ambivalent meanings from the interplay between the different political forces: aristocratic, demotic, and utopian (eschatological).

The question of who shall act on behalf of this holy city seems to call for a divine actor to appear on the stage. Instead, in the following, I will consider three political factors of human action on behalf of Jerusalem that play a role in biblical history and literature, namely, the ruling elites, the people, and the utopian movements that emerged late in biblical history and precipitated the end of ancient Jerusalem. Each of these factors or agencies is complex, diverse, and its legitimacy contested within biblical literature, creating a highly dynamic legacy of theological-political possibilities that has been passed on to later ages. This tradition bequeathed to Jews, Christians, and Muslims a range of types and models of acting on behalf of the Holy City, sanctioned by ancient precedent, prophetic utterance, and holy writ.

Notes

1. See Fustel de Coulange (1980 [1864]).
2. Mumford (1961).
3. The phrase appears 21 times in Deuteronomy 12–31, four times in 1 and 2 Kings, and twice in Zechariah. It is thus particularly associated with the Deuteronomistic school and is absent from other sources of the Pentateuch, which emphasize other places, such as Hebron (Judahite), Shekhem, and Bethel (Israelite).
4. Jerusalem may be intended as the place where the four rivers of Eden have their origin. In Genesis 14:18 Abram meets Melchizedek, priest-king of the Most High, in Salem, which may or may not be a reference to Jerusalem. Jewish tradition identifies Mount Moriah (Genesis 22) with the Jerusalem Temple Mount.
5. Cf. Assmann (1999).
6. See Weippert, Hübner, and Knauf (2002), 31–42.
7. See Ahituv (1984).
8. See Moran (1992).
9. See Trémouille (1997).
10. See Liverani (2005).
11. See Na'aman (2007), Finkelstein and Silberman (2006).
12. A section of the "broad wall" placed on housing built after the fall of Samaria was found and identified by Nahman Avigad when the Jewish Quarter was rebuilt, following the June 1967 Arab–Israeli war.
13. For Sennacherib's inscription see Grayson and Novotny (2012), 96–97.
14. See 2 Kings 23:27.
15. See Isaiah 45, Ezra 1, 2 Chronicles 36. A general order of release of captives and order of rebuilding is found on the "Cyrus Cylinder" at the British Museum. The text is online at http://www.livius.org/ct-cz/cyrus_I/cyrus_cylinder2.html. And see Finkel (2013).
16. See the biblical memoire of Jerusalem's *peha* (governor) Nehemiah.
17. Jacobs (2004).
18. Cf. Zank (2015).

6

Kings, Priests, and the Politics of "One God Alone"

Biblical Jerusalem would not be what it is without King David. The city enters into the purview of biblical history through the agency of David, the eponymous founder of the House of David, a dynastic succession of rulers of Judah seated in Jerusalem, and the progenitor of *mashiah ben david* (literally: the anointed son of David, the one fit to rule), a figure of the theological-political imagination that the early Christians applied to Jesus of Nazareth, and Muslims remade as the *mahdi*, believed to appear at the end. But Jerusalem was not always ruled by kings, and the Jewish sects of the late Second Temple period (roughly: the period of Hasmonean rule and Roman hegemony) imagined a plurality of messiahs, some priestly, some royal. This constitutional ambiguity is due to the fact that ancient Jerusalem underwent a profound change when it was rebuilt, following the Babylonian exile (See Map 6 and Map 7). What used to be a royal city and center of a territorial state became a temple city and sacerdotal center of a far-flung Jewish diaspora. The ideal ruler of biblical tradition, exemplified by Moses, therefore accrued royal and priestly as well as prophetic characteristics. This combination of offices returns in the Christian tradition, where Christ is not just ruler but also high priest and prophet. The economic power behind throne and altar was the *gerousia*[1] of land-owning laypeople represented in the Jerusalem senate or Sanhedrin (Greek: *synhedrion*).

Jerusalem: A Brief History, First Edition. Michael Zank.
© 2018 Michael Zank. Published 2018 by John Wiley & Sons Ltd.

The first Jerusalemite commonwealth (c. 1000–586 BCE) was based on a royal constitution with a king at the head of the social pyramid. The second commonwealth (516 BCE–70 CE) was a temple-state centered on *Yerushalem*[2] that gradually acquired independence and territorial range rivaling, at times even surpassing, the pre-exilic Judeo-Israelite state. At the helm of second-commonwealth Jerusalem stood the hereditary high priest who was the pride of the nation (see Wisdom of Jesus Son of Sirach 50, cited below). When the late second-century Hasmoneans, who ruled over territories that included Macedonian colonies, adopted the *basileus* title, attested on coins, they introduced constitutional ambiguities that, though not uncommon in Hellenistic kingship, were troubling to traditionally minded Jewish circles and engendered an intense scrutiny of the scriptures for signs of the end and a reversion to rightful Davidic rule and Zadokite priesthood, the honorific of a biblical dynasty of priests. These messianic expectations sharpened when the Romans replaced the Hasmonean priest-kings with the Idumean Herod and made him "king of the Jews," a profound though perhaps unintended challenge to the carefully tended Davidic tradition.

The learned Jews of the late second commonwealth were concerned with the proper political order and ritual conduct as measured by the covenantal obligations of the Torah, as well as guided by pious custom and precedent. As high priests began not just to wield symbolic and economic power but also showed military ambitions, their position became ambiguous, entangled in politics, warfare, and international diplomacy. The shift, in the second half of the first century BCE, to Roman client kingship was further cause for concern. Herod's father, Antipater, was the chancellor of the exchequer for the Hasmonean kings, someone who knew how to curry favor with the Romans. He managed the transition of power in difficult times. But it was Herod himself who eventually managed to acquire the trust of the parties that mattered, first Mark Antony and later Octavian, by then Caesar Augustus and sole ruler of the *orbis terrarum* of the Roman Empire. Herod's success in stabilizing and expanding his personal powers as a Roman client king was not something that endeared him or his Roman masters to the Jews. In their eyes he was and remained a usurper, and the tears they cried at his accession to power were justified by the ruthlessness and brutality with which he secured it.

Herod attempted to secure the legitimacy of his rule in the eyes of his Jewish subjects by lavishly rebuilding the Jewish temple in Jerusalem.[3] He was moved to do so by the fact that he could not himself serve as high priest. Josephus, writing nearly a century after the death of Herod, but using contemporary biographic sources, describes Herod as paranoid and self-aggrandizing. From a more neutral perspective, however, one might say that in this and other pious sponsorships, Herod acted in conformity with the Hellenic virtue of *euergetism*, the doing of good deeds on behalf of the public.[4] Along the same lines, he sponsored the Olympic games and acted as a protector of Jewish communities abroad. Herod also emulated his biblical antecedents and cult restorers of earlier ages, not least among them the scions of the house of Hasmon whose pious acts were celebrated in the Books of the Maccabees, widely disseminated in Greek but originally written in Hebrew. In search of Jewish legitimacy, Herod divorced his Samaritan wife, married a Hasmonean princess, restored and enlarged the ancient Jewish sanctuary, and had his good deeds recorded for posterity.

The rebuilding of the ancient sacerdotal grounds of Jerusalem stands out. Cult restoration was one of the oldest tricks in the book of "oriental kingship" and the gesture of doing right by the god who had brought his humble servant from afar (or from the margins) to restore his or her rightful place of worship was invoked by many conquerors and usurpers, not least among them the Hasmoneans themselves.[5] No royal city without shrine, no order without pleasing the tutelary deity. Herod could thus claim to have acted on behalf of the Jews and on behalf of their god who was in Jerusalem (see Map 8).

The first and greatest name of a biblical king associated with the building of a royal shrine in Jerusalem is Solomon.[6] The temple of Solomon (*hekhal sh'lomoh*) is the most important emblem of the Holy City, its sacred center, its divine *raison d'être*. The story of King Solomon, broadly narrated in the succession narrative of 2 Samuel and the account of Solomon's rule in 1 Kings 1–11, is full of ambiguities. Solomon was a Jerusalemite. His mother Bathsheba's first husband was a Hittite warrior and an officer in David's personal guard, and his ascent to the purple came at the expense of the older Hebronite line of Davidids. This usurpation of Judahite kingship by the Jerusalemite branch of David's family required not just the violent extinction of competitors within and without the family, but cultic confirmation of divine pleasure of the rule of Solomon, the peacemaker. The merits of this pious temple builder, famed for wisdom and prowess, are thus balanced by ruthless purges advised by his warrior-father David, and behind-the-scene machinations of his mother, Bathsheba. The text also holds against him the conscription of free Israelites to build the king's cities and stables, just as predicted by Samuel (1 Samuel 8) and Moses (Deuteronomy 17). On the other hand, this lover of many women and not a few horses is the one who inducts the old emblem of tribal warfare, the Ark of the Covenant, into a house built, in all humility, for YHWH's name, to take permanent residence in a place that, by nature, was too small to hold Him, for whom the heavens are a throne and the earth his footstool.) (Solomon knew how to flatter a god.) Solomon's realm is described as vast (from the Euphrates to the River of Egypt), peaceful, and prosperous.

The reign of Solomon, fictitious as it may be, represents the golden age at the beginning of an Israelite kingship unified and centered in Jerusalem. With anthropologist Victor Turner we may call the age of Solomon the "heroic time" of the story narrated in Samuel-Kings, just as the Mycenaean age and its heroes represent the heroic time of Iliad and Odyssey. The biblical account tells us more about what, again with Turner, we may call the "narrative time", i.e. the time when the story was told in the manner in which we have it, though there may have been multiple narrative times, including editorial and scribal stages, since the book was repeatedly worked over before it crystallized into its canonical form.[7] Samuel-Kings is part of what modern scholars have called the Deuteronomistic History because, in language and content, it is related to what we read in the biblical book of Deuteronomy.[8] Deuteronomy, or at least its twelfth chapter with its laws of cultic centralization, has long been associated with the "scroll of instructions" mentioned in 2 Kings 22 that was found in the very temple of Solomon many generations later, by King Josiah. The story of this pious king and the cultic reforms he ordered on the basis of these hitherto unknown and anonymous written instructions found in the temple appears near the end of the Book of Kings, which narrates the story of Israelite and Judahite kingship. We may safely assume that the original version of this story aimed to glorify this particular king and his pious works of unification, expansion, repair, reform, centralization, eradication of competing sanctuaries, and the reestablishment of a state rivaling that of his ancestors David and Solomon.[9] No other king is described in such uniformly panegyrical prose. Josiah is said to have done what was right in the eyes of YHWH, surpassing all of his ancestors, most of whom are in fact condemned for having done what was evil in the eyes of YHWH, referring to the exact opposite of the acts implemented by Josiah. Particularly condemned is Manasseh, who made peace with the Assyrians, following the ill-fated anti-Assyrian rebellion of his father Hezekiah.

Hezekiah as well is foregrounded and praised by the deuteronomistic historians for doing what they believed was right in the eyes of YHWH, when he purged the royal temple of symbols that expressed Judah's loyalty to Assyria. Just as the priests of 66 CE were to do *vis-à-vis* the Romans, Hezekiah asserted independence from the empire and expressed this assertion in cultic terms. In Hezekiah's case, this brief romance of defiance came at great cost to Judah, which was devastated, though Jerusalem survived. Josiah was fortunate to come to the throne after the demise of the Assyrian Empire (640 BCE), at which time the ruling King Amon, a loyalist, was quickly assassinated and replaced with Josiah, a child-king tutored by the Jerusalemite *gerousia*. Scholars date Josiah's reforms to the year 622 BCE, a time when neo-Babylonian claims to the Land Beyond the River, *Eber-nari*, had not yet been staked, allowing Judah to expand into the power vacuum left behind by the Assyrian demise.

Upon reaching adulthood Josiah commanded Jerusalem's royal shrine to be repaired. In the temple, a hitherto unknown scroll is found that the high priest hands to the chief of the royal household who hands it to the king who has it read aloud. When he hears the curses upon those failing to uphold the commands issued in the scroll, he rends his clothes and has the scroll authenticated by the prophetess Huldah, another member of the royal household. Upon her pronouncement of oracles about the fate of king and kingdom, the king has the scroll read in public. 2 Kings 23 lists the measures implemented by Josiah from which we may derive what kind of practices were in place in Jerusalem until these iconoclastic reforms were instituted. It also gives us a clue as to the content and intention of the scroll itself. By virtue of the similarity between the measures described in 2 Kings 22–23 and the commands listed in Deuteronomy 12, along with the blessings and curses listed later in that book, we can be fairly certain that some version of the Book of Deuteronomy corresponds in spirit, if not in letter, to the scroll found by Josiah.

Josiah's measures aimed at a centralization of the cult of YHWH, the god of Israel, in Jerusalem and its temple, as well as the removal of all other cultic objects and practices from that temple and from the city. The list of reforms attests to the fact that YHWH used to be worshiped in many places that therefore rivaled Jerusalem in importance and dignity, and that there used to be many rural cult sites across the land, attesting to the fact that the cult of YHWH was popular and not state-regulated, just as one would expect from biblical stories centered on places such as Shiloh or Shekhem. We also learn that, until that time, the Judahites, or at least their kings, were not exclusively loyal to YHWH, i.e. hitherto the royal shrine had served as a kind of pantheon or ecumenical center that reflected Judah's many alliances and diplomatic obligations toward neighbors and, most irritatingly, toward the Assyrian Empire. These "idols" were now removed as trappings of dependence. Josiah's reforms, as much as they served as the model for many iconoclastic reforms in later history, fundamentally amounted to an official declaration of independence, a covenant with YHWH that was to forestall any future bowing to an imperial yoke of the kind Israel and Judah had suffered at the hands of the Assyrians. The exclusive worship of YHWH became the hallmark of all later forms of Judaism. But in its original context it was a political declaration of independence under the motto of "worshiping YHWH alone, in Jerusalem alone."

Some have called Josiah's measures a move toward monotheism, but there is no indication that Josiah, his historians, or the early version of Deuteronomy thought of YHWH as the only god in existence. Josiah and his theologians were politicians, not metaphysicians. It is therefore more accurate to refer to Josiah's reforms as monolatric and his system as one of monolatrism, which required of "Israel" (now governed from Jerusalem) to worship a single deity as a matter of collective obligation within a particular territory and under the auspices of a divinely sanctioned monarch. Josiah's only successful military campaign was in connection with his acts of centralization and aimed at subduing Bethel, a former Israelite state sanctuary to the north of Jerusalem, where Josiah wreaked utter devastation and desecration with the aim of forestalling any northern Israelite revival that could threaten Jerusalem's claim to exclusive representation of pan-Israelite traditions. All male Israelites were henceforth obliged to make thrice annual pilgrimage to Jerusalem and bring their gifts and tithes to the city YHWH had (now) chosen for his name to reside. The contribution of Josiah (or of his city-branding consultants) to the rise of Jerusalem as a religious symbol cannot be overstated.

Jerusalem's preeminence in Israelite history is, historically speaking, the end-point of a process that entailed the destruction of the northern kingdom of Israel and the establishment of a neo-Israelite state centered on Jerusalem and ruled by Davidic kings. This political resurgence depended on the demise of Assyria, which created the condition for Jerusalem to assert itself, for a few decades, over its immediate neighbors and regional rivals. In a typical example of wisdom in hindsight, the Jerusalemite royal-prophetic historians who tell this story place the co-emergence of Jerusalem and the House of David at the beginning of Israelite statehood to argue that it was the refusal of the Israelites to swallow their pride and bow to the city and its dynasty at its inception that later caused the downfall of Israel. To be sure, justice and the presence of Israelites in Jerusalem required a critique of the early Judahite kings as insufficiently attuned to the freedom of their northern neighbors. This introduces a tone of communal balance and appreciation for the distinguished history of the Israelite north into the picture.[10] The story that culminates in the reign of Josiah, whose advent is presaged by a prophet in an unsubtly panegyric *vaticinium ex eventu* (see 1 Kings 13:2), means to encourage national strength and persistence through unity. The original Deuteronomistic History was most likely written in praise of Josiah, whose measures were hoped to prevent from happening to Jerusalem what had happened to Samaria a century earlier. This hope was dashed a generation later, when it was the very striving for independence and the refusal to accept Babylonian suzerainty that led to the king's exile and Jerusalem's obliteration.

The literary fiction of a golden age of a united Israel, the reign of David and Solomon, peaked with the entry of YHWH to Jerusalem and his presence in the temple. Hezekiah and Josiah served as cult restorers, but both of their stories have strongly anti-Assyrian overtones and illustrate the connection between state and religion in late eighth- to seventh-century Judah. Exclusive YHWH-worship and the centralization of the cult of YHWH in Jerusalem were acts of national proportion aimed at unity and independence. The form in which this state-cult was instituted was the deuteronomistic covenant, formed on the model of the ancient Near Eastern suzerainty treaty familiar in the Levant since the days of the Hittite Empire (mid-second millennium BCE or Middle Bronze Age).[11]

Acts of cult restoration bestow legitimacy on a ruler. This topos is familiar not only from the Bible but also from the Babylonian realm and it was therefore part of a rhetorical *koiné* in the sense of a shared set of widely understood tropes.[12] The most eminent biblical case is also attested outside the Bible, namely, the case of Cyrus of Anshan, founder of the Persian "world-empire." The Cyrus Edict mentioned at the end of Chronicles and variously in the Book of Ezra casts Cyrus as charged by "YHWH, God of heaven," to restore his house in Jerusalem. The anonymous prophet known as Deutero-Isaiah, who was a contemporary of the entry of Cyrus to Babylon in 539 BCE, has YHWH refer to Cyrus as his "anointed" (Isaiah 45). The wording used in this context matches what Cyrus says about himself in the "Cyrus Cylinder," namely, that he was commissioned to restore the proper rituals for Marduk, the Babylonian high god, neglected by Nabonides, to rebuild the sanctuaries destroyed by Nebuchadnezzar, to restore the sacred vessels, and to release the captives. The reason for these measures is clear. Cyrus, anticipating the difficulties of administering an empire of hitherto

unmatched size, could reasonably hope to gain the favor of people who had
suffered under Babylonian rule. He came as a liberator, not as an oppressor.
On the other hand, permission to rebuild Jerusalem did not entail what the
Babylonian Jewish elite may have wished for, namely the restoration of the
status quo ante of national independence, which would have been symbolized in the anointing of a Davidic king. By calling Cyrus YHWH's anointed,
the prophet sides with the new power but places the "king of kings" under
a novel, more supreme divine government: in the hymnic language of later
Jewish prayer, the "king of the king of kings."

In the event, Jerusalem was rebuilt as a temple city, modeled to some
extent on Babylon herself, though without the *ziggurat* (ridiculed in Genesis
10), without the idea of holy matrimony (though this echoes, to some
extent, in the later allegorical interpretation of the Song of Solomon), and
without sacral kingship (though this seems to be alluded to in Psalm 2 and
it surfaces again in the apocalyptic figure of "one like a human being," the
Christian "Son of Man"). The leadership in Jerusalem was divided into
secular officials, such as the governor (*peha*) Nehemiah, and priests, such as
Ezra, also referred to as "the Scribe." Ezra is credited with the first public
reading of the Torah. Some scholars have argued that the Torah read by
Ezra consisted of the so-called Priestly Code, one of the putative literary
sources of the Pentateuch as we have it now. Whether the Torah functioned
as an actual code of law or as more of a compendium of legal studies is not
clear.[13] But the very existence of a written law code underscores the shift
from a royal to a sacerdotal constitution that leaves the position of the king
open and removes kingship to the level of divine rule and world governance.[14] The wisdom of this and similar temporal arrangements[15] was that
it provided a practical solution for the here and now while leaving a more
perfect political order to posterity.

The Torah served as the constitution for Jerusalem as a temple city in
that it provided a meticulous description of sanctuary, vestments, rites of
purification, and cultic sacrifices, and a calendar of daily, weekly, monthly,
and annual obligations centered on a single sanctuary, where the male
Israelites were obliged to appear "before YHWH" thrice annually. At the
top of second-commonwealth Jerusalem society stood the high priest who
officiated at the temple and presided over a priestly aristocracy. The apocryphal Book of Ben Sira (also known as Siracides, Ecclesiasticus, and Wisdom
of Jesus Son of Sirach) gives a lively impression of the regard afforded the
reigning high priest, who represented the order first established under
Persian rule and continued until the destruction of ancient Jerusalem, in

70 CE. The hereditary office of high priest was disrupted in the transition from Ptolemaic Egyptian to Seleucid Syrian rule. The crisis of leadership leads to the expulsion of the Oniad family from Jerusalem, which goes on to establish a rival sanctuary in Egypt. A partisan of the Oniads and a contemporary of the Seleucid conquest of Jerusalem in 198 BCE, the wisdom teacher Ben Sira, composed a song in praise of high priest Simon Onias that shows his regard for the office and the beautiful rites conducted at the Jewish sanctuary. The poem was preserved in a Greek translation prepared by his grandson for the Jews of Alexandria at a time when the Hasmoneans occupied the highest office in Jerusalem. Here is how Ben Sira describes the appearance of Simon, from the Oniad clan of priests.

How glorious he was when the people gathered round him as he came out of the inner sanctuary!

Like the morning star among the clouds, like the moon when it is full; like the sun shining upon the temple of the Most High, and like the rainbow gleaming in glorious clouds; like roses in the days of the first fruits, like lilies by a spring of water, like a green shoot on Lebanon on a summer day; like fire and incense in the censer, like a vessel of hammered gold adorned with all kinds of precious stones; like an olive tree putting forth its fruit, and like a cypress towering in the clouds.

When he put on his glorious robe and clothed himself with superb perfection and went up to the holy altar, he made the court of the sanctuary glorious. And when he received the portions from the hands of the priests, as he stood by the hearth of the altar with a garland of brethren around him, he was like a young cedar on Lebanon; and they surrounded him like the trunks of palm trees, all the sons of Aaron in their splendor with the Lord's offering in their hands, before the whole congregation of Israel. Finishing the service at the altars, and arranging the offering to the Most High, the Almighty, he reached out his hand to the cup and poured a libation of the blood of the grape; he poured it out at the foot of the altar, a pleasing odor to the Most High, the King of all.

Then the sons of Aaron shouted, they sounded the trumpets of hammered work, they made a great noise to be heard for remembrance before the Most High. Then all the people together made haste and fell to the ground upon their faces to worship their Lord, the Almighty, God Most High. And the singers praised him with their voices in sweet and full-toned melody. And the people besought the Lord Most High in prayer before him who is merciful, till the order of worship of the Lord was ended; so they completed his service. Then Simon came down, and lifted up his hands over the whole congregation of the sons of Israel, to pronounce the blessing of the Lord with his lips, and to glory in his name; and they bowed down in worship a second time, to receive the blessing from the Most High. (Ben Sira 50, c. 190 BCE)

The rites reflected in this nostalgic text had been in place since Persian times. The Medo-Persian Empire had no objection to "religious" autonomy and a plurality of national cults. Unlike the Assyrians, the Persian administration refrained from imposing cultic trappings of loyalty and dependence onto the civic sanctuaries of its clients. The Persian Empire was divided into satrapies that were monitored by stoking competition and mutual suspicion among various people, who inadvertently turned themselves into "eyes of the king" by spying on one another. In the case of the Jews, what kept them in check was most likely the suspicion of the prosperous Samaritan governors from the Sanballat family, who were not thrilled to see the erstwhile Judahites return and rebuild Jerusalem. Their perhaps disingenuous offer to help their southern cousins was rejected by the returnees (the *b'ney ha-golah* or "exiles") as inappropriate to the ritual re-founding of a city that prized its memory of independence and preserved Judahite ethnic exclusivity, in distinction from the supposedly mongrelized Samaritans to the north.

Once re-founded as a temple city, Jerusalem developed a new profile and a new aristocracy. Henceforth cult restoration could be necessitated whenever the right rituals were tampered with, when the right lineage of high priests was disrupted, or when the temple was defiled by foreigners and, in the worst case, destroyed. Herod, who, as mentioned before, was excluded from the priesthood and blasphemously usurped the title of "king of the Jews," invented yet another form of cult restoration, namely, megalomaniac temple rebuilding. Though Herod's measures are mocked by the historian Josephus, in his account of the *res gestae* of this most interesting and conflicted of all Jewish kings, the rabbis confirm that he who did not see Herodian Jerusalem has not seen beauty. As Steven Weitzman[16] has shown, the topos of temple restoration was at the heart of Hasmonean propaganda narratives about the Maccabean revolt, and not by accident. Opponents of the Hasmoneans saw their claim to the high priesthood as an act of usurpation. According to Josephus, Hasmonean King Alexander Iannaeus (r. 103–76 BCE) was publicly mocked by the Pharisees when he officiated as high priest, leading to a bloody repression of this purist movement. The rabbis later took their sweet revenge when they curtailed the range of sacred scriptures and excluded the entire body of Maccabean literature as apocryphal (*sefarim hitzoniim*). Maccabean valor, emulated by the Latin Crusaders, for whom the Books of the Maccabees were part of the Bible, languished in obscurity among the Jews until the advent of modern Zionism, which retrieved their heroic narrative of zeal for Jerusalem.[17]

Notes

1. A Greek term referring to an assembly of the (usually) male heads of households.

2. Judging by the consonants in the Hebrew texts and the Greek transcription in LXX, this seems to have been the name of the city in Hebrew prior to the rabbinic age.

3. Our main source of the life of Herod is the works of Josephus Flavius. For modern studies see Dan Bahat in Arav (2008), 117–128, Bloch (2006), Günther (2007), Kasher and Witztum (2007), McCane (2008), Netzer and Laureys-Chachy (2008), Richardson (1996), Schalit (2001), Weber (2003).

4. See Gardner (2007).

5. On cult restoration as a trope in Assyrian, Achaemenid, and Hasmonean sources see Weitzman (2004).

6. See Finkelstein and Silberman (2006).

7. Turner and Turner (1985). I thank my colleague Gina Cogan for having drawn my attention to Turner's literary schema.

8. See Noth (1981a), McBride, Strong, and Tuell (2005).

9. Cf. Eynikel (1996).

10. The history of Israel is largely glossed over in the much later, post-exilic or early Hellenistic Book of Chronicles.

11. On the theory of a correlation between biblical covenant and antecedent suzerainty treaties and its critics see Mendenhall (1955), Perlitt (1969), McCarthy (1972), Brueggemann (1974).

12. See Weitzman (2004).

13. See Heszer (2017).

14. See Oswald (2009).

15. The other striking example is the appointment of Simon Maccabee as king in all but name, with the *caveat* until such time as a prophet might arise to make a more permanent arrangement. See 1 Maccabees. 14:41.

16. Weitzman (2004).

17. On the Zionist reconstruction of the past see Zerubavel (1995).

7

Kinship, Covenant, and Sectarian Divide

In the preceding chapter we considered the character of biblical Jerusalem from the viewpoint of the elites that determined the city's political image and functions. Kings and priests created and maintained the official religion of the state, and they negotiated the often tenuous position of that state in relation to the shifting imperial powers of the Ancient Near East, the Hellenistic age, and Rome. In this chapter, I focus on the communities loyal to biblical Jerusalem – the ancient Judahites and their post-exilic successors, the early Jews. If earlier we focused on politics, here we deal with society. The leaders will inevitably reappear, as our main source, biblical literature, was produced by and for elites, and the perspective of ordinary folk rarely surfaces. Still, we can gain a sense of the communities centered on Jerusalem and their vicissitudes as preserved in scriptures that shaped later Jewish, Christian, and Muslim beliefs about chosenness, inclusion and exclusivity, preconditions of access, historical failure, and the possibility of return, restoration, and permanence. The main focus of this chapter is on conceptions of collective identity and practices centered on Jerusalem.

According to the Book of Genesis, the Israelites were the descendants of a family of semi-nomadic herdsmen from the east, where all of humanity had its origin. This story of origins combines several distinct historical perspectives into a single epic narrative. There are the family relationships between Jacob/Israel and Esau/Edom, Moab and Ammon, and Isaac/Ishmael

Jerusalem: A Brief History, First Edition. Michael Zank.
© 2018 Michael Zank. Published 2018 by John Wiley & Sons Ltd.

located in Canaan and its eastern, southern, and southeastern surroundings. This saga of eponymous patriarchs reflects an Iron Age neighborhood
where the Israelite and Judahite authors of these traditions were at home
and described themselves as related to their neighbors and dependent on
Canaanite and Egyptian urban generosity. The fact that Jerusalem plays virtually no role in the patriarchal narratives of Genesis suggests that the basic
outline of the stories must have been forged prior to the ascent of Jerusalem
to pan-Israelite eminence, i.e. before the destruction of Israel in the late
eighth century.[1] This Iron Age family saga is prefaced by the story of Abram/
Sarai, depicted as the ancestral pair of "many nations" who came to Canaan
from a remote place, specifically mentioning two different Mesopotamian
locations, Ur and Haran. *Ur kashdim* ("of the Chaldeans") connects the primordial migration of Genesis with the experience of the likely first readers
of this expanded version of the family saga, namely the exiles in Babylonia
preparing for their own return to the land of Canaan. Within Canaan,
Abraham is most closely linked to Hebron, the ancient Davidic center.
Jerusalem as well makes a brief cameo appearance in Genesis 14, in the
story about the wars of kings, giving Abraham a somewhat Judahite flair
while maintaining his status of exalted father (*av ram*). The grand narrative
of exodus and conquest ends with Joshua 24, where we hear about a covenant at Shekhem, the ancient Israelite capital, not Jerusalem. This is what I
mean by the relative marginality of Jerusalem in the biblical corpus. In the
Torah, at least, it plays a subordinate, if any, role.

   The complex biblical story of origins became part of the inventory of
Jewish, Christian, and Muslim "social imaginaries."[2] For the most part,
Jews, Christians, and Muslims believe one or another version of these
stories to be simply true. In the second half of the nineteenth century, after
two centuries of literary critical research that had damaged the literal
credibility of Scripture, imperially sponsored biblical archaeologists and
private adventurers set out in search of historical verification of the biblical
past. They surveyed the Holy Land, excavated the tombs of Egyptian kings,
and uncovered the remnants of the great urban civilizations of ancient
Mesopotamia. The results of this research were stupendous but not always
as expected. It changed our view of the ancient world. While providing historical context that sheds light on biblical narratives, archaeology and epig-
raphy are not instruments of biblical verification. The discovery of Bronze
Age remnants sheds light on facts remembered in stories about Israelite
origins. But the stories were not written down with a view to chronicling
verities taken for granted. Biblical literature was produced to explain why

things are the way they are or why certain events came about. The point of biblical historiography was to instill values and to inspire future generations, in light of past experience, to act or behave in a certain way. To borrow a Kantian phrase, biblical history is not so much about "what can we know" and more about "what ought we to do" and "what may we hope." We can still learn a lot from biblical literature as long as we don't ignore the difference between storytelling and history.[3]

In archaeological and epigraphic terms there is no evidence that the Israelites were newcomers to late Bronze Age Canaan when they established their villages in the central hill country of the southern Levant.[4] Judging by the evidence of material culture, such as patterns of pottery glaze, the only early Iron Age people of foreign origin were the Philistines of the *Pentapolis* of Ashdod, Ashkelon, Ekron, Gat, and Gaza. What we know and how we think of these ancient origins matters, since they tend to be invoked in modern "nativist" arguments by Israelis and Palestinians competing for historical priority and settled continuity in the land, that can be particularly confusing when both claim to be descended from the original inhabitants of the land.[5]

As is common in ancient literature, produced at a time when literacy was limited to those near the seats of power,[6] biblical historiography does not give us direct evidence of the ordinary lives and practices of common people. Biblical literature reflects the views and opinions of literate elites. More frequently than not, the texts cast aspersions on the practices of the common people as idolatrous and displeasing to YHWH.

Before it was enshrined in biblical literature, Jerusalem was an ordinary royal city of the ancient southern Levant. Ruled by Hurrian, then Judahite kings and, following its reconstruction, by high priests, the lives, practices, and points of view of its inhabitants were shaped by custom, collective self-interest, and historical vicissitude. There was nothing "scripted," preordained, or exceptional about this history. Even under the early Judahite kings, there were sanctuaries elsewhere, and prophetism paralleled the augury used by other civilizations. Jerusalem was unexceptional. Much like other ancient cities, it was diverse in social stratification and thrived on the division of labor required by constant warfare, the desire of the elites for luxuries, the necessities of tax collection, and commerce. A great number of female figurines found in the ruins of first commonwealth households confirms that ancient Jerusalemites were highly concerned with human fertility, a matter in which the male god of kingship held limited sway. Prophetic polemics against the representatives of the people whom they accuse of corruption, idolatry, self-indulgence, and exploitation, as well as political grandstanding and brinksmanship, indicate that ancient Jerusalem was not a unified or harmonious place but as varied in its occupations and orientations as any other center of power, then or now.

Not only was the city like other royal and temple cities, its inhabitants did not distinguish themselves from other nations by their clothing or appearance. In pre-rabbinic Jewish culture, as in most ancient civilizations, membership in the people of Israel was patrilineal. Shaye Cohen, an eminent scholar of early Judaism, recognized that modern answers to the question of who is a Jew did not apply in antiquity.[7] According to Cohen, it was quite difficult, without the trappings of distinctive clothing or hairstyle, to tell a Jew from a non-Jew. This is obvious, for example, from the paintings of biblical scenes in the synagogue of Dura Europos, which depict people who look exactly like those you might find in Hellenistic Egypt or in the baths of Pompeii.[8] The solemn admonition warning non-Jews from encroaching onto those parts of the temple precinct in Jerusalem that were reserved for Israelite males indicates that, in antiquity, people could not easily tell a Jew from a non-Jew and had to rely on a person's own fear of taboo-violation. On the other hand, the very existence of a "Court of the Gentiles," a Herodian invention, indicates that the Jerusalem temple, like other ancient sanctuaries, generally welcomed the gifts of strangers. The imposition of distinctive garb and markers of separation are the result of centuries of Christian and Muslim discrimination. Today, distinctly "Jewish" clothing is the hallmark only of ultra-orthodox Jews for whom it serves as an expression of loyalty to tradition, similar to what we find among American Mennonites and the Amish.

We don't know a whole lot about membership in the earliest "people of Israel," and most of what we know is based on biblical literature, not historical or epigraphic evidence. The biblical division into 12 tribes (the 12 sons of Jacob = Israel) is somewhat unstable and seems to reflect the division of Israelite territory into administrative provinces, on the model of the ancient Egyptian "nomes" (from a Greek word meaning jurisdiction). The division between Judah and Israel is a political, not an ethnic one, though linguistic differences between tribes or regions may have obtained.[9] According to the Book of Exodus, the Hebrews who escaped Egyptian servitude were not just descendants of Israel but included a "mixed multitude." The notion of a people of Israel as a covenanted nation is a legal category, not an empirical description. There was no Jewish "race." The sages responsible for the composition of the primordial history of Genesis (Genesis 1–11) understood that Israelite history was part of a larger ecumenical world. Their "table of nations" (Genesis 10) indicates an understanding of the relatedness of nations based on linguistic affinities, and it shows a wide geo-political purview that reaches into all three of the ancient continents that were connected through trade routes that intersected in the Levant. The ancient Jews were not ignorant of the world around them, a world connected by trade and imperial competition.

Judging by the books of Ezra and Nehemiah, the Babylonian Jewish leadership of the mid-fifth century BCE was intent on rebuilding Jerusalem as a strictly regulated cultic-covenantal community ruled by a class of priests and Levites. It is in this context that we hear of a tearful dismissal of "foreign wives." Whether this really occurred or not, the intent is clear. Family purity was to be part of the constitution of the temple city. This reconstituted "Israel" centered in Jerusalem was to be distinguished from the "nations" by maintaining ethnic exclusivity as well as ritual purity in a priestly covenant, making membership in the citizenry of the newly established temple city an exclusive affair. It is possible that this rigorous statute obtained only among the priests. The Pharisees, a brotherhood attested since the early days of the Hasmonean dynasty (late second century BCE), applied that rigorous system of ritual purity to themselves and believed every Jew should live this way.

As best we know from the books of Samuel and Kings, things were different under David and his successors. We hear in several places that the "Jebusites" were not expelled from Jerusalem when David took the "Fortress of Zion." Rather, they resided with the Judahites "until this day" (2 Samuel 5). No ethnic cleansing here. David appointed his sons as priests. No ritual purity required. David's palace guard was stocked with foreign fighters, among them Cretans, Philistines, and Hittites. The topoi of the foreignness of the people of Israel to the land of Israel and the separation of the covenanted nation from the ways of Egypt and Canaan enjoined in the Book of Leviticus are absent from the accounts of the early monarchy. The notion, found in the Torah and the Book of Joshua, that the original inhabitants of Canaan had been put "to the sword" seems to be a fiction, designed to explain in hindsight why the monarchy failed. Foreignness of origin is a narrative conceit that appealed to those who returned from the Babylonian exile. Cultic exclusivity was a priestly norm, not an empirical description of the social and ethnic realities of the Israelite and Judahite pasts. The concern with ritual purity is expressed in the laws of Leviticus, which served as the constitution of a "Jerusalem 2.0," after the exile, a city based on sacerdotal practice, not kingship.

The shift in emphasis from kinship, as the primary bond between the people, to covenant, which is a legal bond based on obligation and practice, became an important factor when non-Jews sought to associate with the Jews. The Book of Ruth shows that it used to be possible to associate with an Israelite through marriage rather than ritual conversion. In the second commonwealth, especially in Hellenistic and Roman times, the fame of Jerusalem and the Jewish way of life – though occasionally disparaged by learned Greeks and Romans[10] – attracted people from abroad who wished to pay homage to "the god who is in Jerusalem." It is at this point that association with the Jews for religious reasons becomes possible and desirable for members of other nations. The precondition of legitimate, pious worship of the God of Israel is one of the major questions the gospels, histories, and letters of the New Testament are meant to answer, though in a manner that was deeply contested between believers in Christ and other Jews committed to preserving the ancestral way of life. This polemic became more virulent after the first Jewish uprising against Roman rule, and it became fully operative as a legal and social principle of oppression once Christianity became the official religion of the Roman Empire.

In the Hellenistic age, membership in the body politic of an "Israel" centered on Jerusalem could occasionally be acquired in bulk, namely, when an entire community was integrated peacefully or by force. This was the case under the Hasmoneans who waged wars of territorial expansion that were justified by the biblical fiction of the original conquest. Whether these Maccabean wars took place or unfolded exactly as described or for the reasons given in Hasmonean propaganda literature is not clear. Modern historians and archaeologists are no longer certain whether the wars described in First and Second Maccabees are a reflection of fact or a kind of historical fiction meant to justify the usurpation of the highest offices in Jerusalem by a family of parvenus. What matters in hindsight is that Maccabean literature furnished a literary precedent of just wars waged for the restoration of biblical territory and with the intent of imposing a single form of cultic loyalty on its populations.[11] The Hasmoneans succeeded in associating the Idumeans, the biblical Edomites, with Jerusalem. King Herod was of Idumean descent, but a "Jew" in his devotion to the Judahite cult of Jerusalem. It was Herod who rebuilt Jerusalem's temple on a much grander scale, which we can still appreciate in the massive wall works that support today's Noble Sanctuary. The Hasmoneans did not limit national Jewish identity formation to the collection of taxes. They showed their zealousness for the ancestral laws by promoting distinctly Jewish practices across their realm. This is attested in the elimination of Greek earthenware from Jewish centers of settlement. From an archaeological, material-culture perspective Jewishness was made evident by shunning Greek and Hellenistic images on household goods that, a generation earlier, had been widely disseminated and that vanished, at least temporarily, from the households of the Jews of the Land of Israel.[12] The culture also underwent a Hebraic revival. Imperial Aramaic, attested in the mid-second-century Book of Daniel, vanished as a learned language and Paleo-Hebrew was reintroduced on Hasmonean coins and elsewhere as a marker of the antiquity and autochthony of Jewish civilization, romantically reclaimed by the new dynasty.[13]

In addition to populations forcibly Judaized by the Hasmoneans, the Jewish societies of the early Roman Empire included voluntary converts and "God-fearers," people who associated with the Jews or adopted their way of life by venerating YHWH, sending gifts to his temple, making pilgrimage, observing Sabbath, attending synagogues and houses of study where the Jewish scriptures were read and interpreted, without necessarily converting, or accepting circumcision. The appeal of Jerusalem, temple, Jewish sacred history, and prophetic literature was due, in part, to the fame the city acquired by virtue of its colonies abroad, ranging from Egypt to Mesopotamia to Asia Minor and Rome. The status, character, and (thanks to Herod) ever more expansive architectural design of Jerusalem also helped to attract foreigners, including the royal house of Adiabene in northern Mesopotamia, then part of Armenia. These and other groups translated and disseminated the Jewish way of life and thus, in a sense, invented Judaism as a "religion."

What we refer to as the early Jews (in contrast to the earlier Judahites, about whom we know relatively little), then, are people loyal to the Jerusalem of the second commonwealth, a temple city ruled by priests. Among these early Jews were descendants of the Judahites exiled to Babylonia in 596 and 586 but also descendants of those who had remained or fled north, seeking refuge in former Israelite territory. Others, among them the biblical prophet Jeremiah, had relocated to Egypt, where they might have connected with an earlier Judahite colony on the island of *Yeb* (Elephantine). Following the conquests of Alexander and his Macedonians (333–323 BCE), Jews were settled in the newly established Egyptian capital of Alexandria, where they laid the cultural foundation from which Hellenistic Christianity was to grow later on, namely, by translating the Torah and other sacred Jewish writings into Greek, and by beginning the work of amalgamating Greco-Roman thought (especially Platonism and

Stoicism) with the Mosaic tradition. Jewish diaspora communities in place since before the destruction of the second temple thrived in the Roman, Byzantine, and Muslim Middle East and North Africa until the middle of the twentieth century, when their millennial communities were expelled in retaliation for the Palestinian *Nakba* of 1947–1949. Put differently, with few exceptions, Jewish and other minority communities were able to persist and even thrive in the Middle East and North Africa as long as the generally accepted form of social and political organization across the region was imperial and religiously pluralistic, rather than secular and nationalistic.

The most important indication of the rise of Jerusalem's fame during the late second commonwealth, especially in the days of Herod and his successors, is the considerable increase in pilgrimage to Jerusalem in the days of Roman rule. Israeli scholar Shmuel Safrai, who wrote a seminal study on ancient Jerusalem pilgrimage, concluded that there is no evidence of significant pilgrimage to Jerusalem in Hasmonean times.[14] Things changed with Pompey's entry to Syria (63 BCE) and his conquest of Egypt, when Rome came, saw, and reorganized entire societies. In Judea, Pompey mediated a conflict between two Hasmonean princes, Aristobulus II and Hyrcanus II. Two decades later, Mark Anthony empowered Herod to take the kingship in Jerusalem by force. To assuage Jewish popular discontent, Herod boosted Jerusalem as a major center of pilgrimage that every year attracted hundreds of thousands of visitors who flocked to this "most famous city of the east," as Pliny later called it, with a nod to Titus, its destroyer. When Rome and Jerusalem were at peace, pilgrims included pious and curious God-fearing gentiles for whom accommodations had been made by Herod, who added a "court of the gentiles" to the much enlarged temple area, literally in fulfillment of a biblical prophecy, that all nations were to make pilgrimage to Zion.

Late second-commonwealth Jerusalem was the focal point for a widely disseminated Jewish *demos*. It was also the site of an ongoing struggle for collective self-definition. We know about internal divisions among the Jews from ancient authors, including Philo and Josephus, and from the New Testament, where some of the same groups appear as enemies of Jesus. Our knowledge of late second-commonwealth Jewish sects, parties, and movements has been enriched by manuscript finds, including those from the Cairo Geniza and Khirbet Qumran, though it is not always easy to match knowledge derived from our ancient historians with the provenance of "sectarian" writings. Sects are always in the eyes of the normative beholder, and literature is not always a reliable guide to social reality.

The social world of late second-commonwealth Jerusalem and its satel-
lites across the Roman sphere holds special interest for Christian scholars,
since this is the world from which Christianity emerged. The earliest
Christians were a Jewish group, party, or movement among others. But our
topic is both broader and more specific. We are interested in the inheritance
of Jerusalem's symbolic meanings among Christians and Muslims and we
want to show that the condition for the possibility of such an inheritance
beyond the Jewish community is based, in part, on the nature of the bequest
itself:[15] in this case, by the formation of demotic alternatives enshrined in
biblical and other Jewish literature and traditions that were later appropriated, on the one hand, by rabbinical and non-rabbinical Jews and, on the
other hand, by non-Jewish communities for whom Jerusalem was and
remained a meaningful point of reference and a symbol of the divine in
space and time.

At the time when Jerusalem functioned as a Jewish temple city and
metropolis of a far-flung Jewish diaspora, the definition of "Israel" was contested between Jews (loyal to Jerusalem) and Samaritans (not loyal to
Jerusalem). With the Christian movement, which began to form in the second third of the first century CE, yet another group entered the stage that
understood itself as the "true Israel" (Paul's "Israel according to the spirit";
"free-born children of the promise," etc.), but had no discernible impact
until after Jerusalem's demise.

Late second-commonwealth Jerusalem was beset by a crisis of collective
self-definition that eventually exploded into anti-Roman rebellion and civil
war. This crisis was aggravated by Roman occupation, but it was not caused
by it. The conflict between the Jews and Rome may not have been inevitable,[16] but there were social and ideological forces at work among the Jews of
the early Roman Empire that fueled anti-Roman sentiments and overwhelmed the forces of compromise and accommodation. We will return to
this in the next chapter. For now we will consider the sectarian or social
divisions as part of the diversification of the Jewish *demos* and the proliferation of normative attitudes toward Jerusalem and its institutions.

We have hardly any knowledge about the divisions among the Jews
before the Hasmonean period (mid-second century BCE), and the
knowledge we have about such divisions and movements for the late second
commonwealth is not always solid. Take the rather famous Pharisees, for
example. The late first-century CE historian Josephus has this group appear
prominently as one of Judaism's "three philosophies" (literally *haireses*, i.e.
"manners of discernment"). In contrast to the priestly and aristocratic

Sadducees, the Pharisees stood out by their meticulous observance of the Mosaic Law and their disinterest in luxuries. Josephus distinguishes the Pharisees from the Sadducees and the Essenes, and eventually adds the Zealots as a "fourth philosophy." As Martin Hengel has shown, the Zealots simply distinguished themselves by their embrace of violence, but otherwise recruited themselves from the existing movements and groups.[17] Modern historians have been focusing more on social rather than doctrinal causes for the divisions among the ancient Jews.[18] The Sadducees emerge from the priestly aristocracy while the Pharisees represent a lay-religious movement that aimed to extend priestly purity to every Israelite. To achieve this goal, they established a meal-community of their own, based on meticulous observance of tithing and ritual purity. The name Pharisee (*perush/im*) literally refers to the member (*haver*) of a group of separatists. Josephus, who at one point mentions a group of 6,000 heads of households, also speaks of the fact that they were highly popular among ordinary people. While they are first mentioned as a group voicing opposition to a Hasmonean king who officiated as high priest, they wielded considerable influence under the Hasmonean queen Salome Alexandra (early first century BCE). Jacob Neusner describes the Pharisees as a typical Hellenistic phenomenon, to the extent that they formed an exclusive brotherhood based on philosophical doctrine and careful observance of communal rules. But most scholars see the Pharisees as the representatives of a general trend among the Jews of the Hasmonean Land of Israel toward Torah-based piety and hence as the precursors of the rabbis of Mishnah and Talmud.[19]

Though this characterization dissolves the specific sectarian character of the Pharisees as a distinct movement and makes them into prototypes of "typical" or "normative" rabbinic Jews of a later age, the distinction between Sadducees and Pharisees remains useful, in that it represents the impact on collective self-definition of the two major Jerusalemite institutions of the second commonwealth, namely, temple and Torah.

Though there were other Yahwistic temples or places of animal sacrifice (including the Samaritan sanctuary on Mount Gerizim and the YHWH temple of Heliopolis in Egypt), Jerusalem was preeminent because of its symbolic centrality for the Jews and because of its antiquity. Aside from the cultural and political meanings of Jerusalem as a temple city and the mother city of various colonies, Jerusalem's cultic importance was boosted – and complicated – by the attention of the learned laypeople who measured the cultic practices and the conduct of the priests by the Mosaic Law, i.e. by a written constitution. This became particularly virulent under the conditions of Hellenization, when the Torah could be invoked as a bulwark against "foreign" influence and boosted the claim to rule (or officiate at the temple) of those, who offered the most rigorous loyalty to the text and its increasingly contested meanings. With the institution of the Torah in Persian times, scriptural revelation had displaced the earlier voice of divine guidance, prophecy, or so the rabbis later thought. To determine the will of God, one learned to scrutinize the scriptures, among them many volumes of prophetic writings. Literary production went hand in hand with rewritings of earlier texts and, under Hellenistic influence, with imaginative commentary and allegorical interpretation. What distinguished Jerusalem's sanctuary was not that it was the only place where daily offerings were made to YHWH, but that it was the focal point of learned debates on the right conduct for priests, judges, teachers, and laypeople who, in the eyes of the literate class of "scribes," constituted "Israel." By virtue of Torah being the measure of what constituted a "true Israelite," interpretation took on profound socially constitutive significance. What strikes one most strongly about late second-commonwealth Jewish culture in the Land of Israel are the moments at which the learned clashed with the powerful. One Hasmonean king, Alexander Iannaeus, had thousands of Pharisees massacred for insulting him when he officiated as high priest. Herod, at the end of his life, massacred Pharisees for taking down the imperial eagle, the emblem of Roman loyalty he had installed at the gates of the temple. During the first revolt (66–70/4), the land-owning aristocracy and Herodian royalty sued for peace, while many a learned Zealot rallied for war. Some of the greatest rabbis of the generation following the destruction of Jerusalem were among the martyrs of the Bar Kokhba revolt (132–135), the last great fight for the liberation of Jerusalem, which inflicted significant losses on the Roman legions, but also precipitated imperial measures aimed at preventing any further attempt at restoring the temple.[20] For the next two centuries, an entire Roman legion was stationed at what used to be Jerusalem. Late second-commonwealth Jerusalem seems to have been a paradigmatic case for phenomena that still exist today, a place where *intelligentsia* clashed with *apparatchik*, radical thought adopted violent means, idealism clashed with realism, and rigorous utopian politics with pragmatic accommodation.

As Jerusalem gradually Romanized, demotic alternatives of who or what constituted "Israel" took hold among various groups at the center and in the margins of the Judean commonwealth. All of these groups drew succor and inspiration from sacred literature and ancient prophetic oracles, but some organized in more or less segregated or secessionist meal-associations, and concocted various scenarios of the end. The claim to represent "Israel," a holy nation and a sacred remnant, took on apocalyptic overtones, suggesting that the world as a whole was hurtling toward a final conflagration between the "children of light and the children of darkness."[21]

Notes

1. See Noth (1981b [1948]), Blum (1984).
2. Cf. Thompson (1984).
3. See Finkelstein and Mazar (2007), Liverani (2005).
4. For the debate on Israelite origins see Dever (2003), Davies (1992).
5. See Tamari (2008), 93–112.
6. See Schniedewind (2004).
7. Cohen (1999), Eckhardt (2012).
8. Levine (1987), Gruen (2011).
9. See Judges 12.
10. Schäfer (1997).
11. See Berthelot (2014), Eckhardt (2012), and note the Boston University Maccabees project, directed by archaeologist Andrea Berlin and historian Yonder Gillihan, see http://sites.bu.edu/maccabees (accessed November 22, 2017).
12. See Berlin (2005).
13. Hasmonean revival of Hebrew and other ancient Israelite markers of antiquity indicate a broader struggle for cultural identity and authenticity in the age of Hellenism. See Gardner and Osterloh (2008).
14. See Safrai (1965).
15. On the concept of "inheritance" see Leoni (2016).
16. See Goodman (2007).
17. Hengel (1981).
18. But see Klawans (2013).
19. See Neusner and Chilton (2007).
20. Little did they know that their empire was going to be subverted by a more decisive Jewish institution, "scripture." It would be an interesting contrafactual thought experiment to imagine how world history might have changed had the Romans eradicated all traces of Jewish scripture instead of destroying the temple.
21. Cf. the "War Scroll" (1QM), one of the seven original Dead Sea Scrolls known since 1947 (online edition at http://dss.collections.imj.org.il/war).

8

City and Scenario

The Fortress of Zion, conquered by a shrewd Judeo-Hebronite king and made the seat of his dynasty, became the emblem of Jewish political independence. This city took on greater, pan-Israelite meaning in the wake of the Assyrian destruction of Samaria, absorbing not just some of the Israelite population escaping foreign rule but also the claim to represent "Israel" and its covenantal obligation to "serve YHWH alone." Jerusalem was now the city "YHWH chose for his name to reside." In the name of the God of Israel, King Hezekiah of Judah staged a rebellion against Assyria and survived (the "miracle of 701"). After the collapse of Assyria, Jerusalem undertook a purge of the trappings of all foreign dependence and re-founded itself by renewing the covenant. It is in the context of the reforms of Josiah that we first hear of a "*sefer torah*," a scroll of instructions.

At the time of Josiah, the scroll, "found" in the temple during the repairs commanded by the king, is an instrument of dynastic policy that aims to cement Jerusalem's preeminence, centrality, and dominance in "Israel." At the time of Ezra, the Law of Moses was proclaimed and read aloud, as well as interpreted, so that the Aramaic-speaking Jews could understand it. This "priestly code" stipulated collective commitment to temple and priesthood that served as the constitutive institutions of Yehud, a Jewish sub-province, peacefully integrated into the Persian Empire. In Josiah's time, the "scroll of instruction" represented freedom from imperial dominance, while, in Ezra's

Jerusalem: A Brief History, First Edition. Michael Zank.

time, Torah served to consolidate Jewish life in and around Jerusalem in neighborly coexistence with the Samaritan Israelites, their northern neighbors, insisting on freedom only in a purely cultic sense, without a view to political autochthony.

It is easy to imagine the Jews of Jerusalem, assembled at the temple under the leadership of Ezra, the Judeo-Babylonian priest and scribe; as they listen to the stories of creation and exodus and absorb the laws and admonitions, they understand that it is their own story, the story of a people who, by the grace of God, are given a second chance and opportunity to redeem themselves, by diligently hearkening to the voice of His Law.

The Book of Ben Sira gives us a sense of the pride Jerusalemites derived from their scriptures, as well as from the solemn rituals conducted at the temple in Jerusalem. The book was composed at a time when Jerusalem was undergoing dramatic changes. It is possible that the author wrote because the great institutions associated with Jerusalem, scripture and temple-cult, seemed endangered. In 198 BCE, the Seleucids had expelled Jerusalem's Ptolemaic garrison, and the city came under Seleucid rule. As so often before and after, the Levant had seen a protracted period of battles between regional powers competing for this important gateway to land and sea trade. In 200 BCE, the Seleucid king prevailed at the Battle of Banyas (Greek: *Paneion*), and over the course of the next years consolidated his hold on the Levant. Antioch's ultimate goal was to take control of Egypt and thus restore the unity of the realm conquered by Alexander. In the preceding century, almost exactly from 300 to 200 BCE, the Levant – including *Ioudaia*, as the Persian province of Yehud was called in the Greek administrative language – had been ruled and taxed by the Ptolemies, centered in Alexandria. When the Ptolemies left, the Oniad priests and Tobiad tax farmers, who had dominated Jerusalem for a century, lost office, influence, and property, all of which were claimed by long-time rivals within Jerusalemite society who competed for Seleucid protection. Out of the turmoil that ensued, both internally and in relation to Antioch, rose the sons of Mattathias, better known as the Maccabees, who took power in Jerusalem and usurped the office of high priest. Though in the early days of their guerrilla warfare against the Seleucids these brothers collaborated with pious traditionalists, known in Greek as *asidaioi* (i.e. "pious ones"), who refused to fight on the Sabbath and resisted all trappings of Greek culture, the Hasmoneans, as they are later called, were pragmatists and realists who understood how to exploit various crises of succession at the Seleucid court, and ultimately gained independence for Jerusalem by backing the winning side in this dynastic contest.

To gain popular support, the Hasmoneans cast themselves as vigorous defenders of the ancestral way of life, established under Persian rule, against "Hellenism," the deliberate attempt, cultivated by Alexander and his successors, to amalgamate Greek and indigenous ways of life. But once established as high priests and later as kings, the Hasmoneans triggered dissent over the question of the right to rule. Jewish utopian visions emerged from a widely shared sense that things were not what they ought to be. When Antiochus IV (r. 175–164 BCE) suspended the Torah (perhaps at the behest of Jewish Hellenizers), dissent took the form of apocalyptic visions of a day of judgment when one "like a son of man" will come "with the clouds" and put an end to the reign of the evil beasts on earth; on that day, those who died the righteous death of martyrs for the law and hoped for a restoration to life, were to see their reward, and the evildoers were to be punished (cf. Daniel 12).[1] In those times of tribulation, ancient prophetic oracles found new meaning, including the hyperbolic metaphor, coined by Ezekiel, of a resurrection of the dead (cf. Ezekiel 37:3). Innocuous phrases (e.g. "a young woman will be with child," Isaiah 7:14) were read as signs of the end, the "day of YHWH" (Malachi 4:5), the coming of the kingship of Heaven (*malkhut shamayim*). Davidic kingship and its imminent revival served as a powerful incentive to oppose first Hasmonean and later Herodian claimants to the throne (*al kis'o lo yeshev zar*, says a liturgical prayer still in use today: "no alien shall usurp his throne"). Some seceded from the Jerusalemite temple because of the Hasmonean usurpation of the highest office, others seceded because of differences in the interpretation of a biblical wording that impacted on time-bound commandments, such as the heave offering (*hanifat ha-omer*) following the Passover. Yet others withdrew because of their astrological preference for a solar calendar, in contrast to the lunar calendar observed in Jerusalem.[2]

One particular utopian community from among the late second-commonwealth Jews went on to change the world. The early Christians were radical utopians from the Galilee, then a tetrarchy or sub-division of the Jewish realm ruled, under Roman auspices, by one of the sons of Herod. The followers of Jesus of Nazareth shared with other Galilean dissidents a strong contempt for the riches amassed by the Herodian elite and the high priests who were considered little more than conniving and self-serving collaborators of the Roman hegemon. The gospel stories about Jesus, the son of a Galilean artisan who became a preacher and miracle worker, are set in a milieu of debate, poverty, discontent, and the desire to gather "the lost sheep of the House of Israel" in a movement leading to the establishment of the kingship of God. Herodian rule and Roman power contributed to the destabilization of social order, and increased the sense of an impending day of judgment, in an atmosphere rife with apocalyptic speculation about the day and hour of the end (cf. Matthew 24).

The difference between the followers of Jesus and the Zealots who fomented rebellion against Rome was not always obvious, as the presence of a "knife-man" (Judas Iscariotes) among the followers of Jesus attests. Many early Christians suffered the same fate as other Jewish rebels, who were crucified by Romans or stoned by their fellow Jews, fearful of the disruption of order that emanated from dissent.

Jesus and the early Christians – including Paul, a freeborn Roman citizen from Tarsus in Asia Minor – attest to the vibrancy of the Jewish imagination in areas that were more or less removed from Jerusalem. Though hardly part of the diaspora, the first-century Galilee was a region no longer directly ruled by Jerusalem and a place where Jews, Samaritans, Greeks, and Syrians lived in close proximity to one another and where the purity and devotion of a Jew to the law was frequently tested and interrogated by other Jews, members of societies (*kat, havurah*) like the Pharisees who, much like the modern day *Habad* movement, hoped to strengthen every Jew's resolve to live a life of ritual purity and Sabbath observance. Like other charismatic figures, such as Honi the "circle-drawer" (*ha-meʾagel*), Jesus moved on the margins of the Pharisaic world and was subject to its scrutiny. Clearly the challenges to Jesus we read about in the gospels arose in this mutual testing of one another's respective visions of what it meant to live by the standards of divine kingship. Jesus and the Pharisees were different sides of the same coin of radicalized Jewish living in an age of impending doom.

The utopianism of late ancient Jews took several forms. All were based on discontent with the *status quo* of Hasmonean then Herodian and Roman rule. Some took issue with lax or faulty cultic practice or the usurpation of high sacerdotal office. Others hoped for the restoration of the Davidic monarchy (messianism; freedom from usurpation and foreign rule). Others were devoted to purifying demotic practice and practiced rigorous collective boundary maintenance (holiness movements), or aimed at breaking the stranglehold of elites, in the pursuit of equity and justice (social revolution). For some, the "end" took the form of a restoration of a fondly remembered *status quo ante* and a return to the good old days, however defined; others hoped instead for a new Jerusalem, a new humanity, and even a new heaven and a new earth. Some restricted, while others extended, the definition of "Israel." Some were aristocratic and exclusive, others egalitarian and

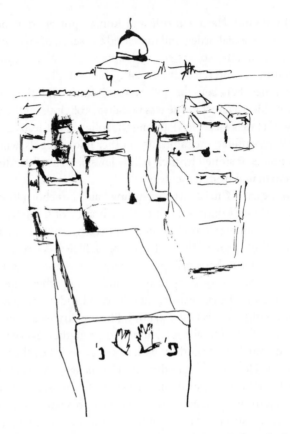

Figure 6   Tombs at the Jewish cemetery on the Mount of Olives look toward the Gate of Mercy, anticipating resurrection. Illustration by Miriam Shenitzer.

expansive. Some embraced asceticism, accusing others of being given over to luxury and vice. Those who saw a meticulously lawful way of life as God-pleasing accused others, who saw themselves as living the *eschaton*, as abominable libertines. Some were violent, others peaceful. Some believed in an afterlife, others did not. Some believed in the immortality of the soul, others asserted the resurrection of the body[3] (see Figure 6). Pretty much everyone believed in angels and feared demons. The unlearned masses took recourse to magic.[4] The sacrosanct name of the God of Israel was a particularly forceful incantation, attested beyond the confines of the Jewish marketplace. The boundaries between "philosophy" and popular religion were permeable.[5] In the end it was the actual *demos* that paid the price for the philosophically driven Jewish wars against Rome, which ended in disaster, destruction, deportation, deforestation, enslavement, banishment, and the obliteration of ancient Jewish Jerusalem.

The Roman destruction of Jerusalem, symbolized by the fire that destroyed the temple, is well remembered as the climactic moment in widely disseminated stories people told about the ancient Jewish city. The destruction was memorialized by three distinct groups to whom this event mattered, albeit for very different reasons: the Jews themselves, who lamented its loss and hoped for its restoration, as in former times; the Christians, who saw the destruction of the temple as a sign of God's displeasure with the Jews for rejecting Jesus Christ, and as evidence of the truth of their own dispensation; and the Flavian house of Roman emperors, who celebrated their victory over the Jews with great bombast for 12 years running, because it was pretty much their only claim to fame in the eyes of the senate and people of Rome, who despised them as *homines novi*.

The event mattered most immediately to the Jews, for whom it meant the loss not just of sovereignty and independence, but also of a central symbol of their collective identity and trans-national cohesion. The rebellion against Rome had failed. But not everyone had participated in this rebellion, many opposed it, and some were forced to stay and withstand the Roman siege against their will. One of the most important Jewish scholars of his time, Rabban Yohanan ben Zakkai, is said to have escaped Jerusalem surreptitiously in a casket. When confronted by the Roman authorities, he turned to them, saying: "Give me a school and ten children!" This is the founding myth of the Synod of Yavneh, the institution that, according to rabbinic tradition, replaced the Great Sanhedrin of Jerusalem after city and temple were destroyed. The story indicates ambivalence toward the rebellion, and Jewish willingness to live in peace with the Romans. This anticlimactic response to the events of the year 70 was forged by the rabbis of the late second to first third of the third century CE, an age of accommodation between the Severan emperors and the Jewish aristocracy. But this attitude was honed only gradually, over the course of the century that followed the destruction, and in light of the failure of a second uprising, the Bar Kokhba revolt (132–135), which – as coins minted by the rebels indicate – was fought for the liberation of Jerusalem. The image imprinted on these coins was the entrance to the holy temple.

The immediate Jewish responses to the events of 70 were less sanguine. Some rebels continued their fight and holed up in Masada, or in caves along the Sea of Galilee. The apocalyptic book of Fourth Ezra (part of the apocryphal 2 Esdras), written a decade or two after the destruction of the temple, hopes for divine intervention and an imminent end to Roman rule. Others calmly prepared for the rematch.

The Galilean rabbis of the early third century were invested in preserving the memory of Jerusalem and the temple. But their task consisted in establishing rules for a Jewish way of life in the absence of a temple that was now no longer a living reality, but a matter of memories to be preserved for the eventuality of its reconstruction. The tannaitic rabbis of Sepphoris, under the tutelage of ethnarch Judah "the Prince," provided the necessary conditions for the continuity of Jewish life within the Land of Israel and beyond. The legal compendium they produced, known as the Mishnah, devotes two out of its six orders to matters pertaining to temple and sacrifice and many of the other legal traditions are also linked to Jerusalemite priestly customs and obligations that the Mishnah invokes as a measure and yardstick for its various ordinances. Reminiscences of Jerusalem, the restoration of the House of David, the ingathering of the exiles, the rebuilding of the temple, and the resumption of the daily sacrifices have remained central to Jewish liturgical prayer. Prayers, hymns (*piyyutim*), works of textual elucidation and homiletics (*midrash*), and literary visions describing the divine throne-world (*hekhalot*), produced in the Land of Israel over the centuries of Roman rule and beyond, preserved the memory of the sanctuary, emulated its functions, and directed prayer and attention to the divine sanctuary, located just above the ruins of the earthly one. This pious imagination, honed over centuries among the Jews of Palestine and adopted across the diaspora, transformed Jerusalem into a grammatical dual: a twice existing city, one in ruins below, and one above and firmly established forever, *yerushalayim shel mata* and *yerushalayim shel ma'la*. Mystical voyages took pious visionaries to the heavenly sanctuary when Rome rendered the lower Jerusalem inaccessible. Under Roman rule, Jews were permitted to approach the city's vicinity only during their annual lament for the destruction of the temple, on the Ninth of Av, a ritual tolerated as well as mocked by Byzantine Christians in whose eyes it reinforced the inferior status of the Jews.

Christians saw the destruction of the temple as a major providential act, confirming the sinfulness of the Jews and, by implication, evidence of the truth of the gospel. For Melito (third quarter of the second century CE *floruit*), quartodeciman Bishop of Sardes, eunuch, and, as some have thought, possibly himself of Jewish descent, Jerusalem's history was completely readable in light of divine justice; in a measure-for-measure interpretation, the razing of Jerusalem was punishment for the murder of Christ at the hands of Israel.[6] The rise and fall of the Jewish commonwealth centered in Jerusalem and its temple were of concern for Christians, especially for those who, like Melito (and Paul before him), saw faith in Christ grounded in the Law and the Prophets, the "books of the old covenant." Once the death of Christ and the destruction of Jerusalem were causally related to one another, the second historic datum, a plain fact, could be invoked as proof of the first. Though Melito himself called for an annihilation of the (other) Jews, presumably to distinguish his own quartodeciman tradition (the then still widely practiced commemoration of Christ's death on the fourteenth day of Nissan, the Jewish Passover) from the "old covenant," what eventually prevailed was something different: following the advice of Augustine, sainted bishop of Hippo, Jews were to be kept alive, though inferior in status, to symbolically attest to the truth of Christianity.[7] Late ancient and medieval Christianity thus ritualized the destruction of Jerusalem no less than did the Jews, though with a completely different semantic. It was inscribed with the meaning of punishment of the Jews as perfidious Christ-killers and deicides, with the Jews themselves (or their representation in form of the synagogue in the guise of a woman with a broken staff) carrying their exile as punishment through time. To be sure, the "razed" Jerusalem could serve as a marker of this rejection of the Jews only as long as the temple was still in ruins. We will see in the next chapter how Emperor Constantine put this doctrine to use when he transformed Jerusalem, then known as *Aelia Capitolina*, into the blueprint for a commemorative landscape. Later on we will have occasion to describe how this Christian triumphalist charade was used and subverted by the early Muslims, using the same means of monumental architecture for the manifestation of similar spiritual claims.

The ill fate of Jerusalem was integrated into a Christian narrative of special providence, retributive justice, and divine power. Early rabbinic Judaism and proto-Orthodox Christianity are related formations distinguished mostly by how they interpreted the destruction of Jerusalem, namely, either as a rallying call for its rebuilding or as a sign of divine retribution for the rejection of Christ. Both took the event seriously. Both grounded their dispensation in the same body of literature, the Jewish scriptures, whose canonization likewise unfolded along the fault line between these competing interpretive traditions. Christians and Jews were both affected by Roman violence and hence had in common that they associated divine election with suffering. In this respect, however, there was to be a more decisive parting of the ways than could be anticipated in the first two centuries following the destruction of the temple. Rabbinic Judaism eventually associated divine suffering with the ongoing Jewish exile, whereas fourth-century Orthodox Christianity was to exchange the suffering Christ for the triumphant *Christos pantocrator*. Their respective attitude toward the Holy City was determined by the very different places their respective theologians assigned to their own community in the economy of salvation.

As mentioned above, Vespasian and his sons Titus and Domitian, who succeeded their father as emperors, shaped another strong and self-interested response to the destruction of Jerusalem. Vespasian was a Spanish-born general who had not shown any political ambitions of his own when Nero sent him to quell the Jewish rebellion that had broken out in 66. Vespasian went about his task methodically, mopping up one Jewish fortress that had joined the resistance after the other. When Nero died in 68, Vespasian withdrew to Alexandria, waiting for further orders. Over the next 12 months no less than three pretenders failed to secure the leadership of the empire, at which point Vespasian accepted the acclamation of his troops, left his son Titus in charge of a swift action against Jerusalem, and went to Rome to secure his new office. The Roman aristocracy regarded the Flavians as *homines novi*, people without pedigree and with little to recommend them for the highest office in service of the people and senate of Rome. In the event, Jerusalem fell and Titus extracted the fabulous wealth that had accrued in the temple. This windfall helped the Flavians to cast themselves as builders on a scale not seen since the days of Augustus. The ruins of the Coliseum, Rome's best known emblem, attest to the riches extracted from Jerusalem. Josephus describes the triumph celebrating the victory over the Jews. The Titus Arch, built by Domitian in honor of his brother and still standing among the ruins of the Forum Romanum, illustrates the exaggerated value his family derived from their association with the fall of Jerusalem. On it, Domitian brags about the fact that Titus had brought down a city no one had ever dared to attack before. Small-denomination coinage, celebrating the capture of Jerusalem in pictures of a bound woman under a palm tree (see Figure 7), brought the same message to millions of illiterate paupers enjoying the blessings bestowed upon them by the divinized emperors who had restored the peace of the fatherland.

Figure 7   Reverse of a Flavian "Ivdea Capta" coin. Illustration by Miriam Shenitzer.

Notes

1. On apocalyptic tradition see Collins (2014).
2. The so-called Temple Scroll of Qumran cave 11 (11QT) presupposes a solar calendar, deviating from what was normative at the time and in later rabbinic Judaism.
3. See Klawans (2013).
4. See Hull (1974), Meyer and Mirecki (2001).
5. Cf. Frankfurter (2003).
6. See Melito of Sardis (2001).
7. Cf. Fredriksen (2008).

Part III
Imperial City

9

Constantine's *Hagiapolis Hierousalem*

In the year 326 CE, Roman Empress Helena Augusta appeared in a provincial city called *Aelia Capitolina*, a place high up in the mountains of Syria-Palaestina, where the Tenth Roman legion (*X Fretensis*) had maintained a veteran's colony and the active legion had been headquartered until just two decades earlier, when it moved south to Aila (Eilat) to guard that sea port against Persian incursions. Helen traveled throughout Syria to promote the policies of her son, Constantine, who had recently succeeded in eliminating his last rival, Licinius Augustus. With the combined military and fiscal powers of the Roman Empire securely in his hands, Constantine began a vast program of religious, legal, and political reform that included the regulation of the Christian faith and the promotion of this newly unified orthodoxy as the dominant religion of the Roman state.[1] Among his measures was the liberation of Roman citizens who had been languishing in exile or laboring in salt mines since the great persecution of Christians instituted by Diocletian and his colleagues in 303, which in some parts of the empire had lasted for more than a decade. The pardoning of Christians involved the restitution of property now in the hands of others who were likely to be upset about this turn of events. Part of Helen's mission was to assuage the concerns of the traditional elites at this reversal, by distributing lavish gifts to all while endorsing the public authority of the Christian bishops. This program included the sponsoring of Christian sanctuaries at

Jerusalem: A Brief History, First Edition. Michael Zank.
© 2018 Michael Zank. Published 2018 by John Wiley & Sons Ltd.

the sites of Christian martyrdom. Her festive *adventus* to *Aelia* – an imperial visit staged with so much pomp and circumstance that it was as if a god or goddess one only knew by hearsay was now appearing in person – elevated both city and empress: the city, proscenium of the most revered miracle of the resurrection of Christ, conferred on the empress the dignity of eyewitness to another resurrection: the miraculous discovery (*inventio* or "coming upon") of the empty tomb of Christ and the finding of the True Cross.

Here is how I imagine Helen's *adventus*. Dignitaries and townspeople, mostly veterans of the *legio fretensis* and their families, are lining the wide cobbled access road leading to the gate of the column cheering the imperial carriage as it is met by the reigning bishop Macarios, who was indeed in luck: the sleepy provincial military settlement over which he presided was about to be turned into one of the major cities of the *oikumene*, the inhabited world. Several panegyric speeches later and imperial favors having been showered on the poor and downtrodden, empress and bishop attend the ceremonial dismantling of a temple of Aphrodite, loathed by the Christians as a vile she-demon, a shrine believed to have been erected by the enemies of Christ on the very spot of his glorious resurrection. The intention of the demons, and of the "wicked men" who were their vessels, had been to obscure "that divine monument to immortality" and token of Christ's victory over death, "at which, brilliant with light, the angel who had descended from heaven had rolled away the stones of those whose minds were set like stone in their assumption that the Living One was still with the dead, when he announced the good news to the women and removed the stone of disbelief from their minds by the information that the one they sought was alive."[2] After tearing down the building to its foundations, a process that must have taken days, if not weeks, the workmen begin to remove the earth and rubble that had supported the shrine and absorbed the blood and libations of two centuries of pagan sacrificial worship. This is when it gets suspenseful. What will they find hidden under the surface? (To this day, excavations in Jerusalem are like that. You never know what you will find when you start digging.) In this case, the Christians seemed to know what they were looking for.[3] A hundred and fifty years earlier, Melito of Sardes reported that he was shown a place in the middle of the city that local guides told him was the place where Christ had been crucified. This testimony has puzzled learned Christian pilgrims and archaeologists in that it put the venerated place of Golgotha within the boundaries of the Roman city of Aelia, whereas the gospels state that Jesus was crucified outside the city walls. Nonetheless, the excavation of the grounds beneath the temple of Aphrodite yielded a powerful discovery that, as Eusebius emphasizes, was entirely unexpected.

What Helen brought to *Aelia* was transformative not just for the Holy City but also for the Roman Empire itself.[4] It was a cult restoration of the first order. Her son, Flavius Valerius Aurelius Constantinus (271/2?–337), better known as Constantine the Great, was the son of Constantius Chlorus, named one of two *caesares* by Diocletian in 293, who served as one of two *augusti* from 305, when Diocletian and Maximinianus Herculius relinquished office, until his death in 306. Helen was a woman of low social origin, known to ancient authors as an "innkeeper's daughter." Late ancient and medieval Christians revered her as the model of a pious empress and a great saint. Constantine was the first Roman Emperor to embrace the Christian religion openly, ushering in a new age in Roman as well as in Christian history, though at the time this was not widely perceived as a major event, and the world historic consequences we tend to ascribe to Constantine's "conversion" are only perceived in hindsight and due to a long history of Christian writing.

After his father's sudden death plunged the empire into a crisis of leadership, Constantine was able to take power by military force. In 312, he defeated the usurper Maxentius. In 324, he took over the eastern part of the empire by defeating his last co-regent Licinius. From that time on, Constantine ruled a unified empire. His subsequent efforts were devoted to securing this unity and passing it on in dynastic succession. He appointed his mother Helena and his wife Fausta as co-regents (*augustae*) and pursued a policy of unifying the empire under the authority of his family. He also leaned on the Christian bishops to agree on a universal creed. His measures were aimed at the consolidation of rule as the single emperor. His motto was "one god, one emperor, one empire." Despite lavish support for the Christians he was unsuccessful in making Christianity the dominant religion of the empire, a feat accomplished only toward the end of the fourth century by Theodosius I,[5] and only at the cost of violently disrupting pagan cults, disadvantaging Greek schools of thought, suffocating Jewish self-governance in what was now the Christian Holy Land, and condemning most sects perceived as deviating from the creed issued by the councils of orthodox bishops that the emperor convened, beginning in 325 at Nicaea.

After 324, Constantine fortified and developed the city of Byzantium on the Bosporus to prepare a new, more central, and better-defended capital for his newly unified empire, as well as to create a residence for himself that was less fraught with ancient aristocratic privilege than Rome.

Constantinople was inaugurated in 330 and it remained the capital of the Byzantine-Roman Empire until it fell to the Ottoman Turks in 1453. Constantine himself died near Nicomedia in 337.

Constantine's turn from the solar symbolism of *sol invictus* to Christ remains a riddle if we only look to the utility of gaining the enthusiastic support of the Christians, whom he openly favored and supported, by casting himself as the one who had ended persecution, defeated the tyrants, freed the captives, restored their property, and exempted the bishops – lifelong leaders of the growing urban Christian communities – from onerous and costly civic duties. In 324, Christians constituted no more than 10% of the population. Constantine was thus not angling for popular support for his reign, but he recognized the symbolic power of the Christian religion, especially if it could be streamlined to serve as an empire-wide, imperially sanctioned way of worshiping the true universal god. The emperor, traditionally the *pontifex maximus* of the Roman rites, became the Vicar of Christ *pantocrator*, the ruler of all.

What predisposed Christ, whom Julian (Constantine's nephew and the last "pagan" emperor, r. 360/1–363) derisively called a "Galilean," to become the object of Roman imperial veneration? Wasn't the "kingdom of god" that Jesus had preached precisely *not* of this world, and had not Jesus taught to render unto Caesar what was Caesar's but to render unto God what was God's? How was the mystery of the death and resurrection of Christ turned from a divine call to eternal life into an ideology sustaining an empire?

From its inception, the Christian movement competed with other religions; in fact, it was outright polemical in its proclamation of the kingdom of God. There were the common astral religions of the east, that had long since been rendered translatable into the pantheon of Greco-Roman religion (e.g. Tyrean Melqart = Greco-Roman Hercules). Christians demonized the traditional gods of the Roman pantheon and, once Christianity acquired imperial protection, effectively expelled the gods from the cities and forced them into the countryside, where they continued to be venerated by *pagani*, i.e. people beyond the pale of civic, civilized, and literate urban life. The remaining urban defenders of the traditional gods and of their religious duties branded the Christians as atheists, because they made people neglect the customary sacrifices to the gods.

When Christianity began to spread, most individuals – both among the elite, but also among legionaries across the empire – would seek personal purification and rebirth in the practices of devotional mystery cults, that were centered on a particular deity (Isis, Mithras, etc.) or located at a particular shrine (e.g. Eleusis). These cults, which required initiation, cut across ethnic divides and thus anticipated some of the broad appeal of Christianity.

Judaism – originally an ethnic religion not unlike others that, as such, posed no threat in Roman eyes – had long since spread beyond its national center. It appealed to many non-Jews, and its dissemination by means of literature and translation prepared the groundwork for the followers of Christ, who claimed that literary inheritance for themselves, while effectively removing the wall between Jews and non-Jews.

Christianity appealed to many people for many reasons. Christian theology appealed to the philosophically trained, because it had much in common with the philosophical schools' criticism of the gods of Hesiod and Homer, without thereby embracing the impiety of the Epicureans who taught not to fear the gods at all. The extravagantly ascetic "contented" life of the Egyptian desert fathers and their gospel of abstemiousness appealed to many because these monks were superior healers and exorcists. Their god even produced results on the racetracks, if saints like Honorius deigned to bless a Christian stable! Christian charity was extensive, and the great masses of the urban poor, orphaned, and widowed were well taken care of by elaborate systems of distribution under the supervision of the local bishops and deacons. Furthermore, the Christian faith offered a path to a type of care for the soul that made the inevitability of individual suffering bearable and even meaningful. Finally, the Christians offered a communal bond of mutual solidarity between people that had hitherto seen themselves as unrelated. It was perhaps this aspect of the Christian religion in particular that made it attractive to an empire that lacked unity, solidarity, homogeneity, and an identifiable common purpose among its citizens.

Constantine's adoption of Christianity was aimed at transforming the empire and it succeeded. Just over 100 years earlier, when Caracalla had extended Roman citizenship to all freeborn citizens of the empire, a legal framework had been created for the many people who found themselves part of a largely accidental empire, that the senate and people of Rome had acquired by military and diplomatic means over the course of two centuries. But the legal fiction of Roman citizenship waited to be filled with a more affective content that might more effectively forge mutual solidarity among the nominally united citizens. While this goal ultimately remained elusive, Constantine's measures nevertheless transformed a city-state ruling many nations into an empire governed by a single and divinely sanctioned authority. The establishment of a New Rome in Constantinople, preferred by the emperor because of its remove from the oversight of traditional Roman aristocracy, was part of that revolutionary strategy, as was the transformation of Palestine into a Christian holy land, and of Aelia into *Hierapolis Hierousalem*.

Much has been written and much more can be said about this world-historic turn in Roman history. Given our focus on Jerusalem, we may add the following consideration. While some of what was said above may explain the persuasiveness of a Christian justification of Roman imperial rule, there are other reasons why the biblical variant of ancient Near Eastern religion turned out to be useful for the Roman imperial theologians.

Christianity saw itself as the culmination of all ancient wisdom, foreshadowed in Greek and Jewish sources and presaged by Virgil and the Roman Sibyl, in a redemptive theology of divine rule that enabled individuals to find remission of sins and entrance into the Kingdom of God, a new humanity where there was room for everyone: rich and poor, male and female, Jew and Greek. But the church was not just a communion of saints. It was a communion of *milites christi*, a body politic tested during times of persecution and now rewarded by imperial support. This combination of divinely sanctioned kingship and a body politic was modeled on the biblical covenant between God and Israel. In scripture, God's covenant was with a people. The role of the priestly aristocracy and of divinely chosen kings was subservient to the idea of one nation under one god. Jerusalem's appeal to the empire was that it could be honored as the place from which this new dispensation had emanated, a place that was central and axial, linking the three ancient continents, as well as linking earth and heaven. It didn't hurt that the message of Christ's resurrection was not just a potent political metaphor but also a popular belief.

Imperial rule was sold to the masses as providential, and the god in whose name Constantine and his successors ruled could be argued to be more caring than the unvanquished sun, which was no more than a metaphor of a supreme power that was necessary for life to exist and, at the same time, blinding if looked upon with the naked eye. More powerful than any natural symbolism was the biblical idea of a creator who, as revealed through his servants, the prophets, and through Christ and his apostles, was superior to nature as well as present in history. This biblical religion had produced scores of martyrs and inspired holy men who could heal the sick and exorcise demons. The Bible provided a redemptive story disseminated through word and image that even the illiterate could grasp and relate to, while it gave infinite room for the learned to expound in elaborate homilies, in concatenations of passages from scripture and other sources that put their erudition on dazzling display, and in church histories and group biographies of saints and martyrs as exemplars of a Christian way recommended for imitation.

The unprecedented position of the church within the Roman state led to an unanticipated sharpening of the dogmatic divisions between Christian schools of thought. The doctrinal fault line coincided with regional and ethno-linguistic divides within the Roman east. The major schools of thought were associated, respectively, with the cities of Alexandria in Egypt (the leading school until c. 450) and Syrian Antioch. The Alexandrians taught, and vigorously fought for, the belief that even Christ's body had been divine through and through (monophysitism), whereas Antiochene theologians argued for the fully human nature of Christ's body. The Antiochene doctrine prevailed at the council of Chalcedon (451) and has since remained the "right teaching" (orthodoxy). In a compromise between extremes, this doctrine argues for the "unmixed" though "inseparable" presence of two natures (divine and human) in Christ. Perhaps not accidentally, it was at the same council that Jerusalem was elevated to the same level as the other chief Christian cities, Alexandria, Antioch, Rome, and Constantinople. It is noteworthy that the theological divide between Alexandria and Antioch mirrored the ancient linguistic and cultural differences between autochthonous Egypt and the multicultural Aramaic-speaking society of Syria. It also anticipated some of the political divisions that were to remain virulent throughout the history of the Middle East and that are still relevant today. Though it was not until the Arab conquest that Egypt and Syria were severed from Constantinople and Asia Minor, the relative autonomy of these Hellenic Christian urban centers with their distinct national-religious cultures did not bode well for the future unity of the Roman Empire. Ironically, Byzantine power and the unity of the region were undermined by the very desire to unify what was left of the Roman Empire, on the basis of Christian doctrine.

The religious revolution triggered by the conversion of the empire exceeded the range of Byzantine orthodoxy and eluded its control. Orthodox Christians were not alone in producing literature in praise of their holy men and spreading collections of wise sayings of the fathers. Jews and pagans boasted martyrs as well. Constantine's elevation of one version of faith and its practices and traditions inadvertently gave rise to a competition among many groups vying for legitimacy and recognition. Instead of creating a unified and homogeneous population of citizens, Byzantium inadvertently generated a "commonwealth of communities"[6] rooted in scriptures, learned traditions, doctrinal assertions, communal practices, and defensive and polemical arguments. It later fell to the Muslims to embrace and foster this plurality of communities under the unifying flag of a prophet who took this plurality of "peoples of the book" (*ahl al-kitab*) for granted.

Under the Byzantines, *Aelia* – aka *Hagiapolis Hierousalem* – developed into a major center of Christian pilgrimage.[7] It is not very likely that many Christians cared for Aelia until its fourth-century transformation.[8] However, once the empire initiated the recovery of biblical places, a lot of intellectual and practical effort went into mapping the Christian *storia sacra* onto the landscape of Palestine. The fifth-century council of Chalcedon's emphasis on Christ's humanity merely confirmed what fourth-century imperial orthodoxy had accomplished when it converted the landscape of Palestine into a *lieu memoire*, reminding believers across the *oikumene* that God had walked on earth in a real body, in a place where traces of His erstwhile presence could once again be found, visited, and venerated.

Notes

1. On the age of Constantine see Lenski (2006).
2. See Cameron (1999).
3. On the history of the Holy Sepulchre see Morris (2005), Walker (1990), Ousterhout (1990).
4. On the following, see Drijvers (1992), Demandt (1989), James (2001).
5. See Lippold (1968).
6. See Fowden (1993), Herbert (1979).
7. See Drijvers in Alston et al. (2013), 309–329, and Elsner (2000).
8. On Aelia before Constantine see Belayche (1999) and (2001).

10

Pax Christiana sive Islamica

The story of the True Cross or Holy Wood, widely disseminated in the
Middle Ages as part of the "Golden Legend" (*legenda aurea*), narrates the
miraculous origin and vicissitudes of this most precious of all divine instruments of salvation.[1] According to the Gospel of Nicodemus and other
apocryphal sources, the Holy Wood was first discovered by Seth,[2] the son of
Adam and Eve, later rediscovered by King Solomon who found it growing
on Mount Lebanon, then attested by the Queen of Sheba at the temple in
Jerusalem. "Thereafter it was found by the Jews in a fish pond."[3] Helen's
rediscovery of the most holy instrument of human salvation helped
St. Macarios of Jerusalem to draw pilgrims to the holy place that
remained under his supervision after Helen's departure, and the object itself
could be easily "translated," i.e. parts of it carried off and displayed elsewhere, including Byzantium, the new Rome and city of Constantine
(*Constantinopolis*). It thus came to represent Christian Jerusalem itself, a
holy city disseminated and emulated all over Christendom. Over time,
slivers of the True Cross, coveted as powerful relics, proliferated to the point
that wits argued one could make an entire Noah's Ark from all the fragments. The two discoveries attributed to Helen, that of the empty tomb and
that of the cross, were enshrined in two buildings Constantine erected in
their place: the *Anastasis* encircling the empty tomb, and the *Martyrium* (a
basilica) that arose over the cave from which the True Cross had emerged.[4]

Jerusalem: A Brief History, First Edition. Michael Zank.
© 2018 Michael Zank. Published 2018 by John Wiley & Sons Ltd.

In between these sites, like the sacrificial altar of the erstwhile temple, was the mount of Golgotha, site of Christ's death, where the True Cross towered, encased in a silver reliquary. In these buildings, moments of the sacred history from Adam to Christ could be seen, touched, and meditated on: Christ's (and our) humanity, suffering, and death, and Christ's (and our) victory over sin, death, and the devil.[5] Without a doubt, it was during the reign of Constantine that Jerusalem attained the extraordinary holiness for Christians that it has enjoyed ever since.[6]

How are we to understand the transformation of Hadrian's *Aelia* into a Christian theme park called *Hagiapolis Hierousalem*? I'd like to consider the wider context of this act of rebranding and the reason why Jerusalem served the interests of this and the later empires that claimed it.

Constantine lavished attention on Jerusalem and on the Christian Holy Land and holy places because he claimed to rule in the name of Christ and his Father, Eusebius's "universal King." We can't be sure what exactly Constantine was thinking. But his measures brought about a revolutionary change in the Roman justification of power and it changed the character of imperial rule. This is not to say that Constantine's decision had no antecedents or that it did not follow, to some degree, on measures that his predecessors had introduced, or that he conceived of the problems of imperial governance in completely different terms. Still, there was something radical and novel about Constantine's adoption of Christ as his patron and Christianity as the faith on which he founded the government, legislation, and administration of the newly unified empire.[7] Edward Gibbon, following the lead of pagan critics of Constantine, foremost among them Constantine's nephew Julian ("the Apostate") and the late fifth- to early sixth- century Byzantine historian Zosimus, dated the decline and fall of the Roman Empire from the conversion of Constantine, arguing that it eroded the Roman military spirit and replaced it with a religion that supported the weak; the other mistake was that the Romans increasingly farmed out the defense of their borders to the barbarians.[8] The nineteenth-century historian Theodor Mommsen saw the "Constantinian turn" (*konstantinische Wende*) as a change in regime: hitherto the emperor had been *princeps* and his realm a "principate"; henceforth the emperor was *dominus* and his realm a "dominate"; a monarchy in all but name.[9] These eighteenth- and nineteenth-century Europeans, weary of religious power, thought of the age of Constantine as the end of a genuinely Roman empire, which they admired and recommended for emulation, and as the beginning of a religiously or biblically motivated type of rule (associated with the name of the new capital at *Byzantium*) that they deplored. Modern scholars may offer a more differentiated assessment of Byzantine rule,[10] but sources contemporary with the Arab conquest suggest that many communities were glad to see the last of the "accursed Chalcedonians." Comparative historians often favor the early Muslim rulers of the Middle East because they were able to negotiate the multi-ethnic, multi-religious pluralism of their realm more successfully and humanely.[11] The Byzantine brand of empire remains implicated in advancing an ideology of religious homogeneity that may have been mitigated by social, military, and economic realities but remained tainted by laws of religious discrimination and policies that failed to curb violently exclusivist religious sentiments. Under Theodosius I (d. 395), the empire stood by when Christians took revenge on pagans, rioting on the streets of Alexandria and elsewhere, wreaking havoc on their gods, their temples, and their libraries; the last Byzantine Emperor to rule Jerusalem, Heraclius (d. 641) (see Figure 8), is known to have attempted an empire-wide conversion of the Jews. Nor should the Muslim rulers be unduly idealized. As their religion became more dominant among the populations of the Middle East and North Africa, the interest in maintaining civic order occasionally gave way to pressures of inter-religious competition infused with a fear of foreign invasion and tinged with religious apocalyptic overtones, leading to waves of persecution of dissenters and minorities. Oppression of religious dissent, though not the rule, was inadvertently part of maintaining a divinely sponsored imperial dispensation.

(a)   (b)

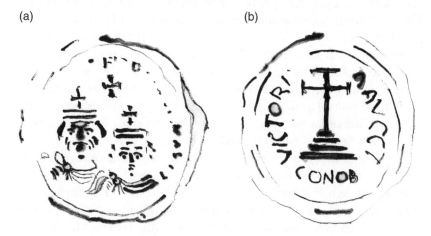

Figure 8 Byzantine gold solidus. Obverse: Emperor Heraclius and his son. Reverse: Cross on steps. Illustration by Miriam Shenitzer.

Jerusalem is implicated in the history of imperial monotheism, an ideology well expressed in Constantine's motto of "one god, one empire, one
emperor," but not limited to Roman rule. Jerusalem mattered, because to
claim Jerusalem meant to claim a divine inheritance while fending off the
odium of usurpation and innovation.

To, as it were, cement this inheritance emperors, caliphs, kings, and sultans sponsored monumental religious buildings (see Map 9). It is for this
reason that Jerusalem looks the way it does, which is a bit like a religious
shrine into which one overly rich patron after the other muscled his or her
outsized votive gift, sometimes placed right next to the gifts of others and
sometimes right on top of them.

Constantine was the first who made Jerusalem into what it became for
Christians, a lavishly appointed city with shrines dedicated to Christian
personages and doctrines. Constantine's design included a visual reminder
of the city's Jewish and pagan pasts: the erstwhile Temple Mount, now in
ruins. In Eusebius's words, the "new Jerusalem" towered over the "old
Jerusalem." This Byzantine strategy of self-representation by means of monumental architecture commemorating moments of holy history and aspects
of divine mystery was later emulated and creatively transformed by the
Arabic and Turkic rulers who inherited the Judeo-Christian Holy Land and
its holy cities.[12] The Jerusalem acquired by the Arabs in the early second
third of the seventh century was that very *Hagiapolis Hierousalem* inaugurated by Constantine and further developed by his successors, a Byzantine
city inhabited predominantly by Greek- and Syriac-speaking Christians of
"Rome" (*rum*). If the invention (in the common sense of that word) of this
"biblicate" Jerusalem belongs to Constantine and Helen, the securing and
perfection of this patent in doctrinal, architectural, military, and legal terms
was accomplished by their successors, the Byzantine emperors and
empresses of the fourth to early seventh century CE, foremost among them
the fifth-century Theodosian Empress Eudokia, who – banished from the
court at Constantinople by her sister-in-law, Pulcheria – became the ruler
of the Holy Land and rebuilt the walls of Jerusalem.[13]

Muslim caliphs as well used symbolic architecture to visualize their claim
to rule in the name of the creator of heaven and earth, who had revealed
himself through his prophets. What Constantine had deliberately left in
ruins, the Temple Mount, was restored by the Muslims to renewed splendor
and advanced as the symbolic center of the earth. Though Muslims and
Christians disagreed on who represented the final dispensation in God's
plan, both built on Jewish/biblical foundations.[14]

If one takes a long view, as Jerusalem's history requires, one is surprised at how stable the city really was, in so many respects, over the course of so many centuries, while Christian and Muslim elites took turns ruling, repairing, and redesigning the city and its holy places. The relative stability of rule and administration accomplished by these empires experiences major disruptions only twice over the course of nearly two millennia. On these two occasions – we will look at them in a moment – imperial powers encroached on one another's territory but failed to make a lasting change in the greater regional balance of power. The immediate effects of these encroachments were episodic, though in hindsight they heralded seismic shifts in geo-political affairs. Experiences of bloody conquest, expulsion, and temporary exile left populations traumatized and resentful of one another. They also called the empire's claim to divinely sanctioned rule into question. Defeat and displacement generated literatures of lament and cast the suffering righteous as tragic heroes who left behind desire and demand for ultimate rectification, the need for which was no less strongly felt by Christians and Muslims than by Jews praying for an end to their exile. Christian and Muslim rulers deciphered moments of defeat in light of antecedent providential history, just as suffering populations could see themselves as a new generation of martyrs. The apocalyptic dimension of antecedent tradition was revived whenever historical events were experienced as harbingers of the end, which was particularly the case when Jerusalem's imperial peace was profoundly disrupted. The apocalyptic imagination always thrived on the margins of power, among the many oppressed and disenfranchised communities that in today's Middle East include Shiite and Sunni minorities locked in proxy wars they hope will lead to a new geo-political order, in place of yet another temporary encroachment on their world, like the one that led to the destruction of the last caliphate.

The Two Disruptions of Imperial Peace: 614 and 1099

In 614, two decades before the Arabs conquered Jerusalem, Roman imperial rule of the east was disrupted when Sassanid general Shahrbaraz took the Holy City after a prolonged siege. This conquest was seared into the memory of Greek Christendom as an unprecedented blood bath. To add insult to injury, in Jerusalem – long since a thoroughly Christianized city from which Jews remained banished – the Persians installed their Jewish allies as governors, an experiment in *status quo* rectification that was soon abandoned due to Christian unrest. The installation of a Jewish government in Jerusalem triggered Christian violence that was, in turn, brutally repressed by the Persians.[15]

The context for these events was the Persian consolidation under the Sassanids, who promoted the fire-religion of Zoroaster as a state cult, just as the Byzantines were promoting the cult of Christ. The memory of 614 lingered among the Christians, who engaged in a violent backlash against the Jews of Syria and Palestine and enshrined their own fallen as a new crop of martyrs. The Persian–Roman wars finally wore out both empires and made them easy prey for the Arabs of the Hejaz, who fell into Syria just a few years after Emperor Heraclius had retrieved the region from the Persians.[16] The Arab conquest of 638, about which we will hear later on, engendered no comparable narrative of resentment. Yet Christian hopes for a reconquest of the Holy Land lingered and were taken up centuries later, leading to the second great disruption in Jerusalem's imperial peace.

This second great disruption took place on the eve of the twelfth century (1099) and it came in the form of the Frankish Crusades in the east. The first Frankish campaign that successfully established a foothold in *outremer* ("overseas") was led by counts Godfrey, Tancred, and Raymond, whose expedition was occasioned by a call from Byzantine Emperor Alexios I Komnenos for military help against the Seljuk Turks. The Franks were following the call, issued by Pope Urban II in 1095 at Clermont in Southern France, to let go of their petty infighting and turn their arms instead against the "infidel Turks," who were rumored to oppress the saints and to defile the most sacred tomb of Christ. The knights vowed not to rest until the "abomination of desolation" was removed and the holy places were back in Christian hands. What drove the Frankish knights, but also women, children, and paupers, to take up the cross must have been a complex mix of motivations, ranging from religious zeal and fear of hellfire to adventurism and the prospect of gain. In the event, Jerusalem was taken in a bloodbath enshrined in several pious memoires of the participants in this act of religious conquest for the liberation of the holy places. For the next 88 years the Noble Sanctuary of the Muslims was the stage for Frankish nobles to play out their neo-Maccabean fantasy of Jerusalem, with the Qibli mosque as their palace and the Dome of the Rock as Solomon's temple (*templum Salomonis*). In 1187, Jerusalem was retaken by a Muslim coalition led by the Ayyubid Sultan Salah ud-Din (Saladin), who defeated the Christians at the

Horns of Hattin.[17] Acre, the last Frankish bastion in the Holy Land, fell to the Cairene Mamluks in 1291, ending the first French foray into colonial expansion. The last Crusader state, on the Island of Malta, was dissolved by Napoleon Bonaparte on his way to Egypt, though the title of "King of Jerusalem" continues to be claimed by several members of the European aristocracy until today.

Crusading and reconquest movements continued in Europe down to the age of the sixteenth-century Protestant Reformation, when crusading was replaced by Counter-Reformation, but the threat to the holy places was never completely forgotten. It was remembered when the Turks laid siege to the eastern-most Latin capital of Vienna (1529, 1683). Jerusalem's loss even echoed among the German rioters of 1819, who blamed the Napoleonic occupation of the Rhineland on the Jews.[18] The profound effect on the European psyche of the loss of Jerusalem may explain the enthusiasm of war-weary Londoners who celebrated General Allenby's December 1917 entry into Jerusalem with the ringing of church bells.

The *Longue Durée* of Imperial/Caliphal Jerusalem

With the exception of the two major violent episodes just mentioned, Jerusalem was overall well integrated into imperial or sub-imperial systems of provincial governance. Beginning in 135 CE, with Hadrian's reorganization of the Roman east, Jerusalem/*Aelia* was part of a sub-province the Romans called *Syria-Palaestina,* a nomenclature adopted by the Arabs as well. The nearest seat of provincial government was Damascus.[19] For nearly two millennia, Jerusalem served as an imperially protected pilgrimage city rather than an administrative center. In Roman times, the administrative capital of Palestine was Caesarea Maritima, a luxurious city built by Herod the Great. The Umayyads established a new, land-based administrative center in *al-Ramla* (*Ramleh*), which served in this capacity until the early nineteenth century, excepting the years of Frankish rule. Roman imperial and early Muslim caliphal rule both lasted for about 500 years (135–635 and 635–1099, respectively), unaffected by changes in the ruling dynasties. Under the Umayyads (661–750) of Damascus, Jerusalem enjoyed a brief period of special significance, a status renewed but not entirely matched under the Cairene Fatimids, Ayyubids, and Mamluks. The Byzantine Empire remained sidelined for 800 years, from the seventh-century defeat of Heraclius until the fall of Constantinople in 1453. But Byzantine rulers and their nominal successors, the Russian czars, always maintained the right to act as protectors of the Orthodox Christians of the Holy Land and occasionally engaged in campaigns for reconquest. Following the century of Frankish rule, the Ayyubids (the family of Salah ud-Din Yusuf b. Ayyub) restored Egyptian hegemony over the Levant, nominally returning it to Sunni Abbasid rule. Shortly before the Mongolian sack of Baghdad (1258), a group of Mamluks took power in Egypt. The Mamluks, a military brotherhood, halted the advance of what remained of the "Golden Horde," took the fortress of Acre (1291), the last Crusader bastion in the Holy Land, and retained control over Syria and the Levant until the early sixteenth-century Ottoman conquest of Egypt (1517). As an institution, the Mamluks continued to dominate Egypt's internal affairs until they were violently crushed by Mehmet Ali (1769–1849), the founder of modern Egypt. As we will see below, Jerusalem was propelled back into history by Mehmet Ali's competition with Constantinople in a century that saw the return of Christian European powers to Jerusalem, this time in the name of an imperial *mission civilisatrice*.

Greco-Roman culture and the Aramaic vernacular persisted on the local and communal level for several centuries even as the Umayyads changed the official administrative language of the western Muslim realm (excepting Persia) to Arabic. The Roman name *Aelia* was in use until the eve of the Crusades. Early Muslim geographers commonly refer to the vernacular name *Ilya* alongside the honorific *madinat bayt al-maqdis* (City of the Holy House). Local Arab knowledge of the distant Roman past is still evident in the names attached to certain places, such as the Damascus Gate, which in Arabic is called *Bab el-Amud*, Gate of the Column, a designation that goes back to Roman times.

Eighteen Centuries of Imperial Rule

Roman/Byzantine *Aelia/Hagiapolis Hierousalem*	135–638
Imperial center: Rome	135
Hadrian builds *Aelia Capitolina* 135	
Imperial center: Constantinople	326
Persian conquest 614	
Heraclius's retrieval 629/631	

Early Muslim *ilya/bayt al-maqdis*	638–1099
Umayyad dynasty (Damascus)	661
Abd al-Malik (r. 685–705)	
Abbasid dynasty (Kufa, Baghdad)	750
[Egyptian hegemony]	
Tulunid, Ikhshidid rule	868
Fatimid (Shiite) rule	969
El-Hakim (r. 996–1021)	
Seljuk sultanate in Anatolia	1077
Egyptian hegemony restored	1096
Latin *Hierosoluma*	1099–1187
Medieval *Al-Quds* [Egyptian hegemony]	1187–1517
Ayyubid sultanate	1187
Mamluk sultanate	1250
Ottoman *Kudus*	1517–1917
Syrian provincial hegemony	16th–19th c.
Egyptian occupation of Syria	1831–1840
Jerusalem independent governorate	Late 19th c.

What was it about the region of Syria-Palaestina, and about Jerusalem as its crown jewel, that attracted the attention of emperors and caliphs, kings and sultans? What compelled them to redesign, develop, and invest in a former Jewish city that Rome had reduced to a provincial military colony? Why, over the course of the centuries were the crumbling monumental buildings of earlier ages repaired time and again, to keep the city attractive for pilgrims, mystics, scholars, and retired courtiers? For centuries, men and women of wealth committed the yield of entire villages, towns, and provinces to endow soup kitchens, public fountains, and religious schools, lavishing charity on the city's poor. Judges were appointed to maintain law and order in the city, and peace between its heterogeneous populations. Many of these characteristics (excepting the pluralism that became the hallmark of the Muslim city and that was alien to the Byzantines) began to take shape when Emperor Constantine sent his mother to *Aelia* to oversee the first in a series of acts of reconstruction that transformed the landscape of Palestine into a biblical holy land, and made *Colonia Aelia Capitolina* into *Hagiapolis Hierousalem*. From then on, Roman and Byzantine, Persian and Arab,

Frankish and Ayyubid, Mamluk and Ottoman elites took turns, vying to show their care and benevolence toward the Holy City. All of them, however, built on biblical foundations, both in a symbolic sense and in reality. Canonical and deuterocanonical scriptures of the Jews provided the imagination of Christians and Muslims with figures, tropes, and precedents by which to establish their claims to legitimate, providentially sanctioned rule. When Byzantine monks were marched into Persian exile in 614, they expressed their longing to return in the words of the Jewish exiles of old, Psalm 137: "If I forget thee, Jerusalem, let my right hand wither." When Caliph Umar b. al-Khattab accepted Bishop Sophronius's surrender of Jerusalem, what he wanted to see was the "holy house." The great Ottoman builder of the walls of Jerusalem, Suleïman the Magnificent, bore the name of the biblical king who had first rebuilt that holy house, the first and last gateway to heaven.

Notes

1. On the popularization of True Cross legends since the age of Emperor Heraclius see Kretzenbacher (1995). Cf. Drijvers (1992).
2. See *The Golden Legend or Lives of the Saints*. Compiled by Jacobus de Voragine (1275). First printed edition 1470. Englished by William Caxton (1483), vol. III, Temple Classics (ed. F.S. Ellis), 1900 (reprinted 1922, 1931). Online: Fordham Medieval History Sourcebook at http://www.fordham.edu/halsall/basis/ goldenlegend/GoldenLegend-Volume3.asp#invention%20of%20the% 20Holy%20Cross (accessed November 21, 2017); Ryan and Ripperger (1969 [1941]), 269–276. On Jacobus de Voragine see Nagy (1971).
3. On the figure of Seth as a mediator of paradisaic flora see Quinn (1962). On the apocryphal Adam and Eve tradition see Anderson, Stone, and Tromp (2000), Murdoch (2009).
4. In the Syriac vernacular of Palestine, the church was known as *k'nisat al-qiyama*, the Resurrection Church. On the history of the Church of the Holy Sepulchre see Morris (2005), Ousterhout (1990).
5. On the classical Christian doctrine of atonement see Aulén (1931).
6. On the fourth-century transformation of *Aelia* into *Hierapolis Ierousalem* see Drijvers in Alston (2013).
7. See Cameron (1991).
8. See Gibbon (1877).
9. See Mommsen (1900). *Princeps* means "first among others." *Dominus* means "lord."

10. On Gibbon see Bowersock (1977). Jones (1986) criticized Mommsen's view of Byzantine rule as "Oriental kingship" and provided the basis for a more differentiated view of later Roman government and administration. For the state of the field see Bowden (2006).

11. See Fowden (1993).

12. On the "rhetoric of power" in late antiquity see Frakes, DePalma Digeser, and Stephens (2010).

13. See Holum (1982).

14. On the symbolic parallels between the Byzantine Holy Sepulchre complex and the Umayyad buildings on the Noble Sanctuary see Busse (1987) and Ousterhout (1990). Both complexes referenced the Solomonic temple and traditions associated with it.

15. On Byzantines and Jews see Cameron (1996) and (2002). On the Persian conquest see Gil (1992), Conybeare (1910). For an archaeological perspective see Avni (2010).

16. Muslim hadith preserves several apocryphal stories about Heraclius holding court in Jerusalem and inquiring into rumors about the Prophet Muhammad. These personages were indeed contemporaries though they never met in person. On Heraclius and the *restitutio crucis* see Drijvers in Reinink (2002), 175–190, Kaegi (2003).

17. The entire period is beautifully depicted, though with some poetic license taken, in the 2005 motion picture "Kingdom of Heaven," directed by Ridley Scott.

18. On the so-called HEP! HEP! riots (for *hierosolyma est perdita*), see Hoffmann (2002).

19. For pagan Palestine (second to fourth century) see Belayche (2001). For Christian Palestine see Wilken (1992) and Dauphin (1998). For the period from the Muslim conquest until the Crusades see Gil (1992). For the Jews of Palestine before 634 see Avi-Yonah (1976).

11

Arab Conquest

In the middle of the fourth decade of the seventh century, only a few years after Emperor Heraclius retrieved Syria and Egypt from the Sassanid Persians and returned the True Cross to Jerusalem, an army burst forth from the south and brought Syria, Egypt, and Mesopotamia under the banner of a Prophet who had arisen among the Arabs of the Hejaz.[1] In 661, about 30 years after the Prophet's death, one of his successors was assassinated, ushering in two rounds of civil war from which the Umayyad governors of Damascus emerged victorious. The Umayyad caliphate (661–750) marks the transition, in early Muslim history, from conquest and wars of succession to consolidation of power, and from inspired warfare to caliphal rule.[2] Jerusalem provided symbolic significance to the Muslim conquest. Like Moses and Joshua, Muhammad and his successors conquered the Holy Land in the name of Allah. For the Umayyads Jerusalem provided a major token of divine legitimacy. It sanctioned their rule over the populations of the Holy Land, cemented their supremacy over the Meccans, and reminded the Byzantines that Jerusalem, not Constantinople, was the center of divine kingship on earth. The Umayyads, foremost among them Caliph Abd al-Malik (see Figure 9), shaped the rhetoric of rule over a diverse, largely non-Muslim patchwork of populations loyal to one version or another of the biblical heritage, by using the tool of monumental architecture and adapting it to their own purposes. To this day, a monument

Jerusalem: A Brief History, First Edition. Michael Zank.
© 2018 Michael Zank. Published 2018 by John Wiley & Sons Ltd.

(a)   (b)

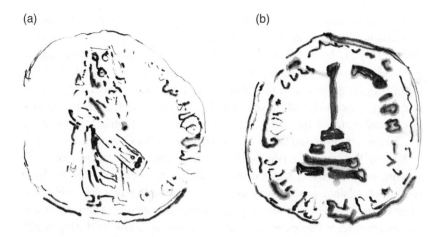

Figure 9 Early Umayyad coin based on Byzantine gold solidus. Obverse: Abd al-Malik with sheathed sword. Reverse: Pole on steps. Illustration by Miriam Shenitzer.

created by Abd al-Malik, the Dome of the Rock, remains the best-known emblem of Jerusalem. It is also the first monumental building in the history of Islamic art.

Legend has it that the Prophet's companion and second successor Umar b. al-Khattab (r. 634–644) accepted the surrender of Jerusalem in person, and led the Muslims in purifying the Noble Sanctuary (*al-Haram al-Sharif*). Umar is also said to have built the first mosque, a modest wooden building on the ancient Herodian platform, a building Abd al-Malik replaced with the present *Qibli* or Friday mosque on the southern edge of the platform, built on an axis with the Dome of the Rock. The design of these two buildings echoes that of Constantine's *Martyrium* and *Anastasis*. To the south of the platform, the Umayyads built palaces that served as their Jerusalem residence. Unlike the Byzantine emperors, who – with the exception of Heraclius – never visited or held court in Jerusalem, the Umayyad caliphs accepted the oath of fealty of their subjects in Jerusalem. Had the Abbasids not driven the Umayyads from Syria, Jerusalem might have turned into the capital of Islam. In the event, Abbasid rule created the conditions for a much wider expansion and consolidation of Muslim civilization by shifting power from Greco-Arab Syria to Persian Mesopotamia with its new capital, Baghdad. For Jerusalem, this meant the beginning of a slow but certain decline from a century of proximity to power to the more marginal position of a merely religious center, a city of pilgrims, scholars, mystics, and retirees, who enjoyed the location's beauty precisely because of its distance from the court.

Most historians consider the Muslim conquest a watershed. It begins a
new chapter in the history of the Middle East. The seventh-century conquest of Syria, Egypt, and Mesopotamia heralded Muslim domination,
eventually, of an area reaching from Spain to Central Asia. Arabic, Persian,
and Turkic languages came to dominate administration, trade, arts, science,
and religious cultures of these newly linked civilizations, where hitherto
Greek and Aramaic had held sway. Heraclius's loss of Syria foreshadowed
the decline and eventual fall of Constantinople to the Ottomans in 1453.

None of the long-term consequences of the Arab conquest were visible to
seventh-century Armenians, Greeks, Syrians, Jews, or even to the Arabs of
the Levant.[3] Islam was not immediately recognizable as a "new religion."
Most of the changes that we may summarily describe as Arabization and
Islamization were implemented over the course of centuries during which
power was consolidated in the hands of dynasties that emerged victorious
from the rivalries over the spoils of conquest. Local elites interpreted the
Arab victory of the Byzantines as a divine punishment for the "accursed
Chalcedonians," i.e. of a Byzantine court that had become onerous to
regions and cities that bore the burden of a top-heavy empire engaged in
perpetual war on several fronts. The learned chronists and historians
among seventh-century Syrians, Armenians, and Jews saw the Arabs as
"Hagarenes" or "Ishmaelites" and assigned them a familiar place in a time-
honored inventory of nations and the usual causes of war. To learned chroniclers, especially from among the repressed monophysite communities who
had suffered under Byzantine intolerance, the Arabs represented an instrument of divine chastisement for the haughty Chalcedonians, foremost
among them Heraclius himself, who – in Armenian sources – is accused of
incest. Jewish observers hopefully embraced "Ishmael" in his fight against
"Edom," a code name for Rome. For both Jews and heterodox Christians
this was a time of divine reckoning for the high and mighty and the pangs
of birth of a final imperial dispensation, a lasting peace on earth. At the
time, people would have been surprised to learn that the Ishmaelites had
arrived to stay.

Abbasid historians – writing after the Umayyads had been muscled
out – developed their own way of remembering the golden days of the
Prophet and his companions, crediting them with unifying the believers
and conquering in the name of Allah. According to the Abbasid historians,
the age of Arab expansion began with the "rightly guided" or *rashidun*
caliphs, the four generals and companions of the Prophet Muhammad who
succeeded him as leaders of the *umma* and led the newly founded "nation

of Islam" from the death of the Prophet in 632 until 661, when Ali, the Prophet's son-in-law and, to Shiites, his only legitimate successor, was assassinated. This conflict of succession is remembered as the first *fitna*, or civil war. What was at stake in this war was the political consolidation of a quickly assembled vast realm of lands that included the major cities, fertile agricultural regions, and long stretches of lucrative international trade routes of Syria, Egypt, and Mesopotamia, lands hitherto divided between the Byzantine Romans and the Sassanid Persians.

The reasons for the sweeping success of the Arab military campaigns across such a vast territory and their ability to maintain control have been the subject of a perennial debate.[4] Some have attributed it to the strength, resolve, discipline, or ruthlessness of the Arabs, others to the weakness of the Byzantines and Persians who had worn each other out after decades of military conflict, excessive conscription, and economic decline. Recent archaeologists have foregrounded other factors to explain the rise and con-solidation of Arab hegemony, including the presence and significance of Arab settlers across Syria, Mesopotamia, and the Levant over the course of the century that preceded the Arab conquest, and the impact of the decline of agricultural settlements, caused by the Roman–Persian wars, on the nomadic populations who found themselves deprived of the symbiotic sources of subsistence on which they had previously relied, such as local and international trade. This decline made them susceptible to using violent conquest as an alternate means of subsistence. What turned the occasional Bedouin raid into a concerted and sustained armed movement was the flag of the Prophet and the religion of Islam.

Muslim folklore couches the days of Muhammad and his companions in the pious and occasionally burlesque terms of extraordinary virtue and piety to be emulated as a "straight path to the watering hole" (*sharia*); these accounts were disseminated by storytellers practicing their craft in a milieu shaped by centuries of Christian, Jewish, and pagan legends about saints and holy men. In purely secular terms, early Muslim history may be char-acterized as a movement of political unification and conquest, and explained by the reorganization of a highly developed interconnected set of agricul-tural and urban regions as a network governed and successfully exploited by a new warrior elite that eventually accommodated itself to the lifestyles of Byzantine and Persian cities.

In the history of Arab conquest, the ensuing conflicts of succession, and the consolidation of power in the hands of a few competing dynastic clans we may discern the echo of an earlier sequence of events, namely, of the famed conquest of Alexander and his Macedonians of the erstwhile Persian empire. The Muslims were able to forge an ideology of rule from the remnants of the earlier amalgamation of Greek and eastern traditions that the nineteenth-century historian Droysen called Hellenism. The Muslims built on the foundations of the Hellenistic east. They were indeed the heirs of Alexander and in many respects constituted the synthesis and apex of late antique civilization.

The realm conquered by the Arabs was virtually identical to that of the Achaemenid Empire that had fallen to the Macedonians in the late fourth century BCE. Just as then, when Greeks had long since ceased to be complete foreigners to the Persian realm, where many of them had served as mercenaries, the Arabs of the seventh century were no longer perceived as the exotic outsiders described by the ancient Assyrians, who were the first to capture and settle Arab tribesmen in the region of Samaria. By the seventh century CE, Arabs were simply part of the mosaic of Syro-Palestinian populations, and as aware as others of the broader history of the Levant and its vicissitudes. Allusions to popular stories about Alexander surface in the Qur'an and later Muslim tradition in the character of *dhu'l-qarnayn* (the two-horned one, an allusion to the ram's horns on ancient coins bearing the likeness of Alexander), indicating that this important antecedent was as clearly remembered in Arabia as it was among Christian historians who compared Heraclius's victory over the Persians to that of Alexander. (Variations of the name Alexander, such as Iskander or Sikander, are popular in many languages and attested in place names across the Middle East to this day.) Similar to the competition between the Macedonian generals and their descendants ensconced in their respective major centers in Syrian Antioch and Egyptian Alexandria, a competition that dragged on for more than a century, conflict arose between second-generation Arab leaders settled in various regional centers, each aiming to bring the entire realm under the rule of a single "commander of the faithful" (*amir al-mu'minin*). In the second half of the seventh century, the opposing regional centers were Damascus, a largely Byzantine city and center of an Umayyad clan of governors, and Mecca, the ancient center of pilgrimage and trade in the Hejaz (western Arabia) that the Prophet Muhammad, in an act of cult restoration, had reclaimed as a *locus* of Abrahamic faith. The ruler installed in Mecca was Ibn Zubayr, who had the distinction of being the first child born to the *muhajirun* in Yathrib/Medina, following the flight of the Muslims from Mecca in 622. The leader of the Umayyads, who eventually vanquished Ibn Zubayr, was Abd al-Malik b. Marwan (r. 685–705), who was to play a significant role in the transformation of Jerusalem into a place of Muslim devotion.

Early Islam functioned as a political religion of unification and divinely sanctioned rule at a time when Arabia served as an important land bridge on a highly lucrative trade route and a link between Christian Axum (Ethiopia) and the Byzantine and Persian empires. As a religion, Islam amalgamated traditional Arab culture with sacred traditions that had long since penetrated the Arabian Peninsula and circulated among the indigenous tribes and itinerant foreigners for centuries. At the same time, as noted above, various Arab communities had fled or migrated in several waves over the centuries and resettled further north, across the Levant, Syria, and Mesopotamia. For example, the Christian Ghassanids, originally from Yemen, migrated to Syria where, under Justinian I, they served as allies of the Byzantines and a buffer against the Persians. Arabs were among the sedentary and nomadic communities crisscrossing the boundaries between the Byzantine and Persian realms.

If we follow the established biography of the Prophet,[5] instead of converting to some form of Christianity or to Judaism, as did the South Arabian Himyarites, Muhammad indigenized the devotion to the one true God when he taught his followers to turn away from Jerusalem and direct their prayers toward Mecca instead. According to several hadith traditions, this occurred about a year and a half after the Muslims had relocated to Yathrib, better known as Medina, in the famous *Hijra* or Hegirah of 622, a kind of "exodus" that marks the beginning of the Muslim calendar. A few years later, following the surrender of Mecca and the purification of the Ka'aba of polytheistic trappings (a Maccabean-like act of cult restoration of a putatively Abrahamic shrine), the Muslims brought the remainder of the Arab Peninsula under their jurisdiction and then carried their fight in the name of Allah onto Byzantine and Persian territories. The impetus for that conquest was both religious and mundane, though it is difficult to say which of these motivations prevailed. The religious cause was not so much a zeal to convert or eradicate the remaining pagans but perhaps a notion that a formula had been found by which to unite all monotheists and establish divine rule on earth. The formula was simple and it is part of the oldest Qur'anic inscriptions, still visible in the Dome of the Rock: There is no God but God, and Muhammad is His prophet. In mundane terms, there were enormous spoils of war to be distributed among those who had suffered for their faith or had been deprived of other sources of subsistence. Neither motivation was unique to the Muslims; in both respects, they matched and, in this case, outdid the ambition and ability of their monotheistic competitors. It was all, as it were, a matter of the "righteous inheriting the earth." The seventh-century Arab unification and conquest movement founded by Muhammad b. Abdallah spoke in the theological-political *koiné* or common language of its time. Moreover, the conquest of Syria and Palestine, the Christian *terra sancta*, could serve as a reenactment of the Israelites bursting forth from the desert, to drive out the infidels and restore the right worship to a land dear to God and men.

In terms of political-religious zeal, Muhammad's contemporary Heraclius provided a proximate example of how one might combine religious power and imperial rule. Following the demise of Sassanid Khosrow II "The Victorious" and the retrieval of the Holy Wood (dated to 629 or 631), Heraclius promoted an empire-wide conversion of the Jews, who were widely charged with having allied themselves with the Persians, and he sought to unify the eastern Christians on the basis of a compromise formula that, in the event, satisfied neither the monophysites nor those who believed in the difference between the two natures of Christ ("duo-physites"). The Byzantines thus provided the most important model for a combination of a religious zeal for doctrinal unification, even homogenization, and the ideological justification of imperial rule.

It should be emphasized that a policy of homogenization could be seriously considered only in a situation where the Christians already constituted the demographic majority. Muhammad and the early Muslims indeed applied the principle of religious homogenization to the Arabs of the desert and among them mostly to the remnants of traditional Arabic religions, which were now forcibly eradicated or forced to voluntarily abandon their traditions, similar to how paganism had been systematically reduced in status and violently obliterated across the Roman Empire. Once the newly united Arabs ventured forth to capture vast swaths of lands populated by Christians, Jews, Samaritans, and Zoroastrians, however, the idea of forced conversion – if indeed it was ever considered – gave way to a deliberately pluralistic system. The conquering Bedouin tribesmen and their sedentary kin established a regime that affirmed the relative legitimacy of a plurality of "people of the book" (*ahl al-kitab*). Byzantine law provided the precedent for regulations that distinguished between the members of the privileged religion and other nations without depriving the latter of their land or livelihood, on which depended the wealth of the empire. In Islamic law, these became the "protected people" (*ahl al-dhimma*) who, though excluded from the spoils of war and subjected to other forms of discrimination, formed a "commonwealth"[6] of tolerated nations under the umbrella of Muslim rule. In the context of empire, Islam originally served not as a means of oppression or enslavement but as a religious justification to rule a broad swath of regions predominantly populated by non-Arabs and non-Muslims. Those of them who chose to convert were integrated as *mawali* (non-Arab Muslims); others retained their traditional ways and still gained or maintained power and influence at court and even dominated regional administrations.

Notes

1. On the Arab conquest see Donner (1981) and (2008).
2. See Donner (1986).
3. See Pentz (1992), Palmer (1993), Hoyland (1997).
4. See Donner (2008).
5. See Ali (2014).
6. Fowden (1993).

12

City of the Holy House (*Madinat Bayt al-Maqdis*)

Byzantine Jerusalem surrendered in 638, following a prolonged siege. Tradition has it that the aged patriarch Sophronius, a distinguished, outspoken, and courageous man, demanded for the city to be delivered to none other than Caliph Umar b. al-Khattab (r. 634–644) himself. The early Muslim historians refer to the city interchangeably by its Roman name *Ilya* (*Aelia*) or by the Arabized Jewish *nom d'honneur, madinat bayt al-maqdis*: City of the Holy House.[1] Traditions about the entry of the caliph into the Holy City are firmly enshrined in Islamic literature. These sources emphasize the modesty and humility of the conquering hero, contrasting the simple Arab clothing of Umar with that of the magnificently bedecked Byzantine patriarch. According to a story passed down in Christian sources, when Sophronius invited the caliph to pray in the Church of the Holy Sepulchre, Umar declined, fearing that Muslims would later make the church into a mosque in his honor. According to tradition, Umar's local informant and tour guide in Jewish antiquities was Ka'b al-Ahbar, a Jewish advisor.[2] When shown the ruins of the Noble Sanctuary, Umar discovered that the hallowed ground of the first *qibla* had been desecrated and turned into a rubbish heap. He then rolled up his sleeves and proceeded to clean up the place with his own bare hands. Following the city's surrender, the Muslims purified the Temple Mount and established a modest wooden mosque near the southern wall of the Herodian platform, facing Mecca.[3]

Jerusalem: A Brief History, First Edition. Michael Zank.
© 2018 Michael Zank. Published 2018 by John Wiley & Sons Ltd.

In comparative religious terms, this was a classic act of cult restoration. In Muslim tradition, as conveyed by late sixteenth-century historian Mujir al-Din, even David and Solomon did not found the sanctuary, but merely restored what had first been built by the angels at the time of creation, "though Allah alone knows what is true."[4]

The *Aelia/Ierousalem* of 638 was a major Byzantine metropolis, though one significantly damaged by the recent Persian invasion.[5] Excepting the decade and a half of Persian occupation, when Jews briefly ruled Jerusalem, no Jews had been allowed to live in the city and its vicinity. This set Jerusalem apart from other places in Byzantine Palestine, where Jews had long since thrived alongside Samaritans, Syrians, Greeks, and others, as attested in the many remnants of late ancient synagogues.[6] Visitors to modern Israel and Jordan are able to admire the remnants of the many churches and synagogues that sprang up over the course of the fourth and fifth centuries and flourished across Palestine, the Judean and Jordanian Desert, and even in the Negev, stretching toward the Gulf of Eilat/Aqaba. Byzantine *Aelia* was one of the best-endowed sites and the object of an exclusively Christian urban development. This included an architecture of symbolic religious contrast between Christian glory and the denigration of pre-Christian cult places, a technique used elsewhere as well. In Apamea on the Orontes, for example, a magnificent temple of Jupiter was partially quarried for new Christian buildings and its remains left to decay, as well as access blocked off by latrines, shifting the center of the city away from its traditional core.[7] Similarly, as attested by Eusebius, the area that had housed the Jewish temple and that, after 135, was dedicated to the Capitoline Jupiter was left in ruins symbolizing the "Old Jerusalem" against which Constantine established his "New Jerusalem" in the form of the splendid *Anastasis* and *Martyrium*, now the Church of the Holy Sepulchre.

We have a pretty good idea what Jerusalem looked like and how it developed over the three centuries preceding the Muslim conquest. To name just a few sources, we have pilgrimage accounts ranging from the Itinerarium Burdigalense produced in 333, shortly before the completion of Constantine's basilica, to the anonymous account of a pilgrim from Piacenza, written around 570.[8] We have letters, including those written by the late fourth-century Latin savant and Bible translator St. Jerome, who disparages Byzantine Jerusalem as a city of actors and buffoons,[9] and we have a visual representation of the city in the Madaba Map, an amazing mid-sixth-century mosaic depiction of Syria, Palestine, and Upper Egypt as seen by a Byzantine Christian artist.[10] Finally, the ever-growing body of archaeological evidence confirms the stunning magnificence of the city, its layout, its impressive Roman colonnaded streets, and its monumental religious buildings.[11]

Byzantine Christianity and its competitors, among them Palestinian Judaism and early Islam, were very much religions of space. The biblical Holy Land (Latin: *terra sancta*; Hebrew: *erets ha-qodesh*; Arabic: *al-ard al-muqadassa*) itself was a sacred space where certain religious laws obtained and from which impurities were banished or where, at least, they were localized in condemned areas, such as the desert, the desacralized ruin, or the Valley of Jehoshaphat (*gey hinnom, jehennam*).[12] Church, synagogue, and mosque enhanced and underscored the sacredness of the landscape and provided sacred space for prayer, contemplation, exposition of scripture, liturgical confession and adoration, and the fostering of communal identities.[13] Connecting holy places were prescribed routes of circumambulation or procession, such as today's *Via Dolorosa*, and similar guidelines for Muslim visitors to the *al-Haram al-Sharif*. Late ancient religions were oriented toward "heaven," taken literally as the highest sphere above the earth. Late antique Hebrew *hekhalot* literature conveyed visions of "descent to the divine chariot" (*merkavah*) that envisaged the divine palaces as hovering above the ruined earthly sanctuary of Jerusalem.[14] Across the various Palestinian, Syrian, Egyptian, Cappadocian, and other urban centers and desert settlements, learned Christians and Jews competed in the production of liturgies, homiletic commentaries, and mystical ascent literature that represented the invisible in visual terms and established a firm connection between heaven and earth.[15] The Arabs, prepared by centuries of cultural and material exchange with Christians, Jews, and others, stepped into this competition and developed their own variation of late ancient spatio-legal piety.[16] To link biblical religious traditions with imperial power meant to assert dominance in space while domesticating the apocalyptic urge. Within early Islam, apocalyptic anxiety is mostly associated with the period of civil war (*fitna*) and imperial competition.[17] The apocalyptic mood lives on, among others, in the doctrine of the "hidden Imam" that characterizes the various Shiite traditions lamenting the break, at one point or another, in the line of Ali. To Sunnis, the institution of the caliphate represented the rule of the representative of God on earth (*khalifat Allah*) and hence a realized *eschaton*, resembling the Christian Orthodox doctrine of the emperor as the Vicar of Christ on earth.

What was the immediate and longer-term impact of the Arab conquest on Jerusalem and the predominantly Christian populations of Syria and Palestine?[18] Byzantine Christians lost their privileged economic position, but the economy of the Byzantine realm had been on the decline since the second half of the sixth century. The archaeological record does not allow us to conclude that the first decades of Muslim rule had a major impact on the economy of the Levant.[19] Greek-speaking Christians continued to constitute the majority population, certainly in Jerusalem, and this changed only very gradually. The Muslims readmitted Jews to the Holy City to live, though only a limited number of families were given permission to settle. Like other non-Muslims, Jews had to accept the responsibilities of a protected people, including the payment of a poll tax (*jizya*), and were required to adopt the somewhat humiliating customs specified in the Pact of Umar, an eighth-century document that continued to be invoked until the early twentieth century and that spelled out the status of non-Muslims living under the protection of the Muslims. In spirit and detail, the Pact of Umar followed Byzantine precedent in regulating the status of non-Christians but, as in that prior dispensation, these laws were not necessarily or uniformly enforced by the authorities.[20] The presence of a plurality of religious communities in Jerusalem led to the emergence, under the Umayyads, of distinct neighborhoods defined by religious affiliation (see Map 10). The location of these quarters changed over time, though the Greeks loyal to Constantinople and to the creed of Chalcedon always remained close to their major sanctuary, the Church of the Holy Sepulchre, and Muslims always resided near the *al-Haram al-Sharif* (Noble Sanctuary). The first Jewish settlement in Jerusalem under the Umayyads was located in the area of the erstwhile City of David, now the village of Silwan, which was then still enclosed within the walls built by Byzantine Empress Eudokia in the fifth century ("Eudokia's wall"). In Fatimid times (tenth and eleventh century CE), the Jewish Quarter shifted to the north of the Haram area. At that time, the Jewish community included Egyptian Karaites and Rabbanites of Babylonian origin whose affairs are well attested in documents that were discovered, 100 years ago, at the Cairo Geniza.[21]

The key dates by which to assess the transformation of Jerusalem under the early Muslims are the beginning and end of Umayyad rule (661–750), and the situation of Jerusalem on the eve of the First Crusade (1099), following three centuries during which times of tranquility, turmoil, and renewed consolidation followed one upon the other in relatively brief cycles, before the city fell to the Franks.

The story to tell here is that of the last centuries in the history of late ancient Jerusalem, a time when the urban character, thoroughfares, monumental buildings, and populations were still based on, and in part identical with, the city built by the Byzantine Romans, i.e. a predominantly Christian city, and yet one that was also decisively altered by the advent of the Muslim Arabs and shrunk by the effects of the great earthquake of 749.[22] Umayyad rule (661–750) entailed a major revival of the city as a kind of secondary or symbolic capital, but the extent to which this project was completed is unclear.

The high-water mark of early Islamic rule of Jerusalem coincided with the flourishing of the Marwanids, comprising the reign of Caliph Abd al-Malik b. Marwan (685–705) and his sons Al-Walid (r. 705–715), Sulayman (r. 715–717), Yazid (720–724), and Hisham (724–743).[23] Following the conquest of Syria-Palaestina and the consolidation of government in the hands of the Umayyad governors of Damascus, the new rulers invested systematic efforts into rebuilding the conquered cities, restoring sea and land trade, encouraging commerce and agriculture, and regularizing relations between the populations of the expanding empire.

Jerusalem benefited from the need of the Umayyads for religious justification of what was essentially a forced arrogation of the caliphate, one that remained debated and contested forever after, not just by the followers of Ali (the Shiites of varying stripes) but also by the Abbasids, who successfully rebelled against the Umayyads in 750 and usurped the caliphate. (Umayyad claimants subsequently established a counter-caliphate in Al-Andalus/ Spain.) Abbasid power, at its peak in the eight to ninth century, but nominally lasting until 1258, when the Mongols destroyed Baghdad, shifted the center of gravity of the Muslim realm, by then a land-based empire of unprecedented size, from Greek- and Aramaic-speaking Syria to the Persian realm, an important shift in terms of the cultural paradigms espoused by the Muslim rulers.

As long as the Umayyads ruled Syria, a region Greeks and Latins had long seen as the center of the *oikumene*, Jerusalem and the Holy Land were the focus of lavish building activities. What is particularly remarkable about Umayyad Jerusalem is that it was not just the location of religious architecture, such as the Dome of the Rock, nodding to its character as a well-established pilgrimage city, but it was infused with the trappings of an emerging second capital, an elaborate palace built just south of the ancient Temple Mount. This palace was unknown until 1968 when, in the wake of massive excavations in the area, Israeli archaeologist Benjamin Mazar stumbled upon the remnants of monumental Umayyad structures that are now on display as part of an archaeological park near the Western Wall plaza.[24] Umayyad attention to Jerusalem is all the more remarkable because the city remained as remote and inappropriate for a wider provincial and military administration of the region as ever. Caesarea Maritima had served

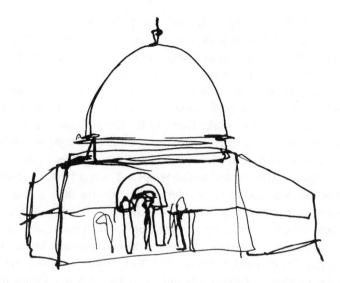

Figure 10   Abd al-Malik's Dome of the Rock (*Qubbat as-Sakhra*). Illustration by Miriam Shenitzer.

this function throughout Roman times, and the town of ar-Ramla served this function under the Umayyads and subsequent Muslim rulers of the *jund filastin* (Palestine). Abd al-Malik and his sons visited the City of the Holy House for reasons of state frequently enough to make it necessary to provide themselves with a stylish residence. It was here that they accepted their subjects' oath of fealty.

The lasting monument of early Muslim rule in Jerusalem is the redesign of the *al-Haram al-Sharif* as a complex sanctuary with several major buildings, foremost among them the Dome of the Rock. There is some debate about the date of the commissioning and construction of the Dome of the Rock. According to Abbasid historians, Abd al-Malik had it built while the conflict with Ibn Zubayr and the Meccans was still raging. Modern historians have called this into question and many prefer 692 as the year of its founding rather than its completion. It was not the only measure Abd al-Malik took to disseminate his right to rule the *oikoumene*. Later Abbasid authors such as al-Tabari, who lists some of the measures taken by al-Malik, surmise that the Umayyad ruler had less than noble intentions in mind when he established the *qubbat as-sakhra*, as the commemorative shrine (sometimes incorrectly referred to, in western sources, as the "Mosque of Omar") is known in Arabic (see Figure 10). Among the Abbasid-age scholars, the question of why the Dome of the Rock was built was commonly answered by surmising that Abd al-Malik's measures aimed to divert attention of pious pilgrims from Mecca, but this theory reflects the growing popularity of pilgrimage among the early medieval Muslims (and the competition between pilgrimage cities) more than the affairs of early Umayyad times. The late Oleg Grabar, one of the foremost historians of early Muslim art, who literally wrote "the book" on the Dome of the Rock,[25] lamented the "occlusion" of the Muslim present in the eyes of modern Christian and Jewish scholars in favor of the city's Jewish and Christian pasts, especially in pursuit of remnants of the ancient Jewish temples. The legitimate concern with the distortions wreaked by the modern interest in the distant past should not distract us from the fact that the first Umayyad caliph built the Dome in its present location precisely because that was the presumed location of the ancient temple of Solomon. Not by accident did the early Muslims refer to *Ilya* as the City of the Holy House. The "Holy House" they were referring to was the temple of Solomon. The *qubbat as-sakhra* was, on some level, a restoration of the Solomonic temple.[26] Its rebuilding at the behest of the divine representative on earth, Caliph Abd al-Malik, was an eschatological act of cult restoration in a place hallowed by the great lineage of saints, prophets, and kings, and in a place that was recognized – by Jews and Christians – to be central on earth and nearest to heaven, a gateway to paradise and the spot from which the Prophet himself had ascended to heaven to converse with Moses and Jesus, just as Jesus – on a different mountain – had once conversed with Moses and Elijah. It is important to note that the Dome of the Rock, as originally conceived, did not erase the Jewish past but confirmed and appropriated it. In subsequent centuries, Muslim attitudes toward the antecedent revealed traditions, collectively referred to as *isra'iliyyat*, became more ambivalent.[27]

Early Muslim devotion toward *bilad al-Sham* (Syria-Palestine, the Jewish and Christian Holy Land), and specifically toward *bayt al-maqdis*, is commonplace in late ancient hadith and early medieval *fada'il al-quds* literature, compilations of legends "in praise of the Holy City."[28] This indicates the lasting interest, among early and medieval Muslims, in the preservation of Jewish and Christian traditions. What Muslim scholars refer to as *isra'iliyyat* represents part of a continuous history of divine revelation, completed and "sealed" by Prophet Muhammad. Like the Christians, Muslims inscribed themselves into the prophetic lineage of biblical Israel. Unlike Christianity, which began as an apocalyptic religion of escape from imminent judgment and only later unfolded its potential as an ideology of imperial rule, Islam arose at a time when that synthesis of otherworldliness and earthly power had been firmly established. For the early Muslims it was therefore a matter of course that the common denominator of the Jewish and Christian dispositions they inherited consisted in the notion of a divinely sanctioned conquest of the land and the establishment of God's rule on earth. Rebuilding Jerusalem and endowing the city's ruined[29] temple area with new splendor and purpose allowed the struggling dynasty of Damascus to derive legitimacy and divine sanction.

Jerusalem suffered in the earthquake of January 18, 749,[30] and it remained in limbo in the aftermath of the rebellion of the Abbasids, which led to the demise of Jerusalem's Umayyad sponsors. Not that the Abbasids were indifferent to the symbolic importance of the Holy City. The ninth-century Caliph Al-Ma'mun went as far as putting his own name in place of Abd al-Malik's founding inscription of the Dome of the Rock (though without changing the founding date), a practice of supersession familiar since the days of the Pharaohs, who replaced the names of their predecessors on monuments they didn't built. But the task of rebuilding the cities across *jund filastin*, which had borne the brunt of the great earthquake, failed to attract sufficient imperial support, leaving many of the great Hellenistic cities in ruins, including for example Scythopolis/Baysan (Beth Shean), which had flourished for nearly a millennium. The Abbasids, whose realm reached from North Africa to Central Asia, had bigger fish to fry. Jerusalem might never have recovered its late ancient glory had it not been for the Fatimids, Franks, Ayyubids, and Mamluks, who did much to revive and rebuild city and region. In the case of the Noble Sanctuary (rather, of *al-haramayn al-sharifayn*, the two sanctuaries of Hebron and Jerusalem), the goals of protection and pious sponsorship complemented one another.

Another major change, more gradual but no less consequential, took place in the centuries between 750 and 1099. Under the Umayyads, Christians still constituted the majority populations of Egypt and Syria. By the time of the First Crusade, following more than a century of Fatimid Egyptian rule, the demographic majority had begun to shift in favor of the Arabized (i.e. Arabic-speaking) and Muslim populations. The decline of Christian power and strength engendered anti-Muslim sentiments among the Christians of the Middle East that are still discernible today. Among the responses to this decline were the Latin incursions that attempted to retrieve the erstwhile Roman East for the Christians. For the Fatimids of the fourth and fifth centuries AH (the tenth to eleventh centuries CE), to invest in *Ilya/bayt al-maqdis* no longer meant, as it had for the Umayyads, to invest in a predominantly Christian city whose sacred places conferred providential dignity on Muslim rulers, but to rebuild a major Islamic sanctuary, one of only three holy cities that the Prophet Muhammad himself had expressly commended as places "to which one ought to set out," i.e. that Muslims were encouraged to visit (in the case of Medina and Jerusalem, in a *ziyara*, not *hajj*).[31] After 1099, the Roman name *Ilya*, until then still used widely and interchangeably with Jerusalem's religious names, gradually vanishes from the Arab dictionary (though the learned Mujir al-Din still mentions it in his sixteenth-century work on Jerusalem and Hebron). After the Crusades, the most common Arabic name of the city is *Al-Quds* (Turkish: *Kudus*), the Holy. In the early eleventh century, Fatimid power and Jerusalem's isolation from Christian influence had progressed to the point that Caliph Al-Hakim (r. 996–1021), in one of his more benighted moments, commanded the dismantling of the Church of the Holy Sepulchre without fearing foreign intervention. After 1244, when the Latins were expelled for the second time, the demographic balance and character of the city permanently shifted away from the Christians, in favor of its Muslim populations, making the city a predominantly Muslim town (until the 1520s, without walls).

Medieval Al-Quds, a city ruled from Fatimid, then Ayyubid, then Mamluk Cairo, shares characteristics with the other chief cities of Syria and the Levant in terms of occupation, demography, architecture, and urban features and functions. It also sees the accrual of a special dignity as the location of more holy places than any other city or town in the district of Palestine or the Syrian province at large. The tenth-century Arab geographer Muqadassi or al-Maqdisi (944–1000) notes that Jerusalem was greater in size than most towns and larger than a few small capitals of the Muslim realm.

There are differences between Fatimid and Mamluk Jerusalem, eras separated by the period of Latin rule. Fatimid Egypt, contemporaneous with a diminished but still significant Abbasid caliphate, is part of a "golden age" of Muslim rule, when lands from Spain to Central Asia were connected, land and sea routes secured, trade from Europe to China flourished, and riches flowed into the capitals of the Muslim empires. The Jerusalem-born Muqadassi, one of the foremost geographers of his time, provides us with a lively impression of the lands, Muslim and non-Muslim, that he had visited, including his own city as it was toward the end of the tenth century, the time of then still unchallenged Fatimid Cairene rule.

The most significant and populous center of the region was Cairo (Arabic: *al-qahira*, "the luminescent"), named in homage to the war planet

Mars. The city was founded in 969 next to *al-Fustat* (now Old Cairo). The builders of this new city were of Libyan origin but claimed to have descended from Ali and Fatima, the daughter of Prophet Muhammad, via Isma'il b. Ja'far, the son of a famous Shii lawyer who, to the Ismailis, was the authentic imam or successor of the Prophet. Even after the political demise of the Fatimids, whose rule came to an end with the seizure of power by Saladin (1171), several branches of Ismaili Islam survived that are alive and well today, among them the Druze populations of Syria and the Levant, who believe that the imamate went into occultation with the disappearance of El-Hakim, and the Nizari Ismailis, a worldwide community loyal to the Aga Khan, which is second in number only to the Twelver Shiites (*Ithna Ashariyyah*), who are at home in Iran, Iraq, Azerbaijan, Bahrain, and many other places.

Any visitor to modern Cairo can admire the beauty and grandeur of the architectural monuments established by generations of Fatimid, Ayyubid, and Mamluk rulers. It is in this wider context that we can assess the recovery of Jerusalem that coincided with the ascendancy of Cairo.

Muqadassi first refers to his birthplace in an introductory passage to the chapter on the realm of *al-Islam* in *The Best Divisions for Knowledge of the Regions* (*Ahsan al-Taqasim fi Ma'rifat al-Aqalim*)[32] where he assures his readers of the trustworthiness of his descriptions of places he saw with his own eyes: "Were I to have concealed the shortcomings of any town I should have concealed the faults of my own native town, because of its great distinction and holiness in the sight of God, may He be exalted, and of His creatures!" (61). The city is first mentioned by name in the introduction to the chapter on Syria, praising the extraordinary beauty and variety of the cities, holy places, and landscapes of *al-Sham*. After calling Damascus "the paradise of this earth" and praising "beautiful Ramla" for the superior quality of its white bread, he refers to Jerusalem as "Ilya the splendid, without tribulation" (128). Muqadassi describes Syria as rich in maritime trade, wealthy, and pleasant. About its inhabitants he says that they lived "as if in a foreign land," in constant dread of "Roman" invasion, their northern borders ravaged and fortifications shattered by constant warfare. This is certainly an interesting observation on the mood of Muslim Syrians a century before the First Crusade. Muqadassi disparages the lack of zeal for education and religion among his countrymen: "Neither are the people here the equal of the Persians in science, religion, and intelligence. Some have apostatized, while others pay tribute, putting obedience to created men before obedience to the Lord of Heaven. The general public is ignorant and churlish, showing no zeal for the holy strife, no rancour towards enemies" (129). To be sure, this good-humored gloss on his fellow Syrians must be taken with a grain of salt. Some of it may, in fact, be a compliment in disguise. Muqadassi was a skillful writer, not a pious fool. Among an overview of the administrative regions and cities of Syria we find the following list delineating the "District of Filastin" (132): "Its capital is al-Ramla. Its towns: Bayt al-Maqdis (Jerusalem), Bayt-Jibril, Ghazza (Gaza), Mimas, Asqalan (Ascalon), Yafa (Jaffa), Arsuf, Qaysariyya, Nabulus, Ariha (Jericho), Amman." Following a section of administrative lists, Muqadassi begins his more detailed descriptions of the major attractions of Syria. The splendor of the great Umayyad mosque of Damascus, which he calls "easily the finest the Muslims now have" (134), provides him with an opportunity to recount a conversation he himself had in his youth where the question is raised that also puzzled us earlier, namely, why the Umayyads established such grand monuments in a land mostly inhabited by Christians.

> Now, talking to my father's brother one day said I: "O my uncle, surely it was not fitting for al-Walid to expend the resources of the Muslims on the mosque of Damascus. Had he expended as much in building roads, or the water tanks, or in repairing the fortresses, it would have been more proper and more to his credit." Said he: "You simply don't understand, my dear son. Al-Walid was absolutely right, and it was open to him to do a worthy work. For he saw that Syria was a country settled by the Christians, and he noted there their churches so handsome with their enchanting decorations, renowned far and wide, such as are the Qumama [viz. Constantine's *Anastasis*; MZ][33] (...). So he undertook for the Muslims the building of a mosque that would divert their attention from the churches, and make it one of the wonders of the world. Do you not realize how 'Abd al-Malik, seeing the greatness of the dome of the Qumama and its splendor, fearing lest it should beguile the hearts of the Muslims, hence erected, above the Rock, the dome you now see there?"

Jerusalem was quickly changing in the century following this description.[34] In 1009, El-Hakim dismantled the beautiful *Anastasis*. Fatimid rule was challenged by the Turkish *Rum* Seljuks who burst forth from Anatolia, took possession of Jerusalem, and threatened Egypt and Byzantium alike. It was against these "accursed Turks" that Pope Urban II called upon the Frankish knights to take up the cross and liberate the holiest places of Christendom.

Notes

1. See e.g. Baladhuri (1968).
2. For a study of traditions attributed to Ka'b al-Ahbar see Twakkal (2008).
3. The tradition about the "wooden" mosque derives from the pilgrimage account of Arculf, who visited the Holy City c. 680, before Abd al-Malik established the Dome of the Rock. It is possible that what Arculf described was scaffolding covering a construction site. See Adomnan, "The Holy Places," in Wilkinson (2002), 170. On the provenance of Arculf's account see Woods (2002).
4. See Little (1995).
5. See Avni (2010).
6. On synagogue architecture in Greco-Roman Palestine see Fine (2010), Levine (2012), 179–197.
7. See Busine (2013).
8. Pilgrimage sources are conveniently given by John Wilkinson (2002). For a historical account of early Christian pilgrimage see Hunt (2002 [1982]), and cf. Wilken (1992).
9. See Jerome, Letter LVIII to Paulinus of Nola.
10. See Donner (1992).
11. See Murphy O'Connor (2008).
12. See the legend of God himself purging the Holy City by means of a September rain following a Christian market day that brings masses of animals into the city, reported by Arculf and recorded by Adomnan, in Wilkinson (2002), 170.
13. For the correlation of landscape and sanctuary in Syrian antiquity see Steinsapir (1998).
14. *Hekhalot* literature was produced in Byzantine Palestine. See Schäfer (1988), Boustan, Himmelfarb, and Schäfer (2013).
15. See Langer and Fine (2005).
16. The spatial aspect of this pious imagination contrasts with an apocalyptic piety focused on catastrophe and the imminence of redemption. The apocalyptic imagination deals with change, including war, conquest, and destruction, whereas ascent/descent literature deals with the eternal invisible order.
17. On the latter see Bashear (1991). On Muslim apocalyptics in general see Cook (2002).
18. On Jerusalem in the early Muslim period see Prawer and Ben-Shammai (1996).
19. See Pentz (1992), 74: "The 7th century 'conquest' of Syria is – in archaeological terms – totally invisible. That is to say, archaeological evidence is abundant, while the archaeologist looking for a break in the material is searching in vain."
20. According to Levy-Rubin (2011), many of the rules developed by the early Muslims to negotiate the parallel existence of multiple tolerated communities were not just based on time-honored precedents but also satisfied the desire for equality among the subjugated communities. In other words, the so-called Pact

of Umar was far less discriminatory in intention and practice than appears in hindsight.

21. For a site seeking to provide access to the fragments from this unique trove of documents, now scattered in museums across the world, see the Friedberg Genizah Project at http://fjms.genizah.org/ (accessed November 29, 2017).

22. On the date of the great earthquake see Tsafrir and Foerster (1992).

23. I am excluding Umar II (r. 717–720) from this enumeration. Umar II was a relative but not a son of Abd al-Malik and the only Umayyad held in esteem by the later Abbasid historians. According to Goldschmidt (1999), 63, it was most likely this Umar who issued the so-called Pact of Umar that imposed various conditions of toleration on non-Muslim populations (*ahl al-dhimma*) while exempting the *mawali* (non-Arab converts to Islam) from the poll tax. Medieval Muslim sources, including Abu Bakr al-Tartushi, *Siraj al-Mulk* (late eleventh to early twelfth century), attributed the Pact of Umar to Caliph Umar b. al-Khattab.

24. For visuals see http://archnet.org/sites/6239 (accessed November 29, 2017). On the discovery of the palaces and the decision to preserve them see El-Haj (2001), 153–162.

25. Grabar et al. (1996), a model of scholarly erudition presented in readable form. See Rabbat (1993).

26. On the meanings associated with the buildings on the *al-Haram al-Sharif* see Busse (1991), Kaplony (2002).

27. See Tohe (2015). On the term and tradition of *isra'iliyyat* see Tottoli (1999), Jane Dammen McAuliffe, "Assessing the *isrā'īliyyāt*. An exegetical conundrum" in Leder (1998), 345–369, and Vajda (2012).

28. On the beginnings of *fada'il al-quds* literature see Sivan (1971).

29. Ruin and neglect of the ancient temple area may not reflect the actual state of the place at the time of the Arab conquest but rather constitute a literary trope. Evidence of buildings in the Golden Gate and possibly the foundations and design of the Dome of Rock may suggest that Heraclius had begun to rebuild the area following the defeat of Khosrow and his triumphant entry into Jerusalem in 629/631.

30. See Tsafrir and Foerster (1992). Others variably dated this mid-eighth-century earthquake to 746, 747, or 748. See Tsafrir and Foerster (1992), 231–235.

31. See Kister (1996). The *ziyara* to Al-Quds and Medina is recommended as meritorious but not commanded as the *hajj* to Mecca is.

32. See al-Maqdisi (2001).

33. Note that Muqadassi uses the derogatory name *al-qumamah* ("dungheap") for the *Anastasis* or Resurrection Church (i.e. the domed Western edifice that was part of the original Holy Sepulchre complex), instead of *kenisat al-qiyama* ("resurrection").

34. But see the 1047 CE description of *Bait al-muqqadas* by Persian traveler Nasir i-Khusraw, in his *Safarname* ("Book of Travels"), transl. Le Strange (1888). Excerpts online at http://nasirkhusraw.iis.ac.uk/site/Jerusalem (accessed November 30, 2017).

13

The Kingdom of Jerusalem: Of Warlords, Popes, and Preachers of *Jihad*

Jerusalem, the walled city, came to an end in the thirteenth century, when Cairo's Ayyubid rulers realized that walls might provide safe haven for the ever-renewed waves of *il-franj*, Frankish armed pilgrims set on retrieving the city they had held for nearly a century, but ignominiously lost in 1187. In this chapter, I take a closer look at the period of crusading and describe how French, English, and German kings and commoners got involved in this first "overseas" adventure and crucible of the European sense of an imperial mission to the "east." This wave of armed missions indicates that the great *translatio* had succeeded: Europe became "hooked" on Jerusalem because Rome was hooked on Jerusalem. Europe was awash with symbols that imprinted Jerusalem, the Holy Sepulchre, and biblical sacred history on the minds of everyone, literate or illiterate.[1] As the barbarians had once fought the wars of Byzantium, Franks, Britons, and Germans – people long since Romanized – now set out to liberate the Christian holy places in the name of the Holy See.

The Crusades, as these armed pilgrimages came to be known, were highly consequential in shaping western societies, institutions, and states. They firmed up the contested superiority of the papacy over the worldly princes of Latin Christendom, and they dominated western imagination until Europe's religious unity fell apart in the sixteenth-century Protestant Reformation. The deeds of Frankish knights and kings reverberated

Jerusalem: A Brief History, First Edition. Michael Zank.
© 2018 Michael Zank. Published 2018 by John Wiley & Sons Ltd.

throughout the centuries in works of romantic nostalgia, such as Tasso's swashbuckling *Gerusalemme liberata*, and they filtered into the nineteenth-century competition between European states to reassert their presence in the Holy Land and the Holy City of a declining Ottoman Turkish Empire.

Broadly speaking, the original quest for the retrieval of the holy places was part of a wider geo-political engagement between Muslim and Christian powers, a struggle for the inheritance of Rome, and for control over the Mediterranean sphere that had once been part of the Roman Empire, but was now divided between the Muslims of North Africa and the Middle East, the Byzantine Greek Empire, and a newly emerging Holy Roman Empire of the German Nation, that was forged, under the tutelage of the papacy, in centuries of sometimes effective, sometimes futile efforts to wrest control of territory from its competitors, while spreading the Latin version of the Christian doctrine. The practical winners of these wars were the maritime centers of Genoa, Venice, Cairo/Alexandria, and the ancient harbors along the Mediterranean seaboard that benefited from the trade relations established between east and west in the wake of religious warfare, a somewhat ironic and unexpected outcome. Trade, in turn, paved the way for a shift in international relations from an economy of warfare and territorial conquest to more peaceful, mutually beneficial mercantile forms of competition.

In the following, I provide a brief overview of the major campaigns of the Latins in the east, before returning to the consequences of these wars. I focus on the interplay between western actions and eastern reactions, most notably the mirror image of repeated western calls for warring in the name of Christ, and the "renewal of *jihad*" preached in the Muslim east.

A Brief Survey of Events

In 1095, at the Council of Clermont in southern France, Pope Urban II called for a campaign against the Seljuk Turks and for a liberation of the holy places from this "accursed race."[2] This appeal was occasioned by a call for help from the Byzantine Emperor Alexios I Komnenos. A similar campaign to retrieve Iberian territory lost to the Umayyads had been proposed by Gregory VII (r. 1073–1085), a great reformer whose political aim, like Urban's, was to subject the secular Frankish princes to the control of the Holy See. The call of the Byzantine Empire for help provided the opportunity to pursue this program further.

Urban's call, directed toward warring factions of southern French knights, was initially heeded by masses of fairly disorganized and untrained peasants, who set out over land in two companies, one led by an impoverished knight, the other by a preacher named Peter the Hermit (People's or Peasants' Crusade, 1096). This poorly organized campaign of a murdering and pillaging mob foundered on the way and never reached the Holy Land, but it left its mark on the popular imagination. It was enshrined in Jewish martyrology for releasing religiously motivated violence on the Jews along the Rhine (especially in the cities of Speyer, Worms, and Mainz), the first incident of this sort in European history. Such outbursts of anti-Jewish violence henceforth occurred with great regularity whenever the crusading movement was stymied, or suffered major setbacks in the east, and the popes ordered new campaigns. The fall of Jerusalem (1187) was followed by a massacre at York in England (1189–1190). The fall of Acre (1291) was followed by the expulsion of the Jews from France (1306).

The so-called First Crusade of 1096–1099 was the first successful Latin campaign in the east. It succeeded in establishing Frankish colonies in *outremer*. These included the County of Edessa, the Principality of Antioch, and the Kingdom of Jerusalem. The capture of port cities, including Tripoli (Lebanon), allowed future contingents of crusaders to reach the Holy Land by sea, which was safer. One of the side effects of sustained campaigning was the creation of an economy of transportation that boosted the fortunes of the major maritime republics of Genoa and Venice, which served as the major ports of embarkation for western traffic to and from the east.

The initial success of these campaigns in the east arose from the weak state of the Abbasids, whose control over Egypt, Syria, and the Levant had long since slipped. Fatimid control of the Levant was threatened by Seljuk Turks based in Asia Minor, who also pressed on Constantinople from across the Bosporus. It was because of this threat that the Byzantines called on the Latins for help, and it was because of the conflict between Seljuks and Fatimids that Jerusalem fell to the Franks like a ripe fruit. For nearly half a century, the Franks became the unchallenged rulers of the Lebanon and the Holy Land, establishing colonies, fortifying cities, and ruling in the name of Latin Christendom. A turning point in the history of *outremer* occurred in 1144, when the County of Edessa fell to Imad al-Din Zangi (or Zengi), Seljuk *atabek* (ruler) of Mosul and Aleppo. This first Muslim victory dispelled the myth of the invincibility of the Franks. The otherwise divided Muslim cities of Syria were henceforth more likely to be swayed by the call for *jihad* preached by Zangi, who increased his own standing among his peers by propagating the need to drive out the Frankish invaders.

The Second Crusade (1145–1149) was called by Pope Eugene III in response to the fall of Edessa and led by Louis VII of France and Conrad III of Germany. At that point, the Byzantine Emperor Manuel I Komnenos entered into an alliance with the Seljuk sultanate to prevent the western coalition from advancing. He thus effectively forestalled the Latin attempt to retake Edessa. This decision had grave consequences for the Byzantine Empire and the Latin Kingdom of Jerusalem. While the First Crusade had been occasioned by the Byzantine emperor's call for help against the Seljuk Turks, now the Byzantines prevented the Crusade of 1145 from advancing through Byzantine territory. One reason for the Byzantine-Seljuk alliance against the Latins was that sustaining masses of western forces in transit was costly, disruptive, and dangerous to Byzantine populations and to Constantinople herself. This fear was well justified, as became evident half a century later (see later in this section, on the sack of Constantinople of 1204). Another reason for the alliance was a fundamental sense of betrayal. Constantinople had expected the Latins to place the eastern territories they had conquered under the sovereign control of the Byzantine Empire. Instead, the Franks had established principalities of their own in the name of the Latin Church, thus deepening the rift between the Latins and the Greeks.[3]

The western coalition made it to Jerusalem but it was defeated in the attempt of engaging the *atabek* in Damascus. The only victory achieved by a crusading contingent at that time was in Portugal, where the Moors were expelled. This, too, was highly consequential for Muslim-Christian-Jewish relations on the Iberian Peninsula in that it precipitated the decline of the tolerant Almoravids of Al-Andalus and triggered a counter-invasion (launched from Morocco) of the radical sect of the Almohads (1147), spelling the end of the Golden Age of Al-Andalus.[4]

Saladin took Cairo in 1171.[5] His family controlled Egypt and the Levant for more than half a century, successfully fending off new western incursions and controlling the fate of Jerusalem through both military prowess and clever diplomacy. Though Saladin's crowning achievement was the toppling of the Fatimids of Egypt, he is better known for the defeat of the Latins at the Horns of Hattin and the conquest of Jerusalem (1187), a moment of great religious import, that involved a cleansing of the Muslim holy places and a famous sermon held at the Al-Aqsa mosque. The Horns of Hattin is the last time we hear of the True Cross, which had been carried into the engagement by Guy de Lusignan, then King of Jerusalem. Later crusades were preached in the name of retrieval not only of the Holy City but also of the True Cross, invoking the feats of Heraclius and making him appear as the first crusader. The loss of Jerusalem was a traumatic event. It did not, however, spell the end of the Latin Kingdom of Jerusalem in name or fact.

In response to the fall of Jerusalem, Pope Gregory VIII (d. 1187) called for a new crusade. The Third or King's Crusade of 1189–1192 involved several French and English kings, including Richard the Lionheart, as well as the aged German Emperor Frederick Barbarossa, who drowned in the Danube before he reached the Holy Land. Though this major campaign failed to take Jerusalem from the Ayyubids, it was successful in retaking many of the erstwhile Latin strongholds in the Holy Land, including the port city of Jaffa and the stronghold of Acre, which remained in Frankish hands until 1291.

With Jerusalem remaining in Muslim hands, Pope Innocent III (r. 1198–1216) vigorously preached for a new crusade to liberate the Holy City. This launched the Fourth Crusade (1202–1204), which culminated instead in the sack of Constantinople and the establishment of a short-lived Latin empire. This state came under constant assault from what remained of the Greek state and it eventually fell in 1261. The conquest and sack of Constantinople involved large-scale theft and transportation of priceless treasures from Greece to Italy and elsewhere in Western Europe. The great library of Constantinople was destroyed. The Byzantine Empire survived, though much reduced, for another two centuries, until it fell to the Ottoman Turks (1453). Emboldened by the capture of Constantinople, the Latins undertook the so-called Fifth Crusade (1213–1221), which succeeded in establishing a foothold in Damietta (Egypt). The attack was motivated by the consideration that Egypt held the key to the Holy Land. Failing to take Cairo, the Franks accepted a negotiated settlement offered by Saladin's nephew, Sultan al-Malik al-Kamil, who allowed the Franks to remain in Damietta for a period of eight years.

At the behest of Pope Innocent III and, after Innocent's death, of Gregory IX, Emperor Frederick II, a reluctant crusader, set out for the Holy Land (Sixth Crusade, 1228–1229) where, instead of taking Jerusalem by force, he negotiated an unprecedented agreement with al-Kamil in 1229. This contract entailed a ceding of authority over Jerusalem, Bethlehem, and a corridor connecting the Holy City with the Mediterranean, much as the British sought much later in the 1937 Peel Commission partition plan, proposed during the period of the British Mandate for Palestine. Under Frederick, Muslims remained living in Jerusalem and in charge of the Noble

Sanctuary. This peace agreement was loathed by Pope Gregory, who excommunicated Frederick, who, in turn, crowned himself "King of Jerusalem." At the expiration of the treaty (1239), Jerusalem – a defenseless city without walls –reverted back to the Ayyubids, but it was soon taken again by force by a new wave of crusaders (1239–1241). A harbinger of geo-political changes, most notably the ongoing campaigns of Mongolian Ilkhanid ruler Hulagu in south-west Asia, Jerusalem fell to Khwarasmian Turkish invaders in 1244. Shortly thereafter, Ayyubid rule in Egypt ended with the uprising of the Bahri-Mamluk slave soldiery, who also defeated the latest wave of French crusaders under Louis IX. In 1250, Damietta surrendered, ending Frankish presence in Egypt, until 1798, when Napoleon Bonaparte appeared at the Delta of the Nile, ushering in the modern history of western engagements in the east.

The great age of Abbasid rule and the Arab civilization associated with the Baghdad renaissance came to an end, not because of the Frankish invasions, which caused local disruptions in an already weakened network of cities and states, but because of the sack of Baghdad (1258) by invaders from Central Asia. The seemingly unstoppable advance of these warriors was halted in 1260 by Mamluk Sultan Baybars at Ayn Jalut ("Goliath's Spring") in the Galilee. Baybars's advance through Latin territory to meet the Mongols was by agreement with the Franks, then still ensconced in Acre and elsewhere across the Levant. With the fall of Acre in 1291 the Egyptian Mamluks gained complete control over Syria and Palestine. The Franks and their institutions retreated to Cyprus, Rhodes, Malta, and elsewhere. The crusading movement continued in Europe until the sixteenth century, when Reformation and Counter-Reformation set in, weakening the political authority of the papacy. The ensuing wars of religion between Catholics and Protestants ended with the Peace of Westphalia (1648), which provided the conditions for the emergence of the modern European political system.

Character and Consequences of the Eastern Crusades

The religiously motivated wars modern historians call the Crusades left behind a legacy of suspicion and resentment between Muslims, Catholic Christians, and Jews. They also introduced Frankish architecture across the Levant, the remnants of which are tokens of what now appears as a distant past or as a futile and quixotic episode. Although the Frankish knights failed to establish lasting colonies in the east, their repeated onslaught had a major impact on how these westerners (*il franj*) were perceived by the populations that took the brunt of these wars fought on behalf of the church. Latin campaigns for *reconquista* in east and west called forth counter-movements that were similarly motivated by religious zeal for sacred territory and holy places, a renewal of the *jihad* or "striving" that had supposedly guided the first wave of Arab conquerors. Just as Urban II rallied Christian warlords at the Council of Clermont in the name of Christ, so his Muslim counterparts in mid-twelfth-century Aleppo and Mosul called on Muslims to set aside their quarrels, renew their faith, and unite in the name of Allah. In the west, divinely ordained warfare boosted the standing of the papacy; in the east, the *jihad* of Zangi, Nur ad-Din, and Saladin temporarily restored Abbasid rule in Syria and Egypt. In both realms, that of the Holy Roman Empire and that of Sunni Islam, shrewd warriors and their spiritual leaders used Jerusalem's place in the religious imagination as a call to arms, a source of solidarity, and an excellent reason to make a supreme effort to fight an enemy who, since religion was in play, could be painted as subhuman, demonic, an enemy of men and God. On the ground, however, western and eastern elites often entered into coalitions and contractual arrangements, mitigating bloodlust by acculturation and accommodation, a fact that often pitted newcomers, not used to distinguishing rhetoric from realpolitik, against seasoned expatriates who had "gone native." Among other things, then, Frankish Jerusalem was a place where ignorant boorish newcomers could be educated in the sophisticated ways of the east.[6]

The Latin campaigns in the former Roman east were wars of divinely sponsored conquest of a particularly symbolic territory, that had been under direct Roman rule since the age of Hadrian, and indirectly since the days of Pompey (63 BCE). It was a land far away from the lands of origin of those who fought for it, yet at the heart of what they thought of as center of the inhabited earth. It was linked to their identity as the heirs of Rome. To the degree that the eastern crusades were driven by a "biblical fantasy" of conquest, they were inspired by biblical saints and heroes, especially by Joshua, with the Pope as Moses sanctioning the effort from afar, but also by the Maccabeans in their zeal to retrieve and purge the temple, and by Christian Emperor Heraclius's retrieval of the Holy Wood. The symbolic prize was the biblical Holy Land, the Holy City, the temple of the Lord, and the tomb of Christ, places utterly familiar from the Gospel, that were mapped on the existing monuments that the frenzied and exhausted Frankish conquerors took over from the massacred population. What motivated these unprecedented campaigns in a far-away place was the fact, that they were preached and perceived as an *imitatio* of biblical acts. And yet these wars were novel, marking a defining moment in the history of the societies that engaged in this violent encounter. Eastern crusading was significant in shaping the self-perception and sense of mission of western societies. Medieval institutions, such as the Knights Templar, the Hospitallers, the Knights of St. John, and other military orders were shaped by the effort and economy of *reconquista*, the concerted retrieval of erstwhile Christian lands in the name of Christ, the fighting off of further Muslim encroachment on Christian territory, and the violent expansion of Christianity, not just in Muslim or formerly Roman territory, but in the lands of the Prussians and Slavs.[7] As wars of conquest, waged in the name of faith and at the behest of a religious institution, rather than simply for the sake of greed or self-defense, the Crusades created the conditions for the consolidation of Western societies into more centralized, better organized, more ambitious states and principalities, that competed with one another for preeminence in Europe and beyond. This legacy was to become virulent again in the nineteenth century, when the Great Powers began to jockey for Ottoman territory, with the Holy Land once again at the spiritual, cultural, and symbolic heart of that declining empire on the land bridge between Africa, Asia, and Europe.

On the ground in Syria-Palestine, along the coast of the Levant, and in Armenian Edessa to the north, the Crusades were no more than a "series of unfortunate events." But the two centuries of proto-colonial warfare between the Latin west and the Muslim east continued to be invoked as a historic precedent and they remained, in the Arab psyche, an ever-present peril and a cautionary tale.[8] No less tangible are the many ways in which this early contact between Latin and Arab civilizations stimulated exchanges of cultural knowledge and civilizational cross-pollination, despite the fact that the Muslim east was never officially integrated into Christian consciousness, other than as an aberration in a linear history of the triple inheritance of biblical religion, Roman power, and Greek civilization.

It is hard to overstate the impact of a movement that changed the equilibrium between religious and secular powers in Europe, that led to the Christianization of Slavic nations, that triggered anti-Jewish violence, and started the wave of Jewish expulsions from western Europe, but also brought the Latin west into close contact with Muslims in east and west. Crusading institutions outlasted the Crusades themselves, though some (including the Knights Templar) were forcibly dismantled, because they became too powerful.[9] French national identity and the royal court's assertion of independence from the papacy are directly linked to the economic and political effects of crusading.[10] The memory of the Crusades, carefully preserved by their contemporary chroniclers, was retrieved and romanticized in the early nineteenth century, when many Europeans, weary of revolution, became infatuated with the Middle Ages, and the Romantic movement took hold of educated elites, no less than it penetrated the popular imagination across England, France, and Germany. In the Muslim east, the memory of *il franj* is associated with the deeply rooted suspicion of all things western, which became an important ingredient in the late nineteenth-century Arab "awakening." In Jewish memory, the Crusades are enshrined as particularly dark chapters in a lachrymose history, triggering acts of collective martyrdom on par with, or even surpassing, those of old.[11] It was the beginning of a life in fear of random violence emanating from frenzied Christian masses, stimulated by the ritualized repetition of anti-Jewish doctrines, blood libel, and charges of well poisoning.[12]

The crusading impulse triggered increasingly violent attitudes toward Jews, Muslims (Moors), and heretics within Europe. Anti-Judaism became endemic in the Latin world, as Frankish invasions of the Middle East were frustrated, giving way to a focus on inner-European conflicts. As France asserted independence from the Pope, England, then still a loyal vassal of the Holy See, entered into a notorious Hundred Years' War with the French crown. Continued pressure on the Jews (expelled from England in 1290 and from France in 1306), led to a migration eastward of German-speaking Jews who took their language with them and created new centers of Jewish life in the Eastern European principalities of Poland and Lithuania, and later also in the Russian "pale of settlement." Moorish and Jewish civilization on the Iberian Peninsula came to an end in waves of persecution, culminating in their expulsion in 1492, which was followed by the reign of terror of the Spanish Inquisition. It was at that time that, for the first time in many centuries, the Holy Land and the Holy City became open to Jewish remigration to the Land of Israel. The invitation to return was issued by Suleïman the Magnificent, heir to the Ottoman sultanate, and newly minted ruler over Egypt and *al-Sham*, builder of the walls of Jerusalem. In this and other respects, the sixteenth century marked a turning point in European and Middle Eastern civilizations and, for better or worse, the dawn of modernity.

Crusading and *jihad* movements were closely linked as acts of warfare that imitated the armed saints of old, while conferring saintliness and forgiveness of sins to those who pursued it. On both sides, this type of war on infidels and heretics was considered a noble, god-pleasing form of devotion.

The effects of these campaigns were far more significant and long lasting in the western societies themselves than in the colonies established by the Frankish knights in *outremer*. Crusading continued within Europe and on its eastern borders until the time of the Protestant Reformation, which triggered internal wars of religion and gave rise to major changes in western societies. Crusader institutions, established to sustain the eleventh- to thirteenth-century campaigns to liberate the holy places, outlasted their original purpose and fixed the image of Jerusalem and "the east" in the European imagination. The capture (1099) and subsequent loss (1187) of Jerusalem were forever enshrined as seminal moments in the ambiguously heroic and tragic story that encapsulated the western sense of mission. The desire for rectification and retrieval rose again in the nineteenth century, the age of nationalism, when the distant past was recalled as a spiritual source of colonialist expansion. In the Arab and Muslim world, the Crusades provided a paradigm by which to decode western intentions and interpret any future encroachment on Arab, Turkish, or Muslim affairs, such as unfolded during the Great War and in its aftermath, which saw the demise of the Ottoman Empire, the abolition of the caliphate, the creation of European client states along artificial boundaries, and the establishment of Jewish- and Christian-majority commonwealths on the territory of the erstwhile Crusader states, Lebanon and *al-Sham* (Greater Syria and the Holy Land). No wonder, then, that twentieth-century European and American politics in the Middle East gave rise to renewed calls for *jihad* against the infidels and for a liberation of the holy places. This explains, to some extent, why *Al-Quds*, the Holy City and the most potent symbol of medieval *jihad*, graces the flags of today's *mujahedeen* and names entire brigades of fighters devoted to bring this age of the new crusaders to an end and reestablish the rule of Islam.[13]

Notes

1. See Wharton (2006), Geary (1990), Brown (2003).
2. Robert the Monk. Source: Munro (1895).
3. Centuries of rivalry between Constantinople and Rome had earlier culminated in the "great schism" of 1054, a rift between Greek and Latin rites that has yet to be mended. See Congar (1959).
4. See Fromherz (2010).
5. On Saladin see Ehrenkreutz (1972), Eddé (2011), and – from a modern Arab perspective – Maalouf (1984).

6. See the account by the Palestinian warrior Usama b. Munqidh, online at http:// sourcebooks.fordham.edu/halsall/source/usamah2.html (accessed November 30, 2017).
7. See Constable (2008), Boas (2001), Hillenbrand (1999), Housley (2006), Riley Smith (1995), Tyerman (2005).
8. See *The Crusades through Arab Eyes*, by Lebanese-born French journalist Amin Maalouf (1984). As recently as 2015, Islamic State propaganda referred to captured Assyrian Christians as "crusaders."
9. On the Knights Templar see Nicholson (2001).
10. See Parsons (2004).
11. See Spiegel (1967).
12. See Haverkamp (1999).
13. Al-Quds and Al-Aqsa remain central to the "monotheistic geography" of modern *jihad* in general, not just for groups, such as Hamas and Fatah, rooted in Palestine. See Devji (2017).

Part IV
Modern City

14

Ottoman *Kudus*

Jerusalem enters modernity in the nineteenth century. This is the age when the city begins to grow beyond its walls. This is true for many cities. European cities, which were walled until the nineteenth century, see their expansion beyond the quaint, dank, and cramped quarters encircled by protective walls and moats. One reason for these expansions is heightened security, due to better, more efficient policing and administration of regions, a kind of pacification of the hinterland; in Jerusalem's case, better Ottoman policing of the Bedouin of the desert. Other reasons include better roads and bridges; centralized administration; political reforms that give more ownership and control to local elites; economic stimulus through foreign investment, immigration, and entrepreneurship. The flipside of urban development is the demise of nature, the loss of that wildness beyond the moat, the freedom of forest brook and mountaintop, cherished and immortalized by the Romantic poets, who gave us the imagery of nostalgia for the Middle Ages, an age of chivalry that prevailed before the rise of the bourgeois middle class, the urban proletariat, and the ubiquitous, indispensable, and despised middleman. Nineteenth-century Jerusalem came to Christian Europe and Christian America through the words of pilgrims, travelers, missionaries, imperially sponsored researchers, surveyors, and archaeologists, and increasingly through the mechanized image of photography, feeding a veritable Bible-land mania that obtains unabated until

Jerusalem: A Brief History, First Edition. Michael Zank.
© 2018 Michael Zank. Published 2018 by John Wiley & Sons Ltd.

today. Why this mania? Why does Jerusalem loom so large in the western imaginary? In this chapter we will look at Ottoman Jerusalem, the city that became prominent among well-meaning Christians and in imperial chambers, in an age when killing the infidels was no longer *en vogue* and crusading took other, more peaceful, forms of geographical penetration and persuasion, an age when religious intolerance gave way (at least officially) to civic equality and the protection of minorities. This was also an age of mission, spearheaded by Protestant pietists who were new to Ottoman territory, but found an object for their zeal in the Jews, with whom they felt a certain Bible-based affinity. Like the Jews, they cared much for the biblical past, and less so for the wrangling between the traditional communities over holy places Protestants regarded with distaste, and increasingly thought of as not just garish in taste but historically inauthentic. The second most important aspect of Christian Holy Land engagement was Christian benevolence that extended to everyone in need. Europeans brought orphanages, hospitals, and schools, they built churches and settlements, struck roots in the Oriental soil, learned the indigenous languages, and contributed to the transformation of Jerusalem, from a quaint Muslim town on the traditional route from Damascus to Mecca, into a modern metropolis in the Syro-Palestinian parts of the Arabian provinces of the once great, but now declining, Ottoman Empire.

Among the factors precipitating change in the urban geography of Jerusalem were the violent invasions of Napoleon Bonaparte and Ibrahim Pasha. The first one, in 1798, led to the founding of modern Egypt, which led to the second one, in 1831, which was the Egyptian occupation of Syria. Restoring Syria to Ottoman rule required European intervention in support of the weakened empire, and thus opened the gates to the "peaceful crusade" of European penetration of Syria, the Holy Land, and Jerusalem in particular. The second precipitating factor in the transformation of Jerusalem consists of innovations in Ottoman law and administration, including the transformation of subjects into citizens[1] (*Tanzimat*), and Jerusalem's administrative elevation to the status of an independent *sançak*.[2] In 1874, the city became the administrative center of the Jerusalem district, which included Gaza in the south and bordered on Egypt, then under increasingly direct British control. The third factor to be considered is the impact of European influence, investment, and immigration, driven by missionary zeal and colonial interests, that was to some extent indulged and encouraged by the High Porte. The result of these factors was the transformation of Jerusalem from a medieval "Islamic city"[3] into a modern "multi-cultural metropolis"[4] or "mixed town,"[5] a character it retained to some extent as late as 1947, when the anticipation of partition led to ethnic separation, expulsion, expropriation, and division. Like India, another formerly British-dominated territory, Palestine ended in a division along sectarian lines.

Ethno-religious segmentation and class differences preexisted the British Mandate, but the British administration, which began in 1917 and marks the end of Ottoman rule, exacerbated these divisions. The British viewed the population of Palestine as divided by religious affiliation, without regard to preexisting structures of communal solidarity, cultural and economic interpenetration, or linguistic affinities. The primary beneficiaries of British rule were the Jews who, in socio-economic terms, were part of a growing middle class that stimulated the economic and demographic growth of Palestine, as evidenced in the building boom of the 1920s, 1930s, and 1940s. As the majority population, Christian and Muslim Arabs benefited from British and Zionist economic activities as well, though more so in the cities and especially if they were willing to invest and build enterprises of their own, and less so in the countryside among Muslim *fellahin*, many of whom lost their traditional means of subsistence without gaining new opportunities outside the building trades, as the country was being transformed and "modernized." Whether it was by design, by preconceived notions of religio-cultural differences, or both, the British way of viewing populations along national-religious lines helped the Zionist pioneers of the Third Aliyah, whose work of colonization and institution building was based on the Balfour Declaration (1917) and the League of Nations mandate for Palestine, which provided the utopian/restorative program of Jewish homeland building in Palestine with an internationally guaranteed charter.[6] When we consider the affinity between Protestants and Jews in evidence from early on in nineteenth-century decisions, taken in various corners of Europe, that directly impacted on the development of Jerusalem, we also need to consider that this affinity may have been based on misconceptions that ultimately led to alienation between the agents of colonization.

This chapter focuses on changes in Ottoman *Kudus* (the Ottoman name for *Al-Quds*) that took place in the nineteenth century and that were driven by competing European interests in the Holy Land. It is these interests, and the Bible-land perspective behind them, that shaped what we now view as modern Palestine, a territory and region whose geographic delineation was based on how modern Bible scholars envisaged ancient Israel and mapped it on modern Syrian territory. Those maps were on the minds and tables of general staff when modern European politicians carved up Ottoman territory into units of interest to competing colonial schemes of development and exploitation. The next chapter deals with Jerusalem after it came under direct British control. British impact on Jerusalem can already be seen in the nineteenth century, especially in the peculiar coalition of interests between Protestants and Jews that transcends the British context and reaches into the story of American ascendancy in the Middle East. But we need to consider nineteenth- and early twentieth-century developments in their own right. As late-Ottomanist Alexander Schölch warned, it would be a mistake to assume the outcomes of the twentieth-century history of Palestine to be predetermined by nineteenth-century developments.[7] Nineteenth-century Jerusalem underwent profound and dynamic changes, but it was and remained a predominantly Muslim Arab city, continuous with its medieval antecedent. As Jerusalem modernized, so did its Muslim and Christian populations, though not necessarily all at the same pace, in the same manner, for the same reasons, and with access to the same resources. Twentieth-century Jerusalem looks very different, for reasons considered further along. Though modern Jerusalem has its nineteenth-century harbingers, it was not fated to unfold as it did. It did so as a result of choices and decisions made by people who had the power to enforce them. These choices may not always have been rational, or entirely perspicacious, and they forced others to place their own hopes and aspirations on hold. What interests me throughout this study of Jerusalem, in its various iterations, are the political regimes and the religious values embraced, promoted, exploited, or repressd by different regimes. In the modern period, with increased agency conferred on local, communal, and trans-national actors, the central imperial regime relinquished control, while maintaining the appearance of an arbiter. After the Great War, new regimes appear that are legitimized by international agencies and contracts, and have as their central mandate the arbitration of competing national claims in a post-imperial realm. We want to understand the combination of religion and politics, and the appeal of Jerusalem as a pawn in the struggle between communities, nations, and empires. As we turn to modern Jerusalem, the question to consider is continuity and change in the religio-political functions of the city, the presence of ancient and medieval symbolism in modern contexts, but also the acutely modern religious and secular meanings of the city, that compel modern and contemporary people to act on behalf of, or in reference to, Jerusalem and its holy places. Why is Jerusalem so important in modern politics? What does it tell us about our sometimes simplistic assumptions about secular modernity, that Jerusalem persists as a religious symbol, and even rejuvenates its symbolic appeal? I raise these questions less in terms of what distinguishes between Jewish, Muslim and Christian views of Jerusalem, but in terms of the degrees of admixture of political and religious, secular and pious, modern and pre-modern types of commitment, boundary formation, rhetoric, and action. The most important differences between modern and pre-modern views of, and commitments to, Jerusalem cut across the religious divides. For example, there is greater affinity today between Evangelical Christians and radically utopian Jews who want to reestablish the Temple, than there is between this Jewish fringe and the Israeli mainstream. Many a liberal Christian finds it easier to identify with secular and moderately religious Muslims among Palestinians than with Christian apocalyptists or traditionalists steeped in turf wars between sects. The list of boundary-crossing solidarity formations goes on.

For 400 years, from 1517 until 1917, Jerusalem was ruled by the Ottoman sultanate, centered in Istanbul (Constantinople). The Ottomans surged onto the European scene with the capture of Constantinople (1453). Half a century later they subdued Egypt and the Hejaz. The flag of the Prophet now waved over all three holy cities, as well as over the eastern capital of Christendom. The lands at the intersection of Europe, Asia, and Africa, with Jerusalem at their symbolic center, had been brought under a single commander again, as they had once been under Roman rule. The Turkish sultans of Constantinople considered themselves heirs of Romans and Arabs alike and took pride in their guardianship of Jewish, Christian, and Muslim communities and holy places.[8] Selim, conqueror of Egypt, also took the title of caliph and bequeathed it to his son whom he named after King Solomon.

At its peak in the late sixteenth century, the Ottomans controlled the eastern Mediterranean from North Africa to Greece and the Balkans, the lands east and west of the Black Sea, and African and Arabian coasts down to the Horn of Africa. In the east they troubled the Safavids and in the west they threatened to take Vienna twice, in 1529 and 1683. The unsuccessful second siege marked a turning point in the fortune of the empire and heralded its retrenchment. At the same time, the European world underwent dramatic changes. In the arts and sciences, the Italian Renaissance, Humanism, and the scientific revolution, put an end to the medieval worldview. In religion, the Protestant Reformation ended the religious unity of the west and unleashed devastating wars of religion. The colonization and exploitation of the resource-rich New World and the global expansion of trade created competition among maritime powers to control and colonize the rest of the world. Mercantilism and industrialization changed the social fabric of European societies, which became increasingly urbanized and socially mobile. In political terms, this was the era of enlightened absolutism and constitutional monarchy, of political revolution and social reform.

Until the nineteenth century, Jerusalem remained largely untouched by these major developments. Ottoman *Kudus* was a nicely walled but sparsely populated, predominantly Arab Muslim city in Syria (*al-Sham*), a spiritual center of pious visitation on the way to Mecca for the annual *haj* (see Map 11). According to Haim Gerber,[9] Jerusalem remained a minor provincial town of no more than 10,000 residents until around the 1830s when its administrative status was upgraded. Until then, the major economic center of Palestine was Acre, which had thrived on the production and exportation of cotton and produced regionally powerful strongmen. Ottoman Jerusalem included Jewish and Christian communities. Greeks and Armenians in particular thrived across the sultanate, because of their significance to Ottoman trade and diplomatic relations with Europe. In the eighteenth and nineteenth centuries, the Georgian and Greek Orthodox churches, protected by the Tsars of Russia, emerged as the largest landowners in the Holy Land and the Holy City. Many of Jerusalem's modern neighborhoods and public buildings were built on land leased from these national churches. In the days of Suleïman the Magnificent (r. 1520–1566), when the Ottomans were at their peak, many Jews expelled from the Iberian Peninsula or fleeing the Spanish Inquisition sought refuge in the east where their skills were welcomed. Some settled in Jerusalem, which was once again a walled city, others in Safed where they were close to the tombs of early rabbis and mystics mentioned in the Book of Zohar, the main text of the medieval tradition of *Kabbalah*.[10] Seventeenth-century mystical messiah Shabtai Tsevi, a flamboyant and manic-depressive Jew from Smyrna, met his prophet, Nathan of Gaza, in Jerusalem. Prophesied to reveal himself in 1666, Tsevi ended up in captivity instead. Given the choice of death or conversion, he and some of his followers converted to Islam, leaving behind a sect of hidden Jews, who persisted until the twentieth century as the Dönmeh of Thessaloniki. Letters from Jerusalem and the Holy Land attest to the fact that, in Mamluk and Ottoman times, the "Ishmaelites" treated their Jewish neighbors with respect and that the routine contempt to which Jews were exposed in Europe was absent here.[11] The Ashkenazi Jewish community of Jerusalem was established by 300 Eastern European *Hasidim* who arrived in 1777, in search of messianic redemption. Shortly thereafter, the relative calm in Ottoman Syria was disrupted by Napoleon's foray into Egypt and the first modern massacres committed in the Holy Land, following the French siege and conquest of Yafo.[12] The French incursion prompted the Ottomans to reorganize Egypt. The man appointed to do so, Albanian-born Mehmet Ali, remembered as the "founder of modern Egypt," destroyed the native Mamluk elite and went on to challenge his Ottoman suzerain when his son, Ibrahim Pasha, occupied Syria and the Levant (1830–1841) and threatened to march on Constantinople. The Egyptian crisis was eventually settled by the intervention of a quadruple alliance of England, Prussia, Austria, and Russia. In exchange for this and later help, the Ottomans began to cede ground in the Holy Land to a sometimes concerted, and often competitive, "peaceful crusade" of Christian powers, that proceeded apace until the eve of the Great War.

Following the French example and currying favor with the Europeans, Ibrahim Pasha (1789–1848) ordered the emancipation of non-Muslims, which triggered a violent peasant revolt in Palestine (1834), the first of several moments of backlash of local populations against Christians as well as Jews that periodically erupted across Syria throughout the nineteenth century. The revolt reached Jerusalem, where the Egyptians holed up in the David Citadel, Christians took refuge in monasteries, and defenseless Jewish residences were pillaged.[13] The Israeli pioneer of Jerusalem's modern urban geography, Yehoshua Ben-Arieh, describes early nineteenth-century Palestine as "a derelict province of the decaying Ottoman Empire."[14] Arab Jerusalemite historian Kamil Asali, on the other hand, emphasizes the fact that the Ottoman walled city was more of a hidden gem, that harbored fields and orchards, describing a pastoral quality of life that was lost to foreign influence and immigration.[15] To Ben-Arieh, the modernization of Jerusalem was the achievement of European colonial powers and Jewish immigrants, especially those of a Zionist persuasion. Israeli Ottomanist Haim Gerber suggests that, on balance, "the effect of the Ottoman government's activities was conducive to modernization."[16]

Beginning in 1838, with the establishment of the British consulate as the first modern diplomatic representation in the Holy City, and accelerating after the Crimean War of 1853–1856, European diplomats gained influence and made Jerusalem an important place for Christian powers to stake a claim in the affairs of the "sick man of Europe," as Tsar Nicholas called the Ottoman Empire. The Crimean War itself broke out over a conflict between France and Russia over Christian privileges in Jerusalem. In 1847, France had renewed the Latin Patriarchate in Jerusalem, boosting the standing of the Roman Catholics and challenging the accustomed superiority of the Greek Orthodox patriarch in Jerusalem, protected by the Russian Czar. Snubbed by the Ottomans, the Russians invaded Ottoman territory in Moldavia and Walachia, but were ultimately satisfied with a diplomatic solution hammered out by a broad European coalition. After the war, the High Porte renewed the reform legislation that gave Ottoman citizens equal rights regardless of their religion, a move that irritated the Muslim populations, especially in the countryside, where Muslims were the overwhelming majority. Over the last half century of Ottoman rule, as the Empire reorganized its military and civilian administration to compete with the other Great Powers, Europeans jostled for influence, and the migration of Jews to the Holy Land from the Yemen, from Central Asian Bukhara, from newly independent (formerly Ottoman) Romania, and from Tsarist Russia, stimulated growth and created need and opportunity to modernize Jerusalem by means of philanthropy and religious missions. International diplomacy, Ottoman politics, and local developments attracted renewed attention to the city. In 1874 Jerusalem was elevated to the status of an independent *sançak*. This move was welcomed by the European powers for whom the Holy Land was of strategic and sentimental value. It was also a concession on the part of the Ottomans, who had suffered state bankruptcy and were heavily indebted to the Europeans. The range of the Jerusalem district was nevertheless limited to southern Palestine, avoiding the creation of too strong an increasingly foreign-dominated wedge within Syria, where the Lebanon, with its strongly Maronite population, was already semiindependent. Though intended to strengthen centralized control, these measures also boosted the status of local Arab notables, who gained direct access to the Ottoman government in Constantinople.[17] The opening of the Ottoman Empire to foreign land purchase allowed European powers and private land agencies to invest in buildings and infrastructure that stimulated economic growth, tourism, and immigration. Foreign-sponsored research institutions, such as the Palestine Exploration Fund, surveyed the land, ostensibly in the interest of geography and archaeology, and tacitly for future military planning. The removal of religious discrimination by imperial decree empowered local Christians and Jews. Foreign schools introduced the children of local elites to western languages and ideas, at a time when the Arab provinces of the Ottoman Empire found themselves in a new situation. With the loss of many of their European territories, the Ottomans began to develop a new, more Muslim and more Turkish, ideology of rule that left the Arab Muslims wondering about their place in the

Turkish-dominated sultanate. What George Antonius memorably called the "Arab awakening"[18] was a complex movement of reorientation, stimulated by European ideas, Islamic conservatism, and Arab nationalism.

Jerusalem saw a first building boom in late Ottoman times.[19] New hospices for pilgrims were added, such as the Russian Compound on Jaffa Road and the Austrian Hospice on the *Via Dolorosa*. Benevolent institutions were founded that brought missionaries and western medical knowledge to what westerners considered neglected "oriental" populations in need of the benefits of modern civilization. These included orphanages, such as the Syrian Orphanage founded by German missionary Ludwig Schneller in 1860, which spawned today's Arab-speaking Evangelical-Lutheran community, hospitals such as the Eye Hospital of the Order of St. John, chartered by Queen Victoria in 1882, churches such as the Evangelical Church of the Redeemer inaugurated by Wilhelm II on his imperial visit in 1898, and the Russian church of Mary Magdalene in the Garden of Gethsemane. The *Mishkenot Shaananim* workers' cottages and windmill, established by the British philanthropist Sir Moses Montefiore, were intended to provide relief to the poor residents of the overcrowded Jewish Quarter. In 1855, Consul James Finn, charged by Her Majesty's government to take the Jews of Palestine under British protection, purchased land to establish the Jewish settlement of Kerem Avraham. Meah Shearim, an intentional community of 100 ultra-orthodox Jewish families, was founded in 1874. In the 1890s, wealthy Bukharan families commissioned German architect and missionary Conrad Schick to build residences in a neo-Gothic style that became known as the Bukharan neighborhood. Leading Muslim families built villas, surrounded by lush gardens, to the north of the Old City,[20] including Sheikh Jarrah, founded in 1865 by the Nashashibis, Jarallahs, and Husseinis. Later Sheikh Jarrah also saw the establishment of an American colony by the Spafford family from Chicago, whose lifestyle also attracted a community of pious Swedish Lutheran immigrants. The Spaffords provided a *pied-à-terre* for US interests, especially during World War I, when most foreigners were expelled.[21] To the south of the Old City, the nineteenth-century Swabian Templer sect built a German settlement, with distinctive red-tiled stone houses and walled orchards, along the road to Hebron. Nearby was the terminus of a single-track French-built railroad, completed in 1892, that connected the coastal harbor of Yafo with the newly burgeoning pilgrimage city of Jerusalem.[22] The late Ottoman urban renewal of Jerusalem was very much a mixture of messianism and modernism.

Modern Ottoman Jerusalem, a burgeoning international metropolis, ground to a halt during the Great War, when expatriates were expelled, Arab men were conscripted or volunteered to defend the Turkish fatherland, locusts ravished the land, and the world of the past gave way to the disruption and brutalization of modern mechanized warfare.[23] Many of the urban, cultural, political, social, and economic trends, started under the Ottomans, continued apace once the dust of war settled, and Jerusalem's multi-ethnic mix of Ottoman populations found itself under a British military administration that raised contradicting expectations.[24] As stated in a 1922 document of a Palestine Arab delegation to the British government in London, making the "Moslem-Christian Case Against Zionist Aggression," the Arabs of Palestine who had pledged themselves to supporting the Allies had reasonably expected the British government to make good on its promise to aid in "the reconstitution of the Arab nation and, as far as possible, of the restoration of Arab influence and authority in the conquered provinces."[25] The Arabs understood that "the object of the Allies in the war (was) the assistance of weaker nations to freedom and self-determination."[26] They were therefore understandably "stunned and horrified"[27] to learn that another promise had been made as well.

Notes

1. Foregrounded by Salim Tamari in Misselwitz (2006), 33 f.
2. *Sançak* (sanjak) or *liva* refers to a second-level division administered by a *sanjakbey* or *mutesarrif* who ordinarily answered to a provincial governor. On Ottoman administrative reforms in nineteenth-century Palestine see Al-Salim (2015).
3. Liebeschuetz (2001), Hinds (2004).
4. Tamari (1999).
5. Rabinowitz and Monterescu (2008).
6. See http://avalon.law.yale.edu/20th_century/palmanda.asp (accessed November 30, 2017).
7. See Schölch (1986), 17–24.
8. See Fetvacı (2013).
9. See Gerber (1985), 5–6.
10. On the hospitality of early Ottoman Jerusalem to Jews escaping Christian Europe see Asali (1994), 41–42.
11. See Cohen (2015), 15.
12. Cohen (2015), 12.

13. See Cohen (2015), 14. On nineteenth-century Palestine see Schölch (1993), Schölch, "Jerusalem in the 19th century (1831–1917 AD)" in Asali (2000 [1990]), Krämer (2008), Gerber (1985), Ben-Arieh (1983).
14. Ben-Arieh (1983), 11.
15. Asali (2000 [1990]).
16. Gerber (1985), 1.
17. See Büssow (2011).
18. Similar processes took place in Egypt and the Lebanon, especially at the urban centers of Cairo and Beirut. See Antonius (2001 [1939]), Hourani (1962), Ajami (1999).
19. For an overview of city quarters, maps, and Ottoman census data for the Ottoman period overall as well as for late Ottoman times, see Arnon (1992).
20. See Kark and Oren-Nordheim (2001).
21. Jacobson (2011).
22. On the urban development of nineteenth- and early twentieth-century Jerusalem see Kark and Oren-Nordheim (2011).
23. On Jerusalem during the Great War see Tamari (2011), Jacobson (2011).
24. See Delegation (1922).
25. The Colonial Secretary in a speech to the House of Commons, June 14, 1921, cited in Delegation (1922).
26. Ibid.
27. Ibid.

15

Ethnic Separation, Partition, and Division

When the Ottoman Empire entered the Great War on the side of Germany and Austria, Great Britain abandoned her century-long policy of propping up the Ottomans and pursued two war aims: to defeat the Central Powers, while preventing her allies (France, Russia) from gaining ground, in case of a collapse of the Ottoman Empire. The secret agreements Britain entered into during the war were virtually impossible to maintain at the same time. These included the Husayn–McMahon correspondence of 1915–1916, the Sykes–Picot Agreement of May 1916, and the Balfour Declaration of November 2, 1917. None of these documents were subject to public review, nor were they widely released until later, in the case of Sykes–Picot only because, after Russia left the war, the Bolsheviks leaked it, with the intention of embarrassing the capitalist powers. The conflicting implications of these documents gave rise to long-drawn-out and bitter debates, and contributed to the decline of British influence in the Middle East, including the erosion of trust in Britain as an honest broker. In consequence of these agreements, Palestine came to be a thrice promised land: once to the Arabs, as part of an independent caliphate centered in the Hejaz, at least as the Arabs loyal to the Hashemites understood it from their interpretation of the Husayn–McMahon correspondence, some of which may have been altered; once to the French, as part of an internationalized holy land, a promise the British reneged on when the war was over; and once to the Jews, as a homeland

Jerusalem: A Brief History, First Edition. Michael Zank.
© 2018 Michael Zank. Published 2018 by John Wiley & Sons Ltd.

open to immigration and development. To deliver on the latter promise, Great Britain obtained the League of Nations Mandate for Palestine, which committed the mandatory power to precisely that goal: to facilitate the establishment of a Jewish homeland in Palestine, though without detriment to the "civil and religious rights of existing non-Jewish communities in Palestine," nor to the Jews residing elsewhere. The two goals, maintaining law and order in Palestine in preparation for the country's independence, and working toward the creation of a Jewish homeland in Palestine, turned out to be irreconcilable. As concerns Jerusalem, neither the British mandatory government, nor the League of Nations, nor its successor organization, the United Nations (UN), considered Jerusalem negotiable. It was always meant to be part of the Christian, or international state, envisaged by European powers since the middle of the nineteenth century. It is interesting to consider that this solution was basically forgotten after 1949, when Jerusalem was divided between the Jewish state of Israel and the Hashemite Kingdom of Jordan. It didn't return to the forefront of the discussion until June 1967, when Israel conquered East Jerusalem and placed it under Israeli civilian administration. UN 242, the basis of all negotiations ever since, committed Israel to withdrawing from occupied territories, including East Jerusalem, but did not return to the internationalization scheme. But the idea has since been floated in negotiations between Israelis and Palestinians for two simple reasons: neither Israelis nor Palestinians want the city to be divided, as it was between 1949 and 1967, and neither Israelis nor Palestinians want to live under the other's sovereign rule. In other words, the only reasonable scenario for Jerusalem that would achieve an equilibrium of unhappiness among the two parties is to do exactly what European powers, the League of Nations, the British Empire, and the UN envisaged for the city, namely, its internationalization. To be sure, as Bernard Wasserstein perceptively wrote in his masterful *Divided Jerusalem*, only those lacking in power to impose their will on Jerusalem argue for internationalization.

On December 11, 1917, General Allenby entered Jerusalem on foot, in a carefully staged act meant to set his conquest apart from Kaiser Wilhelm II's grand entrance of 1898. Though the Anglo-Egyptian Expeditionary Force commanded by Allenby included Arab auxiliaries, these troops and their symbols were not included in the ceremony.[1] Jerusalem was of strategic concern in the conquest of Syria. As the administrative center of southern Palestine, it separated British-dominated Egypt from Ottoman Syria. The city's capture came at an opportune time. The conquest of Jerusalem was much celebrated in the English press, coming as it did shortly before Christmas, after three years of bloody and exhausting conflict, the outcome of which was then still far from certain. Northern Palestine, Lebanon, and Syria remained under Ottoman control until the fall of 1918; loyalty toward the Ottomans remained strong among the local population until the official dissolution of the empire, following the 1923 Peace of Lausanne, and even beyond.[2] As late as November 7, 1918, Britain and France promised the peoples and populations of Syria and Iraq full eman-cipation and self-determination. The Balfour Declaration was as yet to become more widely known. Things changed when the war was over.

From 1918 until 1920 Jerusalem was part of the southern command of the Franco-British Occupied Enemy Territory Administration (OETA). The initial goal, following the war, was relief and rehabilitation. When the League of Nations officially designated Palestine as a British Mandate, it included the wording of the Balfour declaration, charging Britain with the development of a Jewish homeland in Palestine.[3]

Despite the awkward and, to Arabs, irritating commitment of the British to the extravagant project of supporting the Zionists – a minority among the Jews of Europe, a minority among the Jews of Palestine, and a minority among the general population of 1920s Palestine – Jerusalem burgeoned under the British. Until the early twentieth century, Muslims and Christians constituted the majority population of Jerusalem.[4] As agents of the Ottoman administration for southern Palestine, the city's Arab elite wielded economic and political influence across the region. Under the British, middle-class Arab families were able to move out of the Old City and into elegant new Arab neighborhoods, such as Talbiya and Qatamon, adding to already existing Greek, German, and Arab neighborhoods in Baq'a (now Emek Refa'im), as well as to Sheikh Jarrah and Wadi al-Joz to the north.[5] At the same time, modern Jewish garden suburbs, such as Rehavia and Talpiot, accommodated upper-middle-class Jewish immigrants from Germany and Russia, who were either employed by the Mandate or active in Zionist cultural and political organizations. The pre-war Arab neighborhoods outside of the Old City had been initiated by wealthy families, who pur-chased land and built villas surrounded by orchards and gardens. The Greek-Orthodox Arab middle-class families of Talbiya and similar suburbs benefitted from new economic opportunities and took advantage of leases offered by their church, which retained land ownership. The new Jewish neighborhoods were established on land purchased by agencies such as the Jewish National Fund and the Palestine Land Development Company, and designed by architects who made their homes in Palestine, including

Richard Kaufmann and Erich Mendelsohn, who built in the "International style" associated with the Dessau Bauhaus. These new neighborhoods of the British municipality were surrounded, on all sides, by Arab villages such as al-Maliha, Lifta, Sur Baher, Issawiya, Ain Karim, Bet Safafa, Shu'fat, Abu Tor, etc. whose economy had always centered on Jerusalem and provided land sold for development. Looking at a map of Jewish and Arab neighborhoods in Jerusalem on the eve of the war of 1948, one is struck by the virtual parity in land distribution, but also by the prevailing ethnic-religious segregation between residential neighborhoods (see Map 12). Not counting the Arab villages just outside the municipality, about 40% of private property in Jerusalem was Muslim- and Christian-owned.[6] In addition to areas that suggest solid blocs of land ownership along Jewish–Arab lines, there were also areas "along the seams," where property ownership was mixed, as it was in most of the Old City, where Muslims lived everywhere, and only the Armenian Quarter (a closed compound) and a few recent Jewish developments were ethno-religiously solid. The division of the Old City into four quarters was more or less a fiction. Overall, the impression of Jerusalem before 1948 was one of a plurality of thriving communities that lived parallel lives, based more on national and class differences than religion, lives that also intersected and interacted in various public and commercial spaces, and in the context of the British administration, which relied on Jewish and Arab professionals and civil servants, the latter group including Muslims and Christians.[7]

The ordered coexistence of parallel communities scattered across the landscape north, west, and south of the Old City gradually deteriorated because of the ever-growing economic and political pressures the Zionist movement exerted on Arab society. Ethnic separation was presaged by the first countrywide riots of 1929,[8] the General Strike of 1936, and the 1937 Peel Commission report drafted in response, which recommended a division of Palestine into Jewish and Arab areas. The ongoing Arab Rebellion and other considerations prompted the British government to abandon the partition scheme and, in the 1939 White Paper, limit Jewish immigration, forcing the Zionist *yishuv* to organize clandestine immigration and establish new settlements illegally. The shift in British policy in Palestine prompted the Jewish Agency to shift its attention from England to the United States. Abandoning the language of the Balfour Declaration, the 1942 New York Biltmore Conference openly stated the goal of the World Zionist Organization to establish a Jewish state in Palestine. In 1940 right-wing Jewish "Freedom Fighters for Israel" (*Lohamei Herut Yisrael* or *Lehi*) split off from the non-socialist *Irgun Tzva'i L'Yisrael* (*Itzel* or *Irgun*) and began to engage the British through acts of terrorism that culminated in the assassination of Lord Moyne in Cairo (1944). Fully fledged conflict between Arab and Jewish paramilitary groups broke out following UN General Assembly Resolution 181 of November 29, 1947, to partition Palestine at the expiration of the British Mandate, set for May 14, 1948. What swayed the international community on behalf of Jewish statehood in Palestine was the universal recognition of the horrors of the German death camps.

   Israel's 1948–1949 War of Independence was particularly fiercely fought in Jerusalem, especially in mixed areas and around enemy enclaves. While initially fought for the sake of defending the territory the UN had allotted to the nascent Jewish state, the second phase of the war – following a temporary ceasefire that allowed the Israel Defense Forces (IDF) to rearm themselves by way of Soviet-approved aid from Czechoslovakia, and the murder, by *Lehi*, of UN envoy Folke Bernadotte – turned into a struggle for territorial and ethnic consolidation.[9] Surrounded by predominantly Arab areas of Palestine that the UN partition resolution had assigned to the territory of a future Arab state, Jerusalem was exceptional, in that it constituted a mixed metropolitan area with a large Jewish population. Jews lived not just in demographically solid residential suburbs west and north-west of the Old City but also in older mixed neighborhoods like Musrara, outside the Damascus Gate, as well as in Sheikh Jarrah, strategically important to the Arabs as the northern access from the direction of Ramallah, and in enclaves such as the Jewish Quarter of the Old City and the Hadassah hospital and Hebrew University campus on Mount Scopus. At some point in the war, Jerusalem's Jewish defenders were entirely cut off from the only supply route that connected them to the main territory of Israel in the coastal areas north and south of Tel Aviv-Yafo, a dire situation that was resolved by building a relief road (the so-called Burma Road) through the Judean mountains. The Jewish Quarter was surrounded by Arab forces and needed to be evacuated. Hostilities, ongoing since November 1947, caused Arab middle- and upper-class families to leave their homes in what became Jewish West Jerusalem, and seek temporary refuge in the Old City, rather than in one of the UN refugee tent camps set up in Jordan and elsewhere, assuming they would regain access to their homes right after the war. Those who tried to claim property were turned away by the Israeli authorities, which invoked the "Abandoned Areas Ordinance" of 1948 that legalized expropriation in areas under Israeli military control.[10]

Jewish areas and Arab villages, such as Deir Yassin near Jerusalem, were the sites of massacres, speeding up the process of ethnic separation. By the time of the 1949 ceasefire agreement between Israel and Jordan, most of the Arab residents of West Jerusalem had left their homes and those who remained were left to witness unrestrained devastation, looting, and usurpation of abandoned properties, acts mirrored by how Arabs treated the Jewish Quarter and the ancient Jewish cemetery on the Mount of Olives. Over the ensuing decades, each side only cared to remember the damage done to them by the enemy. While Jewish grief for the Old City ended in the exuberance of June 1967, Arab Jerusalemites and their descendants cherish their memories of life as it was until May 1948, and hold out for a return and retrieval of what was lost (see Map 13).

The war of 1948 created a new situation in Jerusalem. Defying UN General Assembly Resolution 181 of November 29, 1947, which had designated the Christian holy cities of Jerusalem and Bethlehem as a *corpus separatum*, the state of Israel and the Hashemite Kingdom of Jordan both annexed to their respective territories those parts of Jerusalem that had come under their military control, and extended their respective civilian administrations, making Jerusalem a city divided along ethnic, religious, and national lines, by concrete barriers, barbed wire, and no man's land. By declaring Jerusalem the capital of Israel, as Prime Minister David Ben-Gurion did in late 1949, the government of Israel officially acknowledged the symbolic centrality of the city for the Jewish state. By doing so, Ben-Gurion not only contravened acute UN pressure to internationalize Jerusalem, but also expressed a deeply and widely held Jewish and Zionist conviction, a consensus hitherto repressed for fear of offending the great powers. Ben-Gurion, a man of consummate political instincts, understood that the nationalization of West Jerusalem would be met by minimal resistance from the international community. More importantly, it would allow Ben-Gurion to make himself the leader of the nation at a time when wounds were still open from the Altalena incident, when the Haganah had opened fire on a boat carrying weapons for its rival, the *Irgun*. For the secular socialist Ben-Gurion, Jerusalem's division was a *fait accompli*, and not a matter waiting to be revised, except perhaps in messianic times. In the meantime, a lot could be done with the part of Jerusalem that remained under Jewish control. To underscore the capital city's importance to the Jewish state, the government moved most ministries from Tel Aviv to Jerusalem. In recognition of Jerusalem's precarious location as a divided border city, the Department of Defense remained in Tel Aviv. In the 1950s and 1960s, West Jerusalem was economically dependent on tax revenue generated elsewhere, as the city still is today. Its predominantly Jewish population included undereducated ultra-religious communities and highly educated western-acculturated professors, intellectuals, and civil servants sustained by subsidized governmental and academic institutions. It was a truncated and alienated town, cut off from the Old City and the Western Wall, which were not just of symbolic value but an important attraction for international tourism that continued to flourish in the Jordanian part of the city. West Jerusalem was also distant from Israel's agricultural heartland and its incipient centers of industry. As a cultural capital, Jewish Jerusalem included the National and University Library, various research centers and archives, concert halls and a symphonic orchestra, cinemas, old-worldly cafés, used-book stores, garden suburbs, and parks. In 1958, the Hebrew University, temporarily housed in part at the Terra Sancta building, at the intersection of King George, Ramban, Agron, and Keren Ha-Yesod streets, moved to the new campus at Givat Ram that was built on land leased from the Greek Orthodox Patriarchate. The nearby Knesset was then dominated by debates between the ruling socialist labor coalition led by Ben-Gurion and Menachem Begin's opposition right-wing *Herut* ("Freedom") party. One of the most hotly contested matters in the early years of the state was whether or not Israel should accept German reparations for the victims of the *Shoah*. While Begin took his moral outrage to the streets, Ben-Gurion's pragmatic "statism" prevailed and Israel established diplomatic relations with Adenauer's Germany, much to the advantage of the Israeli economy.[11] Palestine-born *sabras* who had fought in the War of Independence, many of them kibbutzniks of Ashkenazi descent, came to dominate the Israeli military and civilian elites. Many of these personages remained central to the Israeli establishment until recent years. In the 1950s the country was mostly preoccupied with the tasks of absorbing Mizrahi immigrants, consolidating its industry and economy, and working toward international recognition and diplomatic alliances in the face of a total Arab boycott. The political status of Jerusalem was, in those years, of relatively little consequence.

Jordanian Jerusalem was reduced and truncated as well. It lacked the major modern Arab neighborhoods and villages now abandoned or part of West Jerusalem. On the other hand, Arab "East Jerusalem" included the Old City and the northern suburbs, and it remained connected to most of its rural surroundings, with the Muslim town of Ramallah to the north, predominantly Christian Bethlehem and Bet Jalla to the south, and the ancient oasis of Jericho to the east. The Old City took on greater importance now that it was cut off from the western garden suburbs, severed from the formerly Arab and mixed towns of the coastal areas, such as Yafo and Haifa, and charged with building a union with the Hashemite state of Transjordan.[12] Without the presence of Jews and their economic and religious activities, East Jerusalem was now an exclusively Muslim and Christian city, economically, socially, culturally, and politically reduced, with a population forced to come to terms with the trauma of the *Nakba*, the displacement of a third of Palestine's Arab population, the division of Palestine, and the thwarting of independence. The Jordanian administration tried to dilute the power of the local notables by bringing in officials from Hebron and Nablus, an act that Arab Jerusalemites still remember as a stinging insult. King Abdullah's assassination in 1951 provided further proof, if it were needed, that Palestinian nationalism remained alive and well. Jordanian propaganda disseminated the motto of the "beloved two banks" of Jordan, a country that, in 1946, had successfully transitioned to Arab rule. Palestinian society officially acceded to Jordanian rule but remained internally divided by traditional and new factions, including the large and growing community of refugees who kept the hope alive that the *status quo* would be reversed and they would be restored to their former homes in what was now Israel. Jordan was generally interested in maintaining order and wary of renewing hostilities with Israel, but in 1967 King Hussein yielded to Egyptian and Syrian demands and placed his army under the command of the United Arab Republic, giving Israel a pretext to capture East Jerusalem and occupy the West Bank. Today the Hashemite Kingdom of Jordan nominally continues to maintain guardianship over the Muslim holy places of Jerusalem, though it relinquished responsibility for the population and territory of (Western) Palestine to the Palestinian National Authority (PNA), established in 1994. Jordan frequently raises its voice on behalf of the Muslim holy places and protests any perceived Israeli disturbance of the *status quo*. Most recently, Jordanian King Abdullah II also sponsored the renovations and repair of the Aedicule that surrounds the Tomb of Christ, one of the holy places where the Ottomans had once served as the disinterested imperial broker between competing Christian claims.[13] By the parameters of the Oslo Accords of 1993 and 1994, the status of East Jerusalem remains to be settled in "final status" negotiations. From a popular Palestinian Arab perspective this is only part of the story. The other part is to sue for the restoration of Arab property in what used to be West Jerusalem, let alone in the rest of what used to be Palestine.

Notes

1. Tamari (2011) notes that the number of Arabs participating in the rebellion was small compared to the number of Arabs fighting as conscripts and volunteers in the Ottoman army, suggesting that the role of Arab rebels was largely symbolic while the Arab contribution to the Ottoman war effort was significant. Jawhariyah (2014) mentions deserters from the Ottoman army among his Christian (Greek Orthodox) relatives.
2. See Krämer (2008). As late as the 1929 riots the Arabs of Yafo demanded for a Turkish regime to replace the British Mandate. See Cohen (2015).
3. For the text of the League of Nations Mandate for Palestine see http://avalon. law.yale.edu/20th_century/palmanda.asp (accessed December 1, 2017).
4. On the difficulties of obtaining an exact demographic picture for late Ottoman Jerusalem's populations, see Tamari (1999), 4.
5. On the growth of the Arab entrepreneurial middle class of Jerusalem in the 1930s and 1940s see Khalaf (1991), 52–53.
6. See Tamari (1999).
7. On inter-communal relations in the shared urban spaces of British Palestine see Karlinsky (2012), who argues that, on a dynamic spectrum of relationships, the ethnic relations of pre-1948 Jerusalem were already much more "polarized" than in late Ottoman times.
8. See Cohen (2015).
9. See Morris (2008).
10. The Abandoned Properties Ordinance was replaced by the Absentees' Property Law of 1950. See Fischbach (2003). The question of return or restitution of Arab property in what is now Israel is among the most important issues to be settled in final status negotiations between Israel and the Palestinians.
11. See the text of the reparations agreement of 1952 at http://web.nli.org.il/sites/ NLI/English/collections/personalsites/Israel-Germany/Division-of-Germany/ Pages/Reparations-Agreement.aspx (accessed December 1, 2017).
12. On Jerusalem in Jordanian politics see Katz (2005).
13. See http://www.lastampa.it/2016/04/11/vaticaninsider/eng/world-news/king-abdullah-ii-of-jordan-funds-holy-sepulchre-restoration-work-NalrFqTHD nrSKv62cJWIsM/pagina.html (accessed December 1, 2017).

16

Unholy City

Our brief history of Jerusalem is coming to an end. The Jerusalems considered in this book were layered one upon the other and sometimes existed side by side. Jerusalem – real and imagined – commands the allegiance of a plurality of national and trans-national communities and renders them susceptible to rhetoric of persuasion wielded by imperial and national regimes and militant movements that have written Jerusalem on their banner. *Al-Quds* makes hearts beat faster, *yerushalayim* evokes dreamy looks, *Zion* strengthens the resolve of her lovers. Like Penelope she is surrounded, beset, and depleted by envious suitors. Every one of them believes to be her true husband. Odysseus meets the return of Martin Guerre. Whatever else goes on *in* Jerusalem, it is Jerusalem *itself* that is coveted by our communities for the meanings, hopes, and aspirations they associate with it, hopes and aspirations that range from the mundane desire for a dignified temporal existence of one's family in a place one calls home, to the extravagant expectation of a messianic age, a great reversal of collective fortune, the denouement of history.

What is Jerusalem? Is it "a fiction," as former deputy mayor Meron Benvenisti said?[1] Is it a "frontier city," as Menachem Klein wrote, describing its fluctuating ethnic and political boundaries and its position between Israeli and Palestinian territories?[2] How is it possible that such a beautiful and enchanting place can also be so full of hatred and resentment? Is

Jerusalem: A Brief History, First Edition. Michael Zank.
© 2018 Michael Zank. Published 2018 by John Wiley & Sons Ltd.

Jerusalem the victim of one of those great modern experiments in social engineering that, like socialism, should finally be abandoned and put to rest? At the end of this brief history we are somewhat more informed but we are certainly not finished. Jerusalem, a work in progress.

If holy means "complete" then today's Jerusalem is rather unholy. It is caught in a dynamic struggle between those wishing to preserve the *status quo* and those who wish to rectify it. The desire to rectify *status quo*, to restore a *status quo ante*, or to bring about an ultimate *status quo* rectification, has been present in, and associated with, the Holy City at some times more than others. What makes the modern city "modern" is exactly this: the desire for change. It is this desire that renders the city as it is, the city before our eyes, unfinished – in other words, unholy. But this is true of every city. Every city is unfinished business. Only in Jerusalem the modern desire for change is suffused with biblical revisionism.

For those who experienced Israel's June 1967 conquest of East Jerusalem as a return of the exiles and a dream come true ("When the LORD restored the fortunes of Zion, we were like those who dreamed." Psalm 126:1), the city's return, in the mid-1990s, to the negotiating table[3] unleashed a near hysterical drive to complete the unification and make it irreversible. The Israeli government's aim remains to enlarge, Judaize, Israelitize, modernize, rebrand, and unify the city as the eternally undivided capital of Israel. This peripheral development – peripheral because it mostly takes place (and takes places) around the "holy basin" of the Old City and the sacred landscape to its east – is a kind of temporary compensation. It attests to the fact that, for the most part, the Old City still remains off limits, at least for now. With the exception of the Jewish Quarter, the bulldozing of the Moroccan neighborhood to make room for the Western Wall plaza, the improvement of plumbing and drainage, and a few major archaeological projects, the Arab Old City has remained largely unchanged, frozen in time.

When, in May 1967, Naomi Shemer envisioned the Old City, in her song "Jerusalem of Gold" that became Israel's unofficial anthem, she imagined it empty and devoid of people, because the Jews were then still absent, banished as in days of old, even though East Jerusalem was, in fact, a flourishing center of Palestinian life, culture, scholarship, piety, and international tourism. Even after its "reunification" this eclipse of the actual in favor of the imagined is part of how Jerusalem works. For the most part, modern Jerusalemites manage the plurality of exclusionary outlooks by elaborate strategies of avoidance. The emblem of contemporary Jerusalem is the visual barrier. The mechanism of large-scale avoidance is the bypass road (heir to the safe footpath through hostile urban territory). The chief instrument of the city's segmented horizontal and vertical projects of self-realization is the bulldozer. The tools by which Jerusalem is managed and reshaped are Israeli law and the bureaucracy charged with its implementation, one of those great "iron cages" that provide modern societies with lawful instruments of social control and incremental refashioning.[4] More recently, the "statist" institutions of archaeology and public education have been privatized and outsourced to well-funded religious settler organizations, such as El-Ad.[5] The desire for avoidance is mutual. Without control over urban planning, bound by restrictions on housing development, and virtually cut off from the thriving community of Ramallah, many Palestinian Jerusalemites seek housing and employment elsewhere, risking the loss of their residency permit. Those who remain in the economically and psychologically depressed Old City take some comfort from the fact that staying in place represents a form of resistance. Some resort to violence. One of the common targets of Palestinian attacks is the new light rail system that, to the attackers, symbolizes Israeli urban encroachment on Palestinian territory.

The places where contact cannot be avoided, where communities clash, where seeing and hearing one another and recognizing that one is not alone in this holy city becomes inevitable, are the city's holy places. Greek, Latin, Armenian, Coptic, and Abyssinian Christians clash in the Holy Sepulchre. Muslims and Jews clash on and around the Temple Mount. Ultra-orthodox and modern Jews clash at the Western Wall. Christians and Jews clash at the Tomb of David/Upper Room complex on Mount Zion. Many of these clashes are virtually ritualized brawls between the established communities.

British and Israeli governments pledged their sincere commitment to maintaining the *status quo* of the holy places, established by the Ottomans, even as their very presence significantly altered the semantics of *status quo* preservation. Nor was there ever a clear and universally agreed-on tabulation and regulation of each and all holy places. It was one thing for the ruling Turkish authorities to serve as arbiters of competing trans-national Christian interests in Ottoman territory. It was another thing for Christian and Jewish conquerors to subject the Arab population of Jerusalem to foreign rule, no matter how magnanimous the assurance of respect for their religious freedom. While the British entry to Jerusalem was initially welcomed as an act of liberation,[6] the Israeli conquest came as a shock to Palestinians. While Israel regards its annexation of East Jerusalem as lawful, Palestinians don't differentiate between East Jerusalem and the "occupied territories." In their view, East Jerusalem *is* occupied territory, rendering the municipal expansion and building up of Jewish neighborhoods in East Jerusalem a violation of the Fourth Geneva Convention, which prohibits the transfer of population into occupied territory.

Secular governmental assurances of respect for the holy places and freedom of worship for all religious communities may be sincere, but they may also mask the inherent injustice of the colonial project itself. Thinking of the holy places as separate from power, as merely religious buildings, public parks, or spaces for pious worshippers to convene and conduct innocuous rituals, as commanded by their respective divine sovereign, desacralizes these holy places and transforms them, and the complex relationship that resident and pilgrim communities maintain with their sacred places, into more or less neutral, movable, and manageable platforms for religious functions that could be held elsewhere. In other words, the very essence of the holy place is lost. In its place appears a pale, polite, and civilized location for customary symbolic practices that are thought of as separate from the rest of one's civic commitments; something one does on a Sunday morning, but about which one is not meant to be emotional or ostentatious; a High Church kind of thing rather than a raucous soccer match that might warrant the occasional fisticuffs. It may well be that the *al-Haram al-Sharif* is to Palestinians what Westminster Abbey is to the English, just as the Ka'aba may be to Muslims what St. Peter is to Catholics. But what if Germans patrolled the entrance to Westminster Abbey and admonished the English to conduct themselves respectfully, or what if a British Mandate had been established over the Vatican State and told the Pope to be more respectful of his non-Catholic neighbors who just took over the Sistine Chapel?

Zionism has proved a potent ideology of *status quo* rectification. Like the sorcerer's apprentice, secular Israelis – committed to the liberal values enshrined in the Declaration of Independence proclaimed in Tel Aviv on May 14, 1948 – are finding out that the post-1967 religious national Zionism – wielded by an increasingly religiously devout and nationalistic Jewish public at home and abroad – is committing the state to serving agendas of *status quo* rectification in areas where the secular state has so far feared to tread. The new Zionism, which is more self-consciously Jewish than simply Israeli in its orientation, aims to generate plausibility and support for an annexation of Judea and Samaria, and to routinize Jewish prayer on the Temple Mount. These agendas are openly advocated by members of the current governing coalition and broadly disseminated through public and private educational and cultural projects. Similar projects have already transformed the Old City in significant ways, a development that Palestinian and international protestations have been unable to stop or even slow down. The national-religious, settler-driven City of David archaeological park in the village of Silwan and the Western Wall tunnel in the Old City have literally undermined parts of the living Arab city. These archaeologically impressive, but legally and ethically problematic, works entail carefully curated subterranean displays of biblical history beneath the living city, that serve to authenticate the Jewish past and legitimize the Jewish presence. In this process, which began with the imperially and privately funded Christian scholars and explorers of the nineteenth century, the traditional assumptions of pious conduct that sustained the Holy City for the past 1,300 years are displaced by modern Biblicist attitudes toward experiencing the sacred. Instead of seeking the heavenly Jerusalem above the ever-imperfect earthly one, the gaze of the pious and dazzled visitor is redirected to a Jerusalem that is emerging from the underground. The search for and display of the Jewish past goes hand in hand with the assertion of Jewish sovereignty over all of Jerusalem in the present, shrinking the Arab city in the perception of Israelis and western tourists and pilgrims to something episodic, ornamental, and picturesque. At the same time as this spatial dislocation is taking place, Jerusalem's transformation accelerates, boosting the self-confidence of the dozens of initiatives preparing for the ultimate *status quo* rectification, the rebuilding of the temple on the Temple Mount, the current *al-Haram al-Sharif.* In Herzl's words, if you really want it, this, too, may not be a fairy tale. Jerusalem, a city of biblical fantasies that are the nightmares of the powerless, where one community's utopia is the other community's greatest fear.

Jerusalem's history does not need to end in apocalyptic cataclysm. After a century of conflict between Jews and Arabs in the Holy Land of Israel/Palestine, that for both communities is centered on the Holy City of Jerusalem, it has become clear that only *part* of Jerusalem is at stake. Participants in direct negotiations, contacts, conferences, and initiatives involving Israelis and Palestinians, as well as other stakeholders – including the international community, the Arab League, and the predominantly Muslim countries of south and south-east Asia, as well as the many local and trans-national Christian individuals and bodies involved in Middle East peace negotiations and affected by their outcomes – are aware of the fact that the holy places are the most sensitive issue to be settled in final status negotiations. Nobel laureate Elie Wiesel once argued that, for this very reason, Jerusalem should be "left for last," meaning that perhaps when all other questions have been settled, this too might be resolved. This may be wise counsel. Perhaps, if agreements on less intractable issues can be made, Israelis and Palestinians could build sufficient mutual trust to imagine Jerusalem differently, less exclusively, and more inclusively, as modeled by the legendary Muslim conquerors of old, Caliph Umar b. al-Khattab and Sultan Saladin, and the Prophet Muhammad himself, who made peace with the Meccans. These precedents are important to Muslims. One could similarly invoke King David, who never expelled the Jebusites, who resided among the Judahites "to this day." This could be an important precedent for the Jews.

If things were only so simple. Perhaps they are if we want them to be. But what makes Jerusalem a holy city is more than its holy places. For Palestinians, East Jerusalem, a city formed in the wake of the collapse of Palestine in 1948 and developed under the Jordanian regime, is more than an indifferent surrounding of the holy places. Arab East Jerusalem exists from, with, and for the sake of those Christian and Muslim holy places. It is a city with a rich history and a regional context that has been under siege since Israel annexed it to West Jerusalem in June 1967. East Jerusalem is a living remnant of what Palestine once was, and there's a prevailing and justifiable anxiety among Palestinians that this last vestige of pre-1948 Palestine is being choked and forced out of existence by a plethora of means and measures, each one of them perhaps justifiable in the name of security or other lawful and legitimate rationales, but overall combining into a slow, suffocating avalanche of extinction. It is this reasonable anxiety that magnifies every administrative wrinkle and fiscal burden, every lawful revoking of residency permits, every approval of Jewish housing construction, every demolition of illegal Palestinian housing, every master plan and infrastructure project aiming at Judaization, and any other modification of the *status quo* in and around the city as a breach of good faith, another violation of bilateral agreements and international understandings, another assault on what remains of Palestine. Paranoia? Perhaps. But for good reasons. A workable solution for the holy places must include a workable solution for the Old City and Arab East Jerusalem, which has been the frame and facet of the Christian and Muslim holy places not just in terms of history and architecture but in terms of the many functions of the Old City as a living city of people at home in local and regional contexts that may have been drastically changed but perhaps not irreversibly so. Sophisticated, human-scale, informed, culturally respectful, and ecologically mindful urban planning could, and may still, undo much of the damage that has been done to this city since it became a pawn in the hands of hyper-nationalists and ideologically committed and well-funded mega-developers, enabled by Israeli governments hooked on one-sided and short-sighted national agendas. The question is whether the Israelis and the Jewish community abroad can muster the political will for such a profound reorientation of government policy. In the end, we must assume, everyone just wants to get along; everyone wants Jerusalem to remain – and once again become – an accessible city, a world heritage site, hospitable to Jews and Arabs, Christians and Muslims, and open to business for all. What then stands in the way?

According to the seasoned Israeli negotiator Gilead Sher and the Palestinian survey researcher Professor Khalil Shikaki, what stands in the way of resuming negotiations between Israelis and Palestinians is mutual distrust. In the meantime, Sher suggests for Israel to follow Ehud Barak's lead and act unilaterally, though not just in the interest of imposing the Israeli agenda on the Palestinians. Unilateral action can also mean to act in anticipation of what many reasonable people agree should be the outcome of the final status negotiations: two states for two people and a sharing of responsibility for the "holy basin" of Jerusalem, probably under an international supervisory regime. Israel could unilaterally begin to vacate settlement outposts and incentivize settlers willing to "come home," as Sher put it in a presentation at Harvard University. Removing all post-1967 settlements will not be possible, but reducing the number of settlers and settlements is not just possible, but desirable, if the goal is to allow for Palestinian statehood. While the current Israeli government is divided in its commitment to Palestinian statehood (because of distrust of Palestinian intentions, or in order not to reward the ongoing violence, or because of plans for eventual annexation), at least it is clear what ought to happen. According to Sher, the international community can help by exerting pressure on the Israeli government.

This won't be easy. In the decades since 1967, Israeli society, the global Jewish community, and the world of Evangelical Christian Zionism underwent changes that mirror what has been going on elsewhere. The Iranian revolution of 1979 heralded the end of secular politics and the "re-religionization" (as Moshe Zimmermann put it) of politics across the Middle East. Palestinian Muslims have been increasingly attracted to political Islam as a panacea.[7] The unexpected and resounding June 1967 victory of Israel over its hostile neighbors created a sense of messianic imminence among fundamentalist Jews and evangelical Christians alike. The Gush Emunim settler movement founded in the mid-1970s was based on the belief that G-d himself was waging the wars of Israel, that the biblical homeland of the Jews had now been fully liberated, and that it was incumbent upon the Jews to settle it as in the days of old. The urgency of religious settlement was also fueled by the threat of territorial compromise with the neighboring Arab states based on the formula of "land for peace." This threat first materialized with the return of the Sinai Peninsula to Egypt, following the Camp David agreement of 1978 and the peace treaty of 1979, which entailed the first traumatic evacuation and dismantling of a Jewish settlement, the town of Yamit. Successive decades saw repeated returns of Israeli governments to the negotiating table. Prime Minister Rabin's signing of the Oslo Accords entailed handing over control of territories in Gaza, Judea, and Samaria to the Palestine Liberation Organization (PLO). While the public saw the wave of Hamas-inspired terror attacks that followed the signing of the accords as a direct consequence of Israel's willingness to enter into agreements with the Palestinians, the religious settler movement was even more outraged by a secret letter that Arafat mentioned in a "sermon on *jihad*" he gave in Johannesburg, in which Israeli Foreign Minister Peres had expressed Israeli recognition of Palestinian institutions operating in East Jerusalem.[8] The letter, once made public, confirmed the fears of those who believed that the dovish center-left government was no longer fully committed to keeping Jerusalem united under Israeli rule, that the government was willing to compromise on something the national religious right perceived as sacrosanct. It became clear that significant parts of the Israeli public distrusted not only the Palestinians but also their own government. Ever since then, those right-wing national-religious politicians have commanded greater public respect the more honest and open they have seemed with regard to their ultimate intentions, and the more strongly they have appeared to be committed to keeping Israel safe and Jerusalem united.

The erosion of public trust in the Israeli government was stoked by Likud, then in the opposition, and by the settler community. The perceived selling out of the Land of Israel, and the now no longer tacit recognition of Palestinian rights in East Jerusalem, led to mass demonstrations openly vilifying Rabin and finally to his assassination by a pious Jew. The assassin, Yigal Amir, was empowered by the opinions of the rabbinate of the Yesha Council[9] that considered Rabin a traitor, not just to the state, but to the people of Israel, its divine patron, and the destiny of the Jewish people returning to their ancient homeland, a process that the national-religious right believes, with Rav Kook, has ushered in the end of exile and the beginning of redemption. While one can disentangle the semantic differences between the old nationalist (Revisionist Zionist) agenda of Jewish sovereignty over the "complete land of Israel" (*erets yisrael hashlemah*), which promotes, supports, and incentivizes settlement, and the purely religious and mystical devotion to dwelling in the biblical land of Israel and being near to its holy places, such as the Cave of Machpelah in Hebron and the Temple Mount of Jerusalem, the secular nationalist and religious Zionist agendas coincided in their opposition to vacating territory that has come under the auspices of the *Tz'vah Haganah l'Yisrael* or Israel Defense Forces (IDF). The settler party *Bayit Yehudi*, part of the current governing coalition, advocates the annexation of Judea and Samaria and putting to rest, once and for all, the idea of Palestinian statehood. Naftali Bennett, the party's leader, is popular among voters, because he is willing to say openly what others only think, unhampered by political correctness, a bellwether of the new nationalism that has begun to dominate other countries and communities as well. On the fringe of the settler movement, there are the extremists of the "Price Tag" movement and similar fringe groups that exact violent revenge on innocent Arab civilians and their institutions. There are the soccer hooligans of La Familia, fans of *Beitar Yerushalayim*, who randomly beat up Arabs on the streets of Jerusalem. There are those who promote the demolition of the secular democratic state and its replacement by a messianic theocracy. Yet, there are also settler communities, often inspired by the original Gush Emunim movement, who wish to build bridges between themselves and their Arab neighbors, realizing that if both hope to remain where they are, they will need to learn to coexist for the duration.

The state of Israel of today is not simply a realization of hopes and aspirations articulated by late nineteenth- and early twentieth-century Zionists. Zionists were divided on what they imagined to begin with. Herzl's vision of the Jewish state was devoid of recognizably Jewish symbols. Its language was German, its culture European, its achievements technological and cosmopolitan. Its pride was that it was accomplished by the Jews, then a despised European pariah people. To the degree that Herzl's vision has been realized, Zionism should have come to its end. Israel should have entered a phase of post-Zionism, as many scholars and intellectuals argued. Others, in Herzl's time and until today, have felt that it wasn't worth the trouble to have a Jewish state if that state or, more modestly, that "homeland" was not a center for the renewal of Judaism and the spirit of the Jewish nation. A post-Zionist state of Israel can be satisfied with having a foothold in ancient Jerusalem. It can arrange itself with the Palestinians and accept limited sovereignty over the holy places. A Jewish state, a state committed to Jewish values, and especially a state committed to making room for traditional orthodox Jewish faith, has a stronger stake in making arrangements at the holy places that allow for access and presence of Jewish worship. Jewish romantic and religious attachment to Jerusalem is incredibly strong, and one can understand the urge to return to the Old City, to the Western Wall, the Jewish Quarter, and the ancient cemetery, when the opportunity arose. One can also understand why the majority of Israelis and Jews all over the world are proud of Jerusalem and won't voluntarily yield the Western Wall or relinquish at least symbolic authority over the Temple Mount. But the old Jewish taboo on entering the *al-Haram al-Sharif*, that is still honored by the traditionally orthodox for fear of violating halakhic injunctions, has been attenuated among the younger generation of radical *status quo* revisionists who are now also represented in the Israeli Knesset. Things would be under control if state power and religious hopes for redemption had remained apart. But it so happens that the ideological waters of secular Zionism and orthodox Judaism have long since become significantly muddied.

Israel is a state in transition, an ever-nascent, unfinished project. The source of Israel's strength is its self-image as a young, dynamic, pioneering society, an image touted in the contemporary moniker of Israel as a "start-up nation." This new Israel combines with the idea of ancient Israel and a timeless biblical-Jewish tradition: the Jewish return to the Promised Land, the tropes of loss and retrieval, exile and conquest, survival and hope for future redemption. These forceful notions of a collective identity rooted in biblical exceptionalism contravene the secular Israeli trend toward post-Zionism. The Jewish collective memory vitiates against the secular hope for normalization. Zionism may have solved some problems for some Jews, but it also created new ones, and obviously not just for Jews. Zionism – in need of broad Jewish support – failed to overcome any of the "failings" of Jewish religious tradition that Zionists once diagnosed as detrimental to Jewish political self-determination. As a result, a militarily secure, economically strong Israel watches helplessly as these attributes are becoming more visible and more acute.

Acknowledging that Zionism has accomplished its goals with the establishment and securing of Jewish statehood would mean that the Jewish state could function like other states. It would mean a form of political "assimilation," an attenuation of the original will to power that infused the Jewish Nietzscheans who drained the swamps and armed the *yishuv*. The Jewish state could thus enter into a phase of alienation from the high and lofty goals of national redemption and simply function as a state that could well coexist with others, even Palestinians, and thus open itself up to painful historic compromises. It would lose its heroic character. It would become a bourgeois happiness maximization society that exists for no other purpose than to exist. Jewish statehood, along with the plethora of visions of completion inherited from the Jewish tradition, as well as from the Zionist movement, when it was still the domain of utopian visionaries, has created a more urgent, more focused, and more widely disseminated form of Jewish question than the one it solved: the question of what it means for the state of Israel to be a Jewish state. What does it mean for Jews and Judaism that "the Jews have returned" to "their land," as Zionism proposed? If Zionist striving was not fulfilled and completed in the achievement of Jewish statehood, when will it be fulfilled? Today, nearly 70 years after its founding and 50 years after the conquest of the rest of Palestine, Jews, Judaism, Israel, and Israelis must come to terms with the fact that Zionism, a religiously transgressive and politically dynamic ideology that set in motion the process that led to Jewish statehood, can also lead to the destruction of the state and its society as we know it, a society many have come to love and appreciate, despite its flaws and shortcomings.

The accustomed Jewish role in history, at least in the history of Judaism since the destruction of the second temple, is the role of the loser, the victim of potent imperial forces, the martyr, the wandering Jew. The medieval poet and philosopher Judah Halevi warned that Jews had not been tested in the role of rulers. The "against-all-odds" narrative that attaches to the War of Independence and the Six-Day War was severely tested during the October 1973 Yom Kippur War when Israel's legendary military nearly failed. It triggered the political realization that Israel can survive only if she enters into binding agreements with her neighbors. With the peace agreement between Israel and Egypt, Israel entered the Middle East as a state among others that has since become an important partner to other states as well and plays its role in the complex dynamics of a changing region. Because of its strategic role in a neighborhood divided between Sunni and Shiite centers of power, Israel seems less inclined to worry about solving its internal problems or settling its dispute with the Palestinians. Foreign policy has once again eclipsed the importance of coming to terms with the pressing issue of the occupation. The peace process has been sidelined.

But the peace process itself is of relatively recent vintage. A significant turning point occurred in December 1987, when the so-called First Intifada (literally "shaking off") began and Israel saw itself outmaneuvered by Palestinians who, for the first time, commanded the imagination of the international community as victims of oppression rather than "terrorists."

The jolting images of children using rocks and slingshots in confronting the tanks of the IDF stripped the Israeli military of its pretense of superior morality and revealed its dark side as the instrument of Palestinian suffering and oppression, the tool of a brutal military occupation now in its fiftieth year. Ever since then, the struggle has been between Israel and the Palestinians rather than between Israel and the Arabs in general. The good news for both Israelis and Palestinians was that the Palestinians had for the first time become visible to Israel, to the Jews worldwide, and to the international community. From that moment on the focus shifted, from the struggle for survival of a small and unjustly maligned Jewish state in the middle of a sea of Arabs, to a struggle between two unequal claimants to national self-determination in the same small territory called Israel and Palestine. Shortly after the outbreak of the first Intifada, which coincided with the end of the Cold War, the United States and the Soviet Union jointly convened the Madrid Conference of 1991, where Israelis and Palestinians entered into direct negotiations for the first time.[10] A year later, Bill Clinton defeated George Bush in the US presidential elections and Yitzhak Rabin came to power in Israel. Israel and the United States recognized the PLO, until then still widely shunned as a terrorist organization, as the legitimate representative of the Palestinian people. The initially secret negotiations, brokered by Norwegian Foreign Minister Johan Holst, culminated in the Declaration of Principles, signed on the White House lawn in 1993. The so-called Oslo Accords provided the mutually agreed-on framework for final status negotiations, that were to begin no later than three years hence. They also provided the condition for PLO chairman Yasser Arafat to return to Palestine and establish the first token Palestine National Autonomy administration in Gaza and Jericho.

The Oslo Accords, the peace process, and the two-states solution on which that process was based have long since been eroded. Signs of future trouble for the Oslo process arose almost immediately, when news about the above-mentioned secret letter on Palestinian East Jerusalem surfaced in May 1994.[11] Rejectionist Palestinians poured oil onto the fire by ratcheting up terror attacks on Israeli civilians. From 1993 until the failed Camp David negotiations of 2000, the Jerusalem question, which reappeared at nearly every juncture, could have been thought a mere foible of Arafat's, an instrument he used to generate international pressure on Israel to offer further concessions to the Palestinians, in other words, a Machiavellian tool. There is no doubt, however, that Jerusalem, and in particular the Muslim *al-Haram al-Sharif*, was not just of genuine concern to Arafat but it remained central to Palestinian politics and identity. Opposition leader Ariel Sharon under-stood this well when he arranged for a public visit to the Temple Mount in 2000, after the collapse of the late-second-term Camp David negotiations convened by President Clinton. Sharon's visit, accompanied by 1,000 Israeli policemen, triggered violent Palestinian reactions, playing into the hands of the Israeli nationalist right wing. Sharon's reassertion of Israeli sovereignty, no matter the cost, handily won him the elections. As Prime Minister, he cracked down on the second, or Al-Aqsa, Intifada and reduced Arafat to a prisoner in his own compound. Arafat eventually died in exile, felled by an undisclosed disease. Subsequently, the factional conflict between Hamas and Fatah divided the Palestinian leadership. The Orient House, center of PLO representation in East Jerusalem, was shut down in 2001, leaving Arab East Jerusalem without effective political leadership. Before Sharon entered his own prolonged coma, he outmaneuvered his recalcitrant political allies, created a new centrist party (*Kadimah*), managed the unilateral disengage-ment from Gaza, and set Israel on a path to managing the conflict, by setting its own rules, without having to pretend any longer that it really mattered what the Palestinians wanted. The "separation fence" that now snakes through the desert east of Jerusalem and shuts out about 50,000 Palestinian residents of the municipality, while including large Jewish settlement blocs, has rendered the Palestinians invisible by adding a physical barrier to the political barrier that separates East Jerusalem from the West Bank.

Israel's premise is that Jerusalem was lawfully reunited in 1967; "law-fully," because Jordanian rule of East Jerusalem lacked international recog-nition, and because Palestinians relinquished sovereignty over East Jerusalem at the Jericho Conference of December 1948, when their repre-sentatives called for Jordanian annexation of the West Bank and East Jerusalem. The Jordanians yielded sovereignty over East Jerusalem to the PLO as the only legitimate representative of the Palestinian people. They also signed a peace agreement with Israel. The official position of the United States, the United Nations, and hence the international community is, that the status of Jerusalem and the holy places remains unresolved and should be solved by mutual agreement between Israel and the Palestinians. To this day, the US embassy remains in Tel Aviv, in defiance of the Jerusalem Embassy Act of 1994.[12]

If politics is the art of the possible, what is religion? Earlier we suggested that religion serves as an instrument of social boundary maintenance. The example of Jerusalem shows that – in the case of Judaism and its global heirs, Christianity and Islam – religion also serves as a justification of rule and control. The righteous will inherit the land, or the earth, depending on the translation. Politicians and rulers like to invoke religion, as religion moves the hearts of many people. It serves as an instrument of persuasion. But it cannot be completely controlled by politicians. It is stronger and more than politics in that it goes beyond what is possible. It reaches from "is" to "ought," from the real to the imagined, from the ordinary to the extraordinary, from the mundane to the sacred and holy. From a secular perspective, it seems dangerous and foolish for politicians to try to harness religious sentiments and beliefs to political power. The great achievement of the European Enlightenment was the separation of church and state. That separation is not universally accepted in modern Jerusalem. In Jerusalem, the great symbols of nationhood – history, language, and religion – are often pitted against the values of peaceful coexistence and sustainable development. Archaeology, a scientific instrument of historical retrieval, is too often used to foreground the past of some, while erasing that of others. The administrative necessity of naming the city and its neighborhoods often devolves into an exclusionary imposition of a single identity, an exercise in domination. Just and equitable urban planning for all is often distorted by national agendas of self-assertion. In none of these respects is Jerusalem unique. Examples of bad politics can be found everywhere. But nowhere else is it so easy to use the Bible to justify bad politics, and nowhere else are the three great Abrahamic religions pitted against one another so acutely and so virulently. For Jews, Christians, and Muslims, Jerusalem is therefore the ultimate test of good faith, for faith in the face of the politics of domination and exclusion. Jerusalem raises the question of whether our "biblicate" religions are more and better than instruments of political control and collective self-assertion. It raises the question of whether religion is more, other, and better than politics.

Jerusalem has been around for 4,000 years. It has given the world a unique legacy of hopes and ideas. It is human to love and pray for Jerusalem, and to hope it will be built and rebuilt again, in the future. There are many Jews, Christians, and Muslims who would join such a rebuilding, who already collaborate in planning and dreaming of a future based on a common good: Jerusalem, its people, its landscapes, its holy places, and its many memories – a common good for all who hold her dear. There are Israelis and Palestinians, Jerusalemites and friends of Jerusalem, who maintain that a common future is not merely a dream but a necessity and a possibility. It is also the condition for Jerusalem to become whole and attain, once again, the status of a holy city.

Notes

1. See Misselwitz and Rieniets (2006).
2. See Klein (2001) and (2008).
3. See Klein (2001), chapter 2: "The Curtain Rises: Jerusalem in the Israeli-Egyptian Peace Negotiations" of the 1970s. On the status of Jerusalem in the Madrid Conference of 1991 see the documents collected in the *Journal of Palestine Studies* 21/2 (Winter 1992), 117–149, and Klein (2001), 118–137.
4. See Khalidi (2006). The term "iron cage" was coined by sociologist Max Weber.
5. See http://www.haaretz.com/settlementdollars/.premium-1.707158 (accessed December 1, 2017).
6. Cf. Tannous (1998), 50, speaking of Haifa, where he experienced the end of the war: "There was jubilation for weeks." Similarly, for Jerusalem, Jawhariyah (2014).
7. See Cohen (2011), 131–132.
8. See Musallam (1996), 21–48.
9. See http://www.myesha.org.il/ (accessed December 10, 2017). The motto of this council of the "Jewish Communities of Judea and Samaria" is "It's realistic. It's vital. It's Jewish."
10. See the documentation in *Journal of Palestine Studies*, Vol. 21, No. 2 (Winter, 1992), 117–149.
11. See Musallam (1996), 37–48.
12. See Zank (2016b), Neff (1993).

Jerusalem: A Timeline

2000–1500 BCE	Middle Bronze Age. Dominated by Egypt, Jerusalem appears among other fortified cities of the southern Levant.
1500–1200	Late Bronze Age. Hurrians, Hittites, and Egyptians take turns at ruling the Levant. Hurrian ruler of Jerusalem (*urushalim*) Abdi-Heba attested in Amarna letters (1360–1340). Threat of marauding *hapiru*.
c. 1209	"Israel" mentioned in Merneptah Stele. Time of the biblical "judges."
1200–1000	Collapse of Canaanite city states. Jerusalem declines.
1050–930	Iron Age I. David and Solomon *florent*.
930	Divided kingdom of Israel and Judah. Davidic dynasty continues in Jerusalem only.
722/1	Shalmaneser V or Sargon II destroys Samaria, capital of Israel. Jerusalem expands. Hezekiah's tunnel and fortification ("broad wall").
701	Sennacherib and Hezekiah of Judah. Assyrian siege of Jerusalem.
640–609	Age of Josiah of Judah. In 622: major reforms, cult centralization.
598/7	Nebuchadnezzar II of Babylon (r. 605–562) takes Jerusalemite King Jehojachin and others captive to enforce vassalage.

Jerusalem: A Brief History, First Edition. Michael Zank.
© 2018 Michael Zank. Published 2018 by John Wiley & Sons Ltd.

587/6	Punitive conquest and temple destruction. More Judahites deported. Pro-Babylonian administrator Gedaliah assassinated.
539	Cyrus of Anshan enters Babylon, leading a coalition of Medes and Persians. Beginning of Achaemenid Persian Empire.
516/5	Jerusalem re-inaugurated by returnees from Babylon. Initial governors are members of the House of David (Sheshbazzar, Zerubbavel).
445	Persian Jewish courtier Nehemiah appointed governor (*peha*). Rebuilds walls of the city and institutes program of resettlement. Time of Ezra "the Scribe"?
403–359	Age of Artaxerxes II. Alternate age of Ezra "the Scribe," who institutes the Torah as a public constitution (see Nehemiah 8).
333–323	Alexander "the Great" of Macedonia conquers the Persian Empire.
300–198	Jerusalem under Ptolemaic rule, based in Egyptian Alexandria. Tobiad tax farmers and Oniad priests. Greek-speaking Jewish community in Alexandria. Torah translated into Greek (Septuagint).
198–129	Jerusalem under Seleucid rule, based in Syrian Antioch.
175–164	Reign of Antiochus IV "Epiphanes."
167–164[1]	Maccabean revolt. Rise of the Hasmonean family in Judah. Alternate dates of revolt: 168–165.[2]
142–135/4	Simon Maccabee appointed as *nasi* (prince).
134–104	John (Yehochanan) Hyrkanos I succeeds his father Simon as high priest and ethnarch. Hasmonean dynasty established.
129–63	Independence and expansion of Judah under the Hasmoneans.
63	Roman *imperator* Pompey conquers Syria and Egypt. Settles Hasmonean rivalry and, in an act of sacrilege, enters the inner sanctum of the Jewish temple.
47	Julius Caesar confirms Hasmonean high priest Hyrkanos II and his Idumean *majordomus*, Antipater (father of Herod).
40	Parthian (Persian) invasion installs Antigonos, son of Aristobulos, in Jerusalem. Mark Antony appoints Herod "king of the Jews" and charges him with reconquest on behalf of Rome.
37	Jerusalem captured by Roman commander Sosius. Antigonos executed. Herod installed.
31	Major earthquake shakes Jerusalem. Herod's patron Mark Antony defeated by Octavian at the Battle of Actium.
30	Herod, partisan of Mark Antony, seeks and finds Octavian's forgiveness. His kingship is confirmed and his area of rule increased.

20–19	Jerusalem temple rebuilt on a grander scale. Construction in Jerusalem continues until 66 CE.
4 BCE	Death of Herod the Great. Approximate time of the birth of Christ.
6 CE	Herod Archelaus deposed and exiled. Judea administered by Roman military prefects, governing from Caesarea Maritima. Time of the census of Quirinius, mentioned in the Gospel of Luke as the time of the birth of Christ.
26–36	Pontius Pilate military governor of Judea. Responsible for the execution of Jesus of Nazareth.
41–44	Agrippa I, grandson of Herod, friend of Gaius ("Caligula") and supporter of Claudius, appointed as king of Judea. The apostle Paul, imprisoned in Caesarea, defended himself before Agrippa.
66	Anti-Jewish riots in Caesarea. High priests quit sacrifices for the well-being of the emperor. Beginning of anti-Roman rebellion.
68	Death of Nero in Rome. Year of four emperors. Titus Flavius Vespasianus takes power in Rome, sends his son Titus to finish off Jerusalem.
70	Siege, conquest, and temple destruction. Captives and loot from Jerusalem paraded in Rome. Eye-witness account by Josephus Flavius.
74	Fall of Masada.
132–135	Bar Kokhba revolt "for the freedom of Jerusalem."
135	Direct Roman rule begins. Emperor Hadrian has the city ploughed under and rededicated as *Colonia Aelia Capitolina*. Jews banished from Aelia.
c. 200	Restoration of privileges to Jewish patriarch (in Sepphoris, Galilee, later Tiberias) under the Severan emperors. Judah "the Prince" promulgates a new Jewish code of law, the Mishnah.
250	Christians persecuted under Emperor Decius.
303–311	Empire-wide repression of Christians under Diocletian and his successors.
312	Constantine (r. 306–337) victoriously battles co-Emperor Maxentius at the Milvan Bridge and takes the city of Rome. Embraces Christ as his champion. Monumental church building begins.
313	Edict of Toleration issued by Constantine and co-Emperor Licinius. Ends persecution.
324	Battle of Chrysopolis. Constantine eliminates Licinius and henceforth rules as sole emperor, unifying the empire under the patronage of the Christian god.
325	Council of Nicaea. Unifies Orthodox Christian worship and doctrine across the empire.

326	Empress Helena Augusta arrives in Syria, presides over the dismantling of pagan shrines in Jerusalem and excavation of the empty tomb. Construction of *Anastasis* and *Martyrium* begins.
330	Constantinople (formerly Byzantium) consecrated.
335	Consecration of *Anastasis* and *Martyrium*.
337	Death of Constantine, succeeded by his sons.
360–363	Julian the "Apostate," Constantine's nephew, tries to roll back Christian innovations. Encourages an abortive attempt for a rebuilding of the Jewish temple in Jerusalem.
363	Christian privileges restored by Emperor Jovian.
381	Theodosius I (r. 379–395) elevates cult of Christ to official religion of the Roman Empire. Repression of non-Nicene Christian and pagan cults begins. Christian mobs attack pagans in Alexandria and elsewhere. Olympic games abolished.
402	Western Roman capital relocated to Ravenna.
410	Sack of Rome. Western Empire declines.
408–450	Theodosius II. The real power is his sister, Pulcheria.
443–460	Empress Aelia Eudokia, banished from court by Pulcheria, flourishes in Palestine. Expands and fortifies Jerusalem.
451	Council of Chalcedon. Patriarchy of Jerusalem recognized on the same level as Rome, Constantinople, Antioch, and Alexandria.
476	Western Roman Empire falls.
527–565	Justinian I and Theodora (d. 548). Last great age of Eastern Roman rule.
565–578	Justin II. Beginning of conflict between Rome and the Sassanid Persians.
578–582	Tiberius II.
582–602	Emperor Maurice reorganizes the western provinces (Carthage, Ravenna) and defeats the Slavs. Peace with Persia. Deposed and slain by usurper Phocas.
602–610	The reign of Phocas. Sassanid Persians, under Khosrow II, renew hostilities.
610–641	Reign of Heraclius. Captures Constantinople and defeats Phocas. Continues war with Persia. In Arabia: Formation of early Muslim movement.
614	Sassanid Persian conquest of Jerusalem. Jews return. Christians revolt. Persians slaughter Christians but remove Jewish governors, forestalling attempt to rebuild the temple. Distress for the Orthodox Patriarchate: the True Cross is moved to Ctesiphon.
622	Muslim exodus (*hijra*) from Mecca. Find refuge in Christian kingdom of Ethiopia (Axum) and in the predominantly Jewish city of Yathrib (Medina).

622–628	Heraclius's campaign of reconquest.
629 or 630	Victory near Ctesiphon, peace with Persia, True Cross triumphantly returned to Jerusalem. Jews expelled in restoration of the *status quo ante*.
635	Arab conquest of Syria begins.
636	Battle of the Yarmuk: Romans defeated.
638	Jerusalem's patriarch Sophronius opens the city after a prolonged siege. Christian privileges prevail undiminished.
661–750	Umayyad caliphate, governed from Damascus. Jerusalem as symbolic center.
692	Dome of the Rock built. Reform of Umayyad coinage.
746 or 749	Great earthquake. Eudokia's wall collapses.
750–969	Abbasid rule of the Levant.
969–1099	Fatimid rule, intermittent Seljuk incursions.
1009	Fatimid Caliph Al-Hakim dismantles Constantine's *Anastasis*.
1049	Persian traveler Nasir i-Khusraw in Jerusalem.
1095–1096	Al-Ghazali teaches in Jerusalem on his way to Mecca.
1095	Council of Clermont. Pope Urban II calls for a liberation of the holy places from the "infidel Turks."
1096	People's or Peasants' Crusade.
1099	First Crusade. Frankish colonies in *outremer* ("overseas") established. Jerusalem violently conquered. Dome of the Rock consecrated as a Christian sanctuary (*templum domini*). Friday mosque becomes royal palace, based on the biblical antecedent of King Solomon's palace and temple. *Anastasis* and *Martyrium* rebuilt as the Church of the Holy Sepulchre.
1144	County of Edessa falls to Imad al-Din Zangi, Seljuk *atabek* of Mosul and Aleppo.
1145–1149	Second Crusade, called by Pope Eugene III in response to the fall of Edessa and led by Louis VII of France and Conrad III of Germany.
1171–1250	Ayyubid rule in Egypt
1171	Salah ud-Din Yusuf b. Ayyub removes Fatimid regime in Cairo and returns Egypt to Abbasid Sunni rule.
1187	Fall of Jerusalem to Saladin after Franks are crushed at the Battle of Hattin (Horns of Hattin).
1189–1192	Third or King's Crusade.
1193	Mosque of Omar established next to the Church of the Holy Sepulchre.
1202–1204	Fourth Crusade and sack of Constantinople.
1213–1221	The Fifth Crusade takes Damietta, an Egyptian port city.
1219	Jerusalem's walls torn down by Ayyubid al-Mu'azzam 'Isa.

1228–1229	Crusade of Emperor Frederick II. Sultan al-Malik al-Kamil (r. 1218–1238) cedes authority over Jerusalem, Bethlehem, and a corridor connecting the Holy City with the Mediterranean. Frederick excommunicated.
1239	Jerusalem reverts back to the Ayyubids. New wave of crusaders takes possession of the city.
1244	Jerusalem falls to Khwarasmian Turkish invaders who are pushed into the Levant by the Mongols advancing from Central Asia.
1250–1382	*Bahri* (Turkish) Mamluk rule of Egypt.
1250	Damietta surrenders, ending Frankish presence in Egypt.
1258	Mongolians under Hülegü sack Baghdad, ending Abbasid rule. The Abbasid family, reduced to a symbolic role, moves to Cairo.
1260	Mamluk Sultan Baybars, allied with the Franks of Acre, halts Mongol advance at Ayn Jalut ("Goliath's Spring") in the Galilee.
1291	Fall of Acre. Secures Egyptian Mamluk rule over Syria and Palestine, whose realm includes all three major holy cities (Mecca, Medina, and Jerusalem). Crusader states reduced to Cyprus, Rhodes, and Malta.
1326	Death of Osman I, founder of the Ottoman state in Anatolia (*Rum*).
1382–1517	*Burji* (Circassian) Mamluk rule.
1453	Fall of Constantinople and rise of the Ottomans. End of the Eastern Roman (Byzantine) Empire.
1480–1483	Dominican Friar Felix Fabri makes pilgrimage to Jerusalem and writes a detailed account of the experience.
1495	Jerusalemite Mujir al-Din al-Ulaymi (1456–1522) writes *al-Uns al-Jalil bi-tarikh al-Quds wal-Khalil* (The Glorious History of Jerusalem and Hebron).
1497	Vasco da Gama finds the southern passage around the Cape of Good Hope, enabling European traders to circumvent Ottoman territory.
1500	Flemish painter and Palestine pilgrim Jan Provost creates a realistic painting of Jerusalem in his "Crucifixion."[3]
1517	Egypt conquered by Ottoman Selim I. Protestant Reformation begins in Europe.
1524	Franciscans evicted from *Cenaculum* (Upper Room) on Mount Zion.
1529	Turkish Siege of Vienna.
1535	Capitulation offers protection to subjects of the French king.

1536–1540	Jerusalem's walls rebuilt. Water supply improved.
1551	Hospice of *Khasseki Sultan* founded by Roxelana, the sultan's Russian wife. Jerusalem's population: c. 14,000.[4]
1566	Death of Suleïman the Magnificent.
1618–1648	Thirty Years' War.
1666	Year of Jewish Messiah Shabtai Tsevi.
1672	Ottoman adventurer Evliya Celebi Effendi describes Jerusalem as a flourishing city.
1673	French capitulations renewed. Latin privileges at the Holy Sepulchre restored.
1683	Second Turkish siege of Vienna.
1699	Peace of Karlowitz. Austrians represent Latin Christian interests at the holy places.
1789	French Revolution.
1798	Napoleon invades Egypt.
1801	Mehmet Ali (1769–1849) occupies Egypt for the Ottomans.
1821	Greek war of independence. Mehmet Ali assists, then falls out with the Ottomans.
1827	Italian born British banker/philanthropist Moses Montefiore (1784–1885) has a religious awakening during his first of seven visits to Palestine.
1831–1840	Syria under Ibrahim Pasha (1789–1848). Introduces French-influenced social reforms. Aided by Russia, England, Prussia, and Austria, the Ottomans prevail against Egypt. In exchange, Ottomans boost the standing of the Christian communities and offer rights of representation to foreign powers (capitulations).
1838	Free trade agreement with Great Britain. Britain establishes the first modern European consulate in Jerusalem, then still under Ibrahim Pasha. The consulate's task, then and later: to protect the Jews of the Ottoman Empire and ideally to convert them. American biblical archaeologist Edward Robinson (1794–1863) visits the Holy Land, publishes *Biblical Researches in Palestine and Adjacent Countries* in 1841.
1839	Edict of Reform (*Tanzimat*), *Hatt-ı Şerif* of Gülhane ("Noble Edict of the Rose Chamber"). Emancipation of non-Muslims, basis for Ottoman citizenship, equitable conscription and taxation, secularization of education (based on Prussian law).

1840	The quadruple alliance bombs Acre, forcing Ibrahim Pasha to withdraw. Christian powers pursue "peaceful crusade" in Palestine.[5] British Foreign Minister Palmerston, influenced by Anthony Ashley-Cooper, seventh Earl of Shaftesbury, lobbies the Ottomans for a return of the Jews to their ancient homeland.[6] Damascus blood libel. Anti-Jewish violence.
1841	Jointly funded by England and Prussia, Bishop Alexander is appointed as the first Anglican bishop of Jerusalem, beginning a wave of competing missions.[7] Schemes for an international Christian state of Jerusalem discussed across Europe.
1843	French and Sardinian consulates open.
1844	American consulate opens. In London: Alexander Kinglake publishes his bestselling travelogue, *Eothen*, marking transition from pilgrimage accounts to travel literature.
1846	Polyglot Swiss missionary Samuel Gobat (1799–1879) appointed as the second Anglican bishop in Jerusalem. Serves for 33 years and – with German missionary and builder Conrad Schick (1822–1901) and Swiss banker Johannes Frutiger (1836–1899) – helps to build German Protestant institutions. Second British Consul James Finn and his wife Elizabeth Ann (1825–1921) arrive in Jerusalem where he serves until 1863.[8]
1847	First Protestant school founded by Bishop Gobat. Latin Patriarchate of Jerusalem renewed for the first time since the fall of Jerusalem (1187).[9]
1848	Protestant cemetery established on Mount Zion.
1849	Austro-Hungarian consulate opened. Christ Church (Anglican) inaugurated.
1850s	Total population of "Palestine" (in its later borders): c. 350,000. (Jerusalem region: 180,000).
1852	Ottoman *firman*, regulating the *status quo* at the Christian holy places. Confirmed in 1856.[10]
1853	Correspondents of the weekly newspaper of the Southern-German pietistic "Friends of Jerusalem," the later "Templers," begin to report from the Holy Land, where the group wants to create the seed for a new, better humanity.
1853–1856	Crimean War between Russia and Turkey over *status quo* at the Christian holy places. Turkey supported by France and Britain. Ends with the Treaty of Paris.
1856	Affirmation of reforms (*Tanzimat*), including non-discrimination based on religion. Anti-Christian riots in Nablus and Gaza.

1857	Imperial Russian Ecclesiastical Mission established in Jerusalem.[11]
	French Catholic proselyte brothers Ratisbonne establish Notre Dame de Sion/Ecce Homo convent on the *Via Dolorosa*.[12] Herman Melville visits Jerusalem, takes an unromantic view.[13]
	Sephardic rabbi Judah Alkalay publishes *Goral la-Adonai*, arguing for an active return of the Jews to the Land of Israel and improvement of their living conditions. Joins the short-lived *Kolonisations-Verein* (Frankfurt/Oder) founded by Chaim Lorje (Luria).
1858	German "Friends of Jerusalem" begin land purchase exploration.
1860	Land purchase for a large Russian pilgrimage center outside the Old City (Russian Compound/al-muskubiya/*Nuva Yerushama*).
	Syrian Orphanage founded by German Evangelical missionary Johann Ludwig Schneller,[14] to aid child survivors of the Druze Maronite massacre in the Lebanon, part of a larger anti-Christian backlash.[15]
	Sir Montefiore establishes the workers' cottages of Mishkenot Shaananim, the first modern Jewish settlement outside the Old City of Jerusalem, funded by the estate of American Judah Touro.
1861	Lebanon semi-independent under European protection.
	German "Temple Society" established by Johann Hoffmann, a leading Swabian pietist. Aim: to build a new "temple" in the Holy Land, to usher in a new humanity through model colonies.
1862	The Prince of Wales (later King Edward VII) visits the Holy Land.[16]
	Rabbi Tzvi Hirsch Kalischer publishes *D'rishat Tsiyon*, advocating Jewish land purchase and agricultural settlements in Palestine, to hasten redemption.
	German socialist Moses Hess publishes *Rome and Jerusalem*, arguing for Jewish nationhood in Palestine.
1863	Abd al-Rahman Efendi al-Dajani al-Dawudi appointed as the first mayor of the newly established Jerusalem municipality.[17]
1864	Sir Charles Wilson's Ordnance Survey of Jerusalem.[18]
1865	Palestine Exploration Fund established.[19]
	First direct telegraphic line between Jerusalem and Istanbul.
1865–1866	Cholera epidemic. Sheikh Jarrah (Husseini family) neighborhood established north of the city.

1867	Sir Charles Warren begins archaeological and topographical research in Jerusalem, especially on and around the *al-Haram al-Sharif*.[20] (Completed in 1870.)
	Mark Twain joins an American sea voyage to Europe and the Holy Land, publishes the best-selling *Innocents Abroad* in 1869.
1869	First German Templer colonies founded in Haifa and Yafo. Others follow: Sarona 1871, Jerusalem 1873, Wilhelma near Lod, Galilean Bethlehem 1906, and Waldheim 1907, the latter founded by dissident Templers who returned to the bosom of the Protestant church. Altogether, by 1914, about 2,200 settlers.[21]
	Jewish neighborhoods of Mahaneh Yisrael (Moroccan) and Nahalat Shiv'ah established.
1870–1876	Yusuf Diya-uddin Pasha al-Khalidi (1842–1906)[22] mayor of Jerusalem.
1870	Alliance Israélite Universelle establishes *Mikveh Israel* agricultural school.
1871/2	Jerusalem households: 730 Christian (Greek Orthodox: 299, Latin: 179, Armenian: 175), 630 Jewish, 1,025 Muslim. District of Jerusalem: 6,118 Muslim, 1,202 Christian, no Jewish.[23]
1872	Redrawing of provincial boundaries briefly elevates Jerusalem above Acre and Nablus and makes Palestine an independent *vilayet*. Midhat Pasha, upon his appointment as grand *wazir*, reverses the decree and subjects Jerusalem to Damascene supervision.[24]
1872–1874	Conder and Kitchener produce Survey of Western Palestine.[25]
	Hungarian pilgrim Stephen Illes creates scaled model of Jerusalem shown at the Ottoman pavilion at the Vienna World Fair of 1873.[26]
1873	Stock market crash. Period of uncertainty.
1874	District of Jerusalem (southern Palestine) elevated to status of independent *sançak*. Jaffa-Jerusalem carriage road completed (begun in 1868). Eases transport of imported building material.
	Ratisbonne Monastery established on a remote hill, now part of Rehavia.
1875	Nebi Musa festival attracts nearly 10,000 Muslim pilgrims from across the region in response to heightened Christian activities.
1875/6	Ottoman state bankruptcy. War and uprising in the Balkans. Palestinian cities in a virtual "state of war." Christians fear another wave of massacres.[27]
1876	Constitution proclaimed by Caliph/Sultan Abdul Hamid II.

1877/8	Russian–Turkish war.
1877	First parliamentary elections. Jerusalem mayor Yusuf Diya-uddin Pasha al-Khalidi represents the Jerusalem district.[28] German Society for the Exploration of Palestine established.[29]
1878	Abdul Hamid suspends the constitution. Britain occupies Cyprus.
1880s	Total population of "Palestine" (in its later borders): c. 460,000, not including the Bedouin of Southern Palestine.[30] (*Liva* of Jerusalem, i.e. city and region: 230,000)
1881	Reorganization of Ottoman state debt, 40% of which is held by France, 29% by England, the rest by other European nations. Horatio Spafford and family move from Chicago to Jerusalem to lead a simple Christian life. Beginning of American Colony.[31]
1881–1882	Russian pogroms cause wave of Jewish refugees. Massive immigration to the United States and South/Latin America. First wave of Russian Jewish immigrants and "Friends of Zion" (*hovevey tsiyon*) to Palestine (first *aliyah*), founding of philanthropically funded agricultural settlements. About 35,000 persons arrive between 1882 and 1903. Rishon LeZion, Rosh Pina, Zikhron Ya'akov founded in 1882. Petah Tikvah becomes permanent in 1883.
1882	British military occupation of Egypt.
1886	German Catholic Schmidt-Schule established outside Damascus Gate.
1892	Jaffa-Jerusalem railroad opened.[32]
1897	First Zionist World Congress convened in Basle, Switzerland.
1898	Wilhelm II and Augusta Victoria imperial visit. In preparation, roads and bridges repaired.[33] Wall near Jaffa Gate opened for the imperial carriage. Inauguration of the German Church of the Redeemer.[34]
1905	Russian revolution, followed by anti-Jewish pogroms. Second *aliyah* begins, which brings young Russian Jewish idealists and utopians to Palestine.
1907	Construction starts on the Augusta Victoria church and hospital on Mount Scopus, completed in 1914.
1908	Young Turks (Committee of Union and Progress, CUP) take power, restore the constitution. Clock tower erected over Jaffa Gate.
1909	Abdul Hamid II forced to relinquish power.
1914	Turkey enters the war allied with Germany and Austria-Hungary.

1915–1917	British wartime promises: Husayn–McMahon Correspondence of 1915–1916 (details not made public until 1939), Sykes–Picot Agreement of May 1916 (not widely known until April 1918, leaked by the new Bolshevik Russian government to embarrass capitalist powers), and the Balfour Declaration of Nov 2, 1917 (not officially posted in Palestine until 1920).
1917	Dec 9: Turkish troops and German advisers leave. Jerusalem mayor Hussein Bey al-Husseini submits script of surrender.[35] Population celebrates the end of Ottoman rule associated with forced conscription, starvation, disease, and the cultural offense of pan-Turanianism; welcomes the British as allies of the Amir Faisal b. Husayn (1885?–1933).
	Dec 11: General Allenby enters Jerusalem. Occupied Enemy Territory Administration (OETA) government established.
1918	Oct 5: Amir Faisal, military leader of the Arab rebellion against the Ottomans and ally of the British, installed as King of Syria.
	Nov: Joint Christian and Muslim committee of Palestinian notables formed in Jerusalem with the goal of obtaining French support for an inclusion of Palestine into an independent Syrian Arab state.
1919	Jan 3: Russian-born British citizen, Zionist leader, and favorite of British Prime Minister Lloyd George, Chaim Weizmann (1874–1952) enters into an agreement with King Faisal, who pledges concessions to Jewish interests in Palestine, in return for British guarantee of Arab independence, and protection of Faisal's future, in light of French designs on Syria.
	Jan 19: Paris Peace Conference formally opens.
	June–August: Commissioned by US President Woodrow Wilson, Oberlin College President Henry King and businessman Charles Crane travel to Syria and Palestine. Their report is repressed by the Wilson administration.[36]
1920	Mar 8: General Syrian Congress proclaims Faisal king of a Syrian Arab state.
	April 4–7: Nabi Musa riots (9 dead, 244 wounded). Haj Amin al-Husseini (1895–1974) urges union of Palestine with Syria under Faisal. In response to the riots, the British depose Musa Kazim al-Husseini (1853–1934) as mayor of Jerusalem and appoint his rival, the more pliant Raghib Bey al-Nashashibi (1881–1951).
	April 19–26: San Remo Conference of the Supreme Council of the Paris Peace Conference finalizes the division of the Middle East mandates between France and England.

July 1: Sir Herbert Samuel, a well-connected politician and devoted Zionist, installed as the first High Commissioner for Palestine.

Jul 24: France defeats Faisal's army and takes charge in Syria.

1921   March: Winston Churchill colonial secretary. Makes Faisal king of Iraq and installs the Amir Abdullah, Faisal's brother, as caretaker of Transjordan (hitherto part of the Arab Kingdom of Hijaz).

May 1: Jaffa riots.

May 8: Sir Herbert Samuel appoints Haj Amin "Grand Mufti" of Jerusalem.

1922   July: British Mandate for Palestine confirmed by League of Nations.

Sept: Churchill White Paper limits Jewish settlements to Cisjordan, leading to anti-British sentiments among right-leaning Revisionist Zionists, led by Vladimir Jabotinsky (1880–1940).

1923   Jul 24: Treaty of Lausanne recognizes Turkish independence (replaces ill-fated 1920 Treaty of Sèvres).

Sep 29: Palestine and Syria mandates take effect.

1925   April 1: Ibn Saud takes Mecca, ending Hashemite rule in the Hejaz. In Jerusalem, the Hebrew University is officially opened.

1929   Aug 28/29: Riots at Western Wall spread across the country. First major lethal conflagration between Jews and Arabs in Palestine, leaves 133 Jews and 110 Arabs dead.[37]

1930   British commission submits report on the situation in Palestine to the League of Nations' Permanent Mandates Commission.

1931   Jerusalem Muslim International Congress. Husayn b. Ali buried in Jerusalem.

1933   Jan 31: Hitler elected in Germany. Pressure on Jews to emigrate. *Haavarah* agreement with the German government enables Jews to redeem cash for German-made machine tools to be transferred to Palestine, boosting the *yishuv*'s industrial development.

1934   Hussein al-Khalidi (1895–1966) appointed as mayor. Deposed in 1937 and, with other notable leaders of the Arab rebellion, deported to the Seychelles in 1939.

1936   Arab General Strike protesting increased Jewish immigration. Jewish National Fund land purchase and Hebrew labor ideology of the Jewish Agency lead to unrest among the *fellahin*.

Apr 25: Haj Amin initiates Arab Higher Committee (AHC). Disbanded by the British in September 1937.

1937	Peel Commission Report recommends partition of Cisjordanian Palestine into a Jewish and an Arab state, with Jerusalem remaining under the control of a new mandatory power or international regime.
1938	Woodhead Commission works out partition plan but remains skeptical of pacification of Palestine by means of partition.
1939	May 21: MacDonald White Paper on Palestine (commissioned Nov 9, 1938) sets aside partition, limits Jewish immigration, and proposes proportional participation of Arabs and Jews in transitional government. Opposed by both Jews and Arabs.[38]
	Sept 1: Germany attacks Poland. England declares war on Germany. Beginning of World War II.
1944	Nov 6: British Minister of State Lord Moyne assassinated in Cairo by members of *Lehi* ("Freedom Fighters for Israel").
1945	May 8: Germany's unconditional surrender ends World War II in Europe. Palestine descends into a three-way war between Zionist paramilitary, Arab fighters, and the British.
1946	May 25: Hashemite Kingdom of Jordan declares independence.
	July 22: Southern wing of King David Hotel, home of the British military headquarters for Palestine, blown up by *Lehi*.
1947	April: Founding of UNSCOP (UN Special Committee on Palestine).
	Nov 29: UN General Assembly votes (33 to 13) to partition Palestine. Triggers escalation of the war between Jewish and Arab paramilitary groups, jockeying for territory.
1948	Accelerated flight from urban neighborhoods and expulsion of Arab populations from villages the Jewish paramilitary organization Haganah wants to bring under the control of Israel before the expected attacks from outside. Estimates of the number of Palestinian refugees vary between 650,000 and 1 million (Arabic: *al-Nakba*, the catastrophe).
	May 14: In a ceremony held in Tel Aviv, a provisional government headed by David Ben-Gurion declares the independence of Israel.
	May 15: Mandate ends and the last British convoy leaves Palestine. The haphazard departure leaves populations to fend for themselves. No governing institutions in place to establish Arab statehood. British commanders of the Arab Legion of Jordan (trained by Sir John Bagot Glubb aka "Glubb Pasha") fight under the Jordanian flag.

1948/49	First Arab–Israeli War. In Israeli parlance, the "War of Independence."
1948	Sept 17: UN mediator Swedish Count Folke Bernadotte assassinated by *Lehi*.[39]
1949	Between Febr and June: General Armistice Agreements between Israel, Egypt, Jordan, Lebanon, and Syria.
	Dec 8: UN Relief and Works Agency (UNRWA) established for Palestinian refugees in Jordan, Egypt, Syria, and Lebanon.
1952	Egyptian revolution. End of British-installed monarchy. Beginning of military autocracy in the name of a pan-Arabic revolution against colonialism.
1953	Oct 15: Qibya massacre: cross-border raids and massacre among Palestinian refugees by Unit 101, commanded by Ariel Sharon.
1954	Febr 25: Gamal Abdel Nasser sworn in as second president of Egypt.
1956	July 26: Gamal Abdel Nasser nationalizes the Suez Canal, precipitating the "Suez Crisis."
	Oct 29: Encouraged by Britain and France, Israel invades Egypt.
1958	Formation of the United Arab Republic, linking Egypt and Syria. Syria quits in 1961 but Egypt retains the name until 1971.
	Yasser Arafat (1929–2004) and Khalil Ibrahim al-Wazir ("Abu Jihad," 1935–1988) meet in Kuwait and found a Palestinian national liberation movement by the name of *al-Fatah*.
1964	Jan 13–17: First official summit of the Arab League convened in Cairo.
	May 4–June 2: Palestine National Council convened in East Jerusalem. Palestine Liberation Organization (PLO) established, chaired by Ahmed al-Shukeiri (1908–1980).
1965	Fatah operates on Jordanian territory. First attacks on Israeli targets.
1966	Baath Party seizes power in Syria. Civilian administration replaces military rule of Arab villages in Israel.
1967	June: Following Egyptian, Syrian, and Jordanian threats, Israel preemptively attacks Egypt, Syria, and Jordan, captures Sinai, Gaza, West-Bank, and Golan Heights. Hundreds of thousands of Palestinians flee, adding to the millions already living as refugees in UNRWA-managed camps across the region. Israeli civilian administration extended to East Jerusalem, municipal boundaries extended.

1967–1970	Israel–Egypt war of attrition.
1968	Mar 21: Following a Fatah terror attack on a civilian bus in Israel, Israel Defense Forces (IDF) enter Jordanian territory at Karameh. Fatah defensive success boosts Arafat's reputation and leads to greater assertiveness of Fatah and other, more radical paramilitary groups (Popular Front for the Liberation of Palestine – PFLP; Democratic Front for the Liberation of Palestine – DFLP) in Jordan. Cross-border raids provoke Israeli reprisals on Jordanian territory.

July: PLO adopts amended National Charter, calling for violent struggle for the liberation of Palestine. The program of Fatah prevails. Ahmed al-Shukeiri resigns.

Several airliners hijacked and blown up by the PFLP, a Marxist revolutionary group led by George Habash. |
| 1969 | Fatah establishes military presence in the Lebanon. Arafat elected chairman of the PLO. His image makes the cover of *TIME Magazine*.

An Australian Christian torches Saladin's *minbar* at Al-Aqsa mosque. |
| 1970 | July: United States mediates end to War of Attrition. Recognizes Jordanian sovereignty over the West Bank and East Jerusalem. Palestinians feel betrayed by Nasser and start a campaign against him, costing them Nasser's protection and prompting King Hussein to launch a violent crackdown on Palestinians in Jordan.

Sept 6: PFLP hijacks several airliners, forcing them to land on an airstrip in Jordan. On Sept 12, the planes are blown up.

Sept 15: After two weeks of Palestinian assassination attempts, King Hussein imposes martial law and begins violent crackdown on the PLO ("Black September").

Sept 28: A day after brokering an agreement to end hostilities in Jordan, President Nasser dies of a heart attack. Nasser's successor, former Vice President Anwar al-Sadat, begins a "corrective revolution." Persecution of the Muslim Brotherhood leads to their dispersion and spread of their version of political Islam across the Middle East. |
| 1971 | July: PLO expelled from Jordan.

Nov 28: "Black September" hitmen – a group formed with Arafat's approval – assassinate Wasfi al-Tal, Jordan's prime minister. |

1972	In Munich, "Black September" terrorists kill two Israeli athletes and take the rest hostage, who are killed during a botched rescue attempt. Nayef Hawatmeh's DFLP moves toward two-state solution for Palestine.
1973	March: US ambassador killed by "Black September" at the Saudi embassy in Khartoum.

Oct 6–26: Yom Kippur War, a surprise attack on Israel's Egyptian and Syrian fronts. Sadat's goal: to reestablish Egypt as a political player.

1974   Jan: Golda Meir forms a new government.

March: Gush Emunim ("Bloc of the Faithful") begins settlement of Judea and Samaria for the sake of a "redemption of the land." The first settlement is attempted at Sebaste, the site of the ancient capital of Israel, Samaria.

April: Agranat commission blames Prime Minister Golda Meir and Defense Minister Moshe Dayan for failure to anticipate Yom Kippur attack. Golda Meir resigns.

May: Yitzhak Rabin, the first native-born prime minister of Israel, forms a new government, replacing Dayan with Shimon Peres.

Oct 17–Nov 23: The General Conference of UNESCO meeting in Paris/France condemns Israel for alterations to the Old City of Jerusalem, which the international community considers occupied territory.[40]

Oct 26–29: The PLO moves from armed to political struggle. The Arab League recognizes the PLO as the only legitimate representative of the Palestinian people. The PLO moves toward two-state solution.

Nov 13: PLO Chairman Arafat addresses the UN General Assembly where he receives a standing ovation.

1975   April: Lebanon civil war begins, pitting politically conservative Maronite Christian Phalangists (pro-Western, anti-Muslim) and Palestinian and Druze Marxists and socialists (supported by the Soviets) against one another.

Sept 4: Egypt–Israel disengagement agreement signed in Geneva, ending hostilities.

Nov 10: UN General Assembly (UNGA) Resolution 3379 declares Zionism racism. Revoked in 1991, as a condition for the Madrid Conference.

Dec: Ma'aleh Adumim established east of Jerusalem as a strategic extension of the city, not a "settlement."

1976	Jan: Christian Phalangists and their allies massacre Palestinians at Karantina. In revenge, Palestinians massacre Christians at Damour. Later that year, aided by Syria, Christian Maronites massacre Palestinians at Tel al-Zaatar.

Mar 30: Palestinian citizens of Israel call for a general strike in protest against massive expropriations of land in the Galilee to make room for Jewish settlements. Many are killed in clashes with the police. Henceforth marked by Palestinian citizens of Israel as "Land Day."

June 1: Syria intervenes in the Lebanon crisis. Its force, stabilizing the conservative Christian regime, is directed against the left-wing coalition of the PLO and the Druze militias of Kamal Jumblatt. Israel as well supports the right-wing Christian Phalangists led by the Gemayel family. Palestinian refugee camps are overrun, fighters expelled, and civilians massacred.

June 27: Wadie Haddad, an associate of George Habash of the PFLP, has an Air France airliner hijacked to Entebbe, Uganda, where the Israelis launch a spectacular rescue operation.

Dec 11: American F15 fighters are received by the Israeli government on a Sabbath, angering religious parties who stage a parliamentary vote of no confidence. Rabin government falls due to charges his family had maintained a dollar account from the time Rabin served as Israel's ambassador in Washington, DC.

1977	May: Menachem Begin (1913–1992) wins Israel's parliamentary elections by a landslide, ending 30 years of left-wing dominance in Israeli politics.

Nov: Sadat visits Israel, addresses Knesset, accepts "land-for-peace" formula, offers recognition. Egypt expelled from Arab League.

1978	Jan: Abu Nidal group, supported by Iraq's Saddam Hussein, assassinates the PLO representative in London.

Mar 14: "Operation Litani" – following a terror attack in Haifa where over 30 civilians are killed, the IDF enters Southern Lebanon, establishes "security zone."

Sep 17: Camp David Agreement between Egypt and Israel, brokered by US President Jimmy Carter.

1979	Jan 22: Israel's spy agency, the Mossad, assassinates Ali Hassan Salameh, chief of Arafat's security, in Beirut.

Mar 26: Egypt–Israel peace treaty signed by Anwar al-Sadat and Menachem Begin.

Apr 1: Ayatollah Khomeini declares Iran an Islamic Republic (Iranian Revolution).

1980   June 2: The mayors of Nablus and Ramallah are severely injured by car bombs planted by Jewish terrorists, members of the radical right or "Jewish Underground."[41]

July 30: Knesset passes "Jerusalem Law," officially annexing East Jerusalem. In response, Venezuela and Uruguay withdraw their ambassadors from the city.

1981   Febr: President Reagan declares Jewish settlements in the West Bank "not illegal."

June 7: Shortly before national elections, Israeli warplanes destroy Iraqi nuclear facility near Baghdad. The act is condemned by the UN Security Council. Begin is reelected.

Oct 6: Anwar al-Sadat assassinated at a military parade commemorating the Yom Kippur War.

Dec 14: Israeli civilian administration extended to Golan Heights.

1982   Apr 11: A recent immigrant from the United States randomly shoots and kills Arabs on the Temple Mount.

April 25: Yamit forcibly evacuated, settlement bulldozed.

May 2: El Al no longer flies on Sabbath.

May 10: Israeli reservists speak out against the brutalization of Palestinian civilians in the occupied territories, accusing Defense Minister Ariel Sharon of incitement to commit atrocities.

May 25: Karp Report on settler violence against Arabs is so critical of the Israeli military occupation that it is repressed by the government.

June 3: Abu Nidal group attempts to kill Shlomo Argov, Israeli ambassador in London. Israeli government uses this crime to act against the PLO in Lebanon, acting on Defense Minister Ariel Sharon's invasion plan (Operation "Peace for Galilee"). Most observers, including the PLO, erroneously assume the Israeli objective was limited to South Lebanon, as in 1978.

June 6: Israeli land invasion begins. Palestinian defense in South Lebanon collapses. Syria agrees to a ceasefire. Israel launches siege of Beirut. Palestinians decide to stay and fight.

July 25: Right-wing Tehiya party joins Begin's government.

August: After heavy bombardment, a compromise is reached in Lebanon, allowing PLO fighters to leave, and keeping IDF out of Beirut. The departure of the PLO leaves Palestinian refugees exposed. President Bashir Gemayel is assassinated, Israeli troops move into West Beirut and encircle refugee camps Sabra and Shatilla, claiming that hundreds of Palestinian fighters had stayed behind. Protected by Israeli forces, Christian Phalangists enter the camps and massacre 800 civilians.

1983   Febr 8: Ariel Sharon resigns after Kahan Commission holds him responsible for Sabra and Shatilla massacre.

Febr 10: Peace Now activist Emil Gruenzweig killed by a hand grenade at demonstration outside the Prime Minister's residence.

April: PLO moderate Issam Sartawi assassinated by Iraq-supported Abu Nidal group.

June: PLO weakened by factional warfare, Arafat expelled from Damascus. Syria's Hafez al-Assad renews Syria's claim to representing the Palestinians as part of a greater Syria, leading to factional split in the PLO.

July: Jewish settlers attack Muslims in a Hebron Islamic college.[42]

Aug 2: A UN Security Council resolution (UNSCR) calling on Israel to dismantle all settlements in territories occupied in June 1967 fails to pass.

Aug 28: Begin announces his intention to resign.

Aug 27: President Reagan calls the building of further settlements an "obstacle to peace."[43]

Dec 22: After more turmoil in Lebanon, Arafat meets with Hosni Mubarak, breaking the boycott against Egypt since peace treaty with Israel.

1984   Jan: Jewish attack on Al-Aqsa mosque thwarted.

Febr 9: Karp Report on settler violence released two years after it was suppressed.

April: Radical settlers caught in the act of wiring five Arab buses with explosives. First time the extent of organized Jewish anti-Arab violence becomes known to the Israeli public.

June: Meir Kahane's extremist Kach party disqualified from participating in the elections.

July: Meir Kahane (1932–1990), charismatic US rabbi and founder of the Jewish Defense League, elected to the Knesset.[44]

September: Jordan reestablishes diplomatic relations with Egypt.

Nov: King Hussein allows the Palestine National Council (PNC) to convene in Amman. Restores Arafat's legitimacy as chairman of the PLO.

December: Shas (Sephardi Torah Guardians) party founded with Rav Ovadiah Yosef as spiritual leader.

1985   Jan: IDF begins withdrawal from Lebanon.

Febr: Amman Accord between Jordan and PLO establishes confederation for purpose of future Arab–Israeli negotiations. Prime Minister Shimon Peres signals willingness to enter negotiations with a Jordanian-Palestinian delegation as long as PLO has no part in it. In response to PLO-Jordan reconciliation, Syria uses Amal militias to wage the so-called War of the Camps, where militias would lay siege to refugee camps in south Lebanon and Beirut and indiscriminately shoot anyone venturing out to seek food or water for their families.

May: City of David archeological park opened.

Oct: In response to a terror attack on an Israeli yacht anchored at Larnaca (Cyprus), Israel bombs the PLO headquarters in Tunis. Soon after, a radical PLO faction (led by Abu al-Abbas) hijacks the cruise ship *Achille Lauro.*

1986   Feb: King Hussein terminates his year-long consultations with Arafat on the peace process.

July 21: Prime Minister Shimon Peres meets with King Hassan of Morocco.

Aug: First direct diplomatic contacts between Israel and Soviet Union since 1967.

Aug 5: Knesset passes law prohibiting racial incitement.

Sept: A survey finds that 90% of Palestinian citizens of Israel believe that the PLO is the sole and legitimate representative of the Palestinian people; 78% hope for the establishment of a democratic Palestinian state.

Nov: Iran-Contra affair. Israel is implicated in covert American arms transfer to Iran but denies any role in the transfer of funds to the Contras in Nicaragua.

1987   Febr: President Reagan publicly recognizes Israel as a major non-NATO ally.

Apr 11: Agreement on outlines of a peace agreement between Jordan and Israel between Foreign Minister Shimon Peres and King Hussein after secret talks in London.

Apr 24: Soviet leader Mikhail Gorbachev recognizes Israel's right to peace and security while criticizing "Tel Aviv's" annexationist policies.

May: Clashes between settlers and Arab residents of Qalqiliya and Nablus. Riots in East Jerusalem.

June 6: Arabs riot throughout the territories on the twentieth anniversary of the Six-Day War.

Aug 26: Faisal al-Husseini, the unofficial PLO representative in Jerusalem, is arrested on charges of inciting civil unrest.

Oct: Riots in Gaza, spreading to East Jerusalem and Ramallah.

Dec 9: A traffic accident in Gaza involving an Israeli truck slamming into Arab cars triggers the first sustained uprising in the occupied territories, known as the Intifada (lit. "shaking off"). Palestinian citizens of Israel are drawn into the wave of protests. During the Intifada, Sheikh Yassin founds Hamas as the Palestinian wing of the Egyptian Muslim Brotherhood.

Dec 15: Ariel Sharon, minister of trade, inaugurates his new home in the Muslim Quarter of the Old City of Jerusalem.

1988   Intifada continues. Local Palestinians take the initiative in a grass-roots uprising characterized in western media by stone-throwing teenagers confronting Israeli tanks.

April 16: Israeli commandos led by Ehud Barak assassinate Abu Jihad, Arafat's second in command, in Tunis. The funeral in Damascus turns into a popular referendum on the PLO. Arafat reemerges as a leading figure.

July 31: Jordan relinquishes all claims to the West Bank, recognizing the Palestinian right to self-determination.

Nov 15: PNC proclaims the State of Palestine with Jerusalem as its capital, accepting UNGA Resolution 181 (1947), the so-called Partition Resolution, and UNSCR 242, which calls on Israel to withdraw to the ceasefire lines that prevailed until June 1967.

Dec: Arafat renounces terrorism, recognizes UNSCR 242 as the basis for a settlement of the Palestine conflict, belatedly legitimizing the 1949 ceasefire line ("Green Line") and recognizing Israel's right to exist. This allowed the United States to enter into a dialogue with the PLO.

1989   Jan: G. H. W. Bush inaugurated as forty-first President of the United States.

Faisal al-Husseini released from detention.

Feb: US report criticizes Israel for human rights violations in the West Bank, deems its security forces inexpert in dealing with civil unrest.

May 14: Knesset approves Shamir peace plan, which calls for elections in the occupied territories but rules out any PLO participation.

May 22: In a speech to the American Israel Public Affairs Committee (AIPAC) conference, Secretary of State James A. Baker III calls on Israel "to lay aside once and for all the unrealistic vision of a greater Israel" and calls on Palestinians to "reach out to Israelis and convince them of your peaceful intentions."[45]

June 5: Members of the Jewish Underground have their prison sentences reduced by President Chaim Herzog.

Between 1989 and 1994, around 800,000 Jews emigrate from Russia. About 500,000 immigrate to Israel. The wave of new immigration levels off after 2001.

1990   August: Iraqi invasion of Kuwait. Arafat attempts to mediate the conflict and is courted by Saddam Hussein.

Jewish immigration from Russia peaks with 183,400 new immigrants in 1990.

1991   Jan: As scud missiles rain on Tel Aviv, Palestinians in the occupied territories can be seen dancing jubilantly on the roofs. This, along with Arafat's failure to condemn the Iraqi invasion of Kuwait, diminishes the Palestinians in world opinion.

March: At the behest of Saddam Hussein, Abu Nidal group assassinates Arafat's close associate Abu Iyad.

Oct: After the Gulf War (Operation "Desert Storm"), the United States, joined by the USSR, convenes Middle East peace talks in Madrid. Though the PLO is not officially invited, the Palestinian representatives from West Bank and Gaza are hand-picked and they adjust their statements with Arafat in Tunis.[46]

Dec: Following a direct appeal by President Bush, the 1975 UN Resolution 3379, equating Zionism with racism, is repealed.

1992   Jan: Extreme right-wing parties leave the government coalition in protest against Madrid talks. New elections scheduled for June.

March 9: Menachem Begin dies.

March 18: Knesset changes electoral laws. Prime Minister is to be elected by direct vote.

April 8: A plane with Arafat on board crashes in the Libyan Desert, making it obvious that no successor for Arafat had been groomed.

June: First suggestions of Oslo process. While Islamist resistance to negotiations with Israel increases, Arafat gives green light to secret direct negotiations with Israel in Oslo.

June 14: Gorbachev visits Israel.

June 23: Labor beats Likud in the elections. Rabin forms government with a comfortable majority. Rabin is the first to float the idea of a clear demarcation between Israeli and Palestinian areas.

1993   Jan: William Jefferson Clinton sworn in as the forty-second President of the United States.

July: After months of secret negotiations, Israel's government announces openly that it is ready to negotiate with the PLO.

Aug 20: Initialed the day before, the Oslo Accords (= DOP or "Declaration of Principles on Interim Self-Government Arrangements")[47] are publicized, spelling out a framework for peace. Hamas denounces the accords.

Sept 13: Handshake between PLO chairman Arafat and Israel Prime Minister Yitzhak Rabin following the signing of the accords on the White House lawn. The Oslo Accords are denounced in the Arab world but welcomed among Palestinians in the occupied territories.

Nov 2: Ehud Olmert defeats the 82-year-old Kollek in the mayoral race in Jerusalem.

Nov 15: US Senate lifts sanctions on the PLO.

Dec 30: Vatican establishes diplomatic relations with Israel.

Arafat and Rabin appear as two of the "peacemakers" as "men of the year" of *Time Magazine*, along with F. W. de Klerk and Nelson Mandela of South Africa.

1994   Febr 25: Dr. Baruch Goldstein, an American-Jewish extremist living in Kiryat Arba, opens fire on Muslim worshippers in the Ibrahim/Tomb of the Patriarchs and Matriarchs mosque in Hebron, killing 29 and wounding more than 100.[48] Two weeks later, Hamas answers with suicide bombings inside Israel. Violence on the rise.

March: Yemenites demand inquiry into abduction of Yemenite children by the Jewish state in the early days of statehood.

May 4: Rabin and Arafat sign the Cairo Agreement on Gaza and Jericho, launching the first partial Israeli troop withdrawal and beginning of Palestinian autonomy in Gaza and Jericho.

May 10: Arafat in Johannesburg, South Africa, for Nelson Mandela's inauguration. Gives "Sermon on *jihad* for Jerusalem," secretly recorded and distributed by the religious settler group "Women in Green" (http://womeningreen.org/), widely criticized (misinterpreted?) as contravening the spirit of the DOP.[49]

July 1: Arafat's triumphant return to Palestine. Palestine National Authority (PNA) charged with administration of limited territories.

July 25: Washington Declaration normalizes relations between Jordan and Israel.

Oct 26: Israel–Jordan peace agreement signed.

Dec 10: Arafat, Rabin, and Peres jointly awarded Nobel Peace Prize.

In 1994, first section of a physical barrier separating West Bank and Israel is built near Tulkarm.

1995   Jan: Rabin makes promise to Arafat to freeze new settlement building in the territories.

May 8: Israel announces land expropriation in East Jerusalem. A week later, an end to such expropriations is declared.

Nov 4: Israeli Prime Minister Rabin is assassinated by Yigal Amir after militant rabbis condemn Rabin for trading away parts of the Holy Land.[50]

Nov 22: Shimon Peres forms new government.

1996   In the first direct elections for Prime Minister, the widely loathed Shimon Peres loses to Binyamin Netanyahu, whose campaign slogan is "peace with security."

Negotiations over final status issues (borders, security, the status of Jerusalem, and the return or compensation of the refugees) are bogged down because the newly elected Israeli Prime Minister Netanyahu fundamentally opposes the Oslo process.

Israel completes a security barrier around the Gaza Strip begun under Prime Minister Rabin to curtail terrorist activity.

1998   Oct: Wye River Memorandum on the implementation of the 1995 Oslo Accords. Brokered by President Clinton to coax Netanyahu and Arafat to advance the peace process.

1999   Newly elected Prime Minister of Israel Ehud Barak offers the Palestinians withdrawal from most of the West Bank but not from all of East Jerusalem.

2000   Barak promotes "unilateral disengagement," launches withdrawal of IDF from South Lebanon, vows to build separation barrier between Israel and West Bank to foster Palestinian independence.

July: Arafat and Barak agree to a summit at Camp David. Following up on the Wye River Memorandum, this summit was the first to address permanent status issues such as borders, the refugees, and Jerusalem. Rapport between Barak and Arafat is poor. Arafat turns down the Israeli offer and is publicly blamed by the United States for the failure of the negotiations.

Sept 28: Opposition leader Ariel Sharon visits Temple Mount, accompanied by hundreds of Israeli security forces, triggers the second or Al-Aqsa Intifada, which derails the peace process.

Dec: Israel rebuilds and fortifies the damaged security barrier around the Gaza Strip.

2001   Jan: George W. Bush sworn in as the forty-third President of the United States.

Feb 6: Ariel Sharon elected as Prime Minister of Israel.

After September 11, Sharon persuades the United States that their fight against terrorism is the same as the one Israel has long been facing on a daily basis. Many Israelis call for a wall of separation for the protection of its citizens from suicide attacks waged through infiltration from Palestinian territories.

2002   Arafat's headquarters in Ramallah surrounded by tanks, PNA offices destroyed or vandalized. Arafat refuses to leave his compound.

Planning for a barrier between the West Bank and Israel begins. Supreme Court of Israel rules on questions of hardship for Palestinians, affirms the legality of the barrier as a security measure.

June 24: George W. Bush calls for the creation of a Palestinian State to live side by side with Israel and introduces a "Roadmap" to peace, supported by the "Quartet" of United States, the European Union, Russia, and the UN.

2003   Jan: Sharon reelected on a platform opposing "unilateral disengagement."

June 4: Summit in Aqaba, Jordan, presided over by US President Bush.

Dec: Release of the Geneva Accord, a non-governmental organization (NGO) proposal addressing permanent status issues. Chief architects: Yossi Beilin and Yasser Abed Rabbo. Updated in 2009.[51]

2004   March: Hamas leader Sheikh Ahmed Yassin assassinated by Israeli helicopter gunship.

October: Arafat (*nom de guerre* "Abu Amar" 1929–2004) evacuated to Paris, dies of undisclosed illness. Successor: Mahmoud Abbas (aka Abu Mazen).

2005   Aug 15–Sept 5: Israel withdraws from the Gaza Strip and evacuates all settlements. 9,000 settlers are offered resettlement and compensation. Those who refuse are removed by force. Protest rallies in Jerusalem and Tel Aviv. Israel retains control of border crossings.

2006   Jan 4: Sharon suffers brain hemorrhage. (Dies in January 2014.)
                Ehud Olmert, member of Sharon's Kadimah party, takes over as
                Prime Minister.
                    Jan 25: Hamas soundly defeats Fatah in the first free elections
                in the Palestinian territories.
                    May: Olmert reelected. Kadimah's success is based on the
                broadly centrist appeal of the policy of unilateral
                disengagement, which *de facto* replaced the Oslo Process.
                    July 12–Aug14: Second Lebanon War. Following Hezbollah
                rocket attacks, IDF responds with massive air and naval strikes
                and a ground invasion of the Lebanon.
2007   June 13: Hamas seizes Fatah headquarters in Gaza.
                    Nov: Annapolis Conference.
2008   April: Khalid Meshal conveys Hamas willingness to enter into a
                long-term truce (*hudna*) with Israel, conditional on Israel's
                recognition of the Palestinian refugees' right to return.
                    Dec 27: Israel military incursion into Gaza. Hundreds of
                Palestinian civilians killed.
2009   Jan: Israel ends its Gaza incursion a day before the inauguration
                of Barak Obama as the forty-fourth President of the United
                States.
                    March 31: Netanyahu sworn in as Prime Minister of Israel.
2013–2014   United States attempt to restart the stalled peace process
                between Israel and the PNA.
2014   July–August: Following the abduction and killing of three
                Jewish teenagers and Israeli crackdown in West Bank, Hamas
                rockets rain on Israeli territory, provoking a severe military
                response, involving air strikes and a ground invasion.[52]
2015–2016   "Stabbing Intifada" begins in Jerusalem during High Holidays.
                Ongoing low-grade terror activity, mostly by young people
                using knives in random attacks. Ongoing revenge attacks
                on Palestinians by Hill Top Youths and acts of "price tag"
                violence.
2017   The number of Palestinian refugees and their descendants has
                grown from 750,000 in 1950 to more than 5 million in 2005.
                According to UNRWA, "Nearly one-third of the registered
                Palestine refugees, more than 1.5 million individuals, live in 58
                recognized Palestine refugee camps in Jordan, Lebanon, the
                Syrian Arab Republic, the Gaza Strip and the West Bank,
                including East Jerusalem."[53]
                    Dec 6: President Trump recognizes Jerusalem as the capital
                of Israel.

Notes

1. Dating according to Bickerman (1937).
2. Dating according to Bringmann (1983).
3. https://www.wikiart.org/en/jan-provoost/crucifixion (accessed December 5, 2017).
4. See Asali (2000 [1990]), 204.
5. Schölch (1986), 52.
6. Schölch (1986), 53. On Shaftesbury, see Mary Grey, "Preparing the Ground for Balfour – the contribution of Shaftesbury" at *Balfour Project* (blog), http://www.balfourproject.org/shaftesbury (originally posted May 4, 2012; accessed December 5, 2017).
7. See Carmel vol. I (1978), 16.
8. See Lask Abrahams (1978), Finn (1866).
9. See Latin Patriarchate of Jerusalem, http://en.lpj.org/ (accessed December 5, 2017).
10. See Economic Cooperation Foundation (ECF), "Appendix 3: Imperial Firman of February 1852, Concerning the Christian Holy Places," http://content.ecf.org.il/files/M00952_Firman1852English.pdf (accessed December 5, 2017).
11. See Russian Ecclesiastical Mission, Jerusalem, http://jerusalem-mission.org/history.html (accessed December 5, 2017).
12. Ecce Homo Jerusalem Pilgrim House, http://www.eccehomopilgrimhouse.com/(accessed December 5, 2017).
13. See Obenzinger (2010). On the American "holy land mania" see Obenzinger (1999).
14. See Eisler (2014).
15. See Schölch (1986), 255, and Finn 1980.
16. Royal Collection Trust, "Cairo to Constantinople," https://www.royalcollection.org.uk/collection/themes/exhibitions/cairo-to-constantinople-early-photographs-of-the-middle-east/the-queens-gallery-buckingham-palace/the-prince-of-wales#/(accessed December 5, 2017).
17. Büssow (2011), 554.
18. The Palestine Exploration Fund, http://www.pef.org.uk/profiles/major-general-sir-charles-william-wilson-1836-1905 (accessed December 5, 2017).
19. The Palestine Exploration Fund, http://www.pef.org.uk/quarterly/ (accessed December 5, 2017).
20. The Palestine Exploration Fund, http://www.pef.org.uk/profiles/general-sir-charles-warren-1840-1927 (accessed December 5, 2017).
21. Carmel vol. I (1978), 7–8.
22. See Schölch (2005).
23. Figures based on Schölch (1986), 25, who views the numbers as an underestimate.

24. The reason: Fear of creating a province that contained all Christian and Jewish holy places. See Schölch (1986), 22.
25. The Palestine Exploration Fund, http://www.pef.org.uk/profiles/lt-claude-r-conder-re-1848-1910 (accessed December 5, 2017).
26. See Tower of David Museum of the History of Jerusalem, http://www.tod.org.il/en/exhibitions/model-of-jerusalem-in-the-19th-century/ (accessed December 5, 2017).
27. Schölch (1986), 256.
28. Institute for Palestine Studies, "Before Their Diaspora," http://btd.palestine-studies.org/content/name-god-let-palestine-be-left-alone-1-0/ (accessed December 5, 2017).
29. German Society for the Exploration of Palestine, http://www.palaestina-verein.de/wp/wordpress/?lang=en (accessed December 5, 2017).
30. Based on Schölch (1986), 42–44.
31. The American Colony Hotel, Jerusalem, http://www.americancolony.com/history/about-the-colony.htm (accessed December 5, 2017) and Library of Congress, "The American Colony in Jerusalem," https://www.loc.gov/exhibits/americancolony/amcolony-jerusalem.html (accessed December 5, 2017).
32. See Büssow (2011), 447.
33. Carmel vol. II (1983): Reports in *Die Warte des Tempels* from Aug 11 1898, Dec 1 1898, Dec 8 1898, Dec 22 1898, and Jan 5 1898. The weekly bulletin appeared in Germany and was not subject to Turkish censorship. The German settlers often discussed the poor state of repair of the roads and other installations and complained about the general indifference of the Syrian administration.
34. See Lion (2011).
35. Details such as location and circumstances of surrender are disputed. See Jawhariyah (2014), 100–103.
36. See Grossi, Milligan, and Maddelow (2011). On Charles Crane's pro-Arab and anti-Jewish attitudes see Brecher (1988).
37. On the events and their implications see Cohen (2015).
38. See ECF, https://ecf.org.il/issues/issue/955 (accessed December 5, 2017).
39. Cf. Stanger (1988).
40. See UNSECO, Records of the General Conference, Eighteenth Session, 60, http://unesdoc.unesco.org/images/0011/001140/114040E.pdf (accessed December 5, 2017).
41. See Pedahzur and Perliger (2009), 39ff.
42. See Pedahzur and Perliger (2009), 62–65.
43. See Weisman (1983).
44. See Council on Foreign Relations, http://www.cfr.org/israel/kach-kahane-chai-israel-extremists/p9178 (accessed December 5, 2017), and cf. Pedahzur and Perliger (2009), 74–97.
45. See Friedman (1989).

46. See "The Madrid Peace Conference." *Journal of Palestine Studies* 21.2 (1992): 117–149 (accessed December 5, 2017).
47. See the text of the DOP at http://avalon.law.yale.edu/20th_century/isrplo.asp (accessed December 5, 2017).
48. See Pedahzur and Perliger (2009), 69–71.
49. For text and analysis of the sermon on *jihad* for Jerusalem see Musallam (1996), 21–36.
50. See Greenberg (1995), Ephron (2016).
51. Geneva Initiative, http://www.geneva-accord.org/ (accessed December 5, 2017).
52. United Nations Relief and Works Agency (UNRWA), https://www.unrwa.org/2014-gaza-conflict (accessed December 5, 2017).
53. See UNRWA, https://www.unrwa.org/palestine-refugees (accessed December 5, 2017).

References

Abu El-Haj, Nadia. *Facts on the Ground: Archaeological Practice and Territorial Self-Fashioning in Israeli Society*. Chicago, Illinois: The University of Chicago Press, 2001.

Ahituv, Shmuel. *Canaanite Toponyms in Ancient Egyptian Documents*. Jerusalem: Magnes Press, 1984.

Ajami, Fouad. *The Dream Palace of the Arabs: A Generation's Odyssey*. New York: Vintage Books, 1999.

al-Maqdisi, Abu 'Abd Allah Muhammad. *The Best Divisions for Knowledge of the Regions*. Reading, England: Garnet, 2001.

Ali, Kecia. *The Lives of Muhammad*. Cambridge, Massachusetts: Harvard University Press, 2014.

Al Jazeera. "PLO-History of a Revolution." 2009. http://www.aljazeera.com/programmes/plohistoryofrevolution/plohistoryofarevolution.html (accessed December 14, 2017).

Al-Salim, Farid. *Palestine and the Decline of the Ottoman Empire: Modernisation and the Path to Palestine Statehood*. London: I.B. Tauris, 2015.

Alston, Richard, Onno van Nijf, and Christina G. Williamson. *Cults, Creeds and Identities in the Greek City after the Classical Age*. Leuven, Belgium: Peeters, 2013.

Amirav, Mosheh. *Jerusalem Syndrome: The Palestinian-Israeli Battle for the Holy City*. Brighton, England: Sussex Academic Press, 2009.

Anderson, Gary A., Michael E. Stone, and Johannes Tromp. *Literature on Adam and Eve: Collected Essays*. Leiden: Brill, 2000.

Antonius, George. *The Arab Awakening: The Story of the Arab National Movement.* Safety Harbor, Florida: Simon, 2001 [1939].

Arav, Rami. *Cities through the Looking Glass: Essays on the History and Archaeology of Biblical Urbanism.* Winona Lake, Indiana: Eisenbrauns, 2008.

Armstrong, Karen. *Jerusalem: One City. Three Faiths.* New York: Ballantine, 1997.

Arnon, Adar. "The Quarters of Jerusalem in the Ottoman Period." *Middle Eastern Studies* 28.1 (1992): 1–65.

Asali, Kamil. "Jerusalem in History: Notes on the Origins of the City and Its Tradition of Tolerance." *Arab Studies Quarterly* 16.4 (1994): 37–45.

Asali, Kamil, ed. *Jerusalem in History.* Brooklyn, New York: Olive Branch Press, 2000 [1990].

Assmann, Jan. *Moses the Egyptian. The Memory of Egypt in Western Monotheism.* Cambridge, Massachusetts: Harvard University Press, 1999.

Auld, Sylvia, and Robert Hillenbrand. *Ottoman Jerusalem: The Living City, 1517–1917.* London: Altajir World of Islam Trust, 2000.

Aulén, Gustaf. *Christus Victor: An Historical Study of the Three Main Types of the Idea of the Atonement.* London: SPCK, 1931.

Avi-Yonah, Michael. *The Jews of Palestine: A Political History from the Bar Kokhba War to the Arab Conquest.* Oxford: Blackwell, 1976.

Avni, Gideon. "The Persian Conquest of Jerusalem (614 c.e.) – an Archaeological Assessment." *Bulletin of the American Schools of Oriental Research* 357 (2010): 35–48.

Azarya, Victor. *The Armenian Quarter of Jerusalem.* Berkeley: University of California Press, 1984.

Baladhuri, Ahmad ibn Yahyá, Philip K. Hitti, and Francis Clark Murgotten. *The Origins of the Islamic State, Being a Translation from the Arabic, Accompanied with Annotations, Geographic and Historic Notes of the Kitâb Futûh Al-Buldân of Al-Imâm Abu-l 'Abu-l, Ahmad Ibn-Jâbir Al-Balâdhuri.* Studies in History, Economics and Public Law, 163–163a. 2 vols. New York: AMS Press, 1968.

Barakat, Rena. "Thawrat Al-Buraq in British Mandate Palestine: Jerusalem, Mass Mobilization and Colonial Politics, 1928–1930." PhD Dissertation, University of Chicago, 2007.

Bashear, Suliman. "Apocalyptic and Other Materials on Early Muslim–Byzantine Wars: A Review of Arabic Sources." *Journal of the Royal Asiatic Society* 1.2 (1991): 173–207.

Belayche, Nicole. "Forget Jerusalem – the Pagan Transformation of Jerusalem into Aelia-Capitolina from the Second Century to the Fourth Century of the Common Era." *Revue Des Etudes Juives* 158.3–4 (1999): 287–348.

Belayche, Nicole. *Iudaea-Palaestina: The Pagan Cults in Roman Palestine (Second to Fourth Century).* Religion der römischen Provinzen. Tübingen, Germany: Mohr Siebeck, 2001.

Bellah, Robert N., and Hans Joas. *The Axial Age and Its Consequences*. Cambridge, Massachusetts: Belknap Press of Harvard University Press, 2012.

Ben-Ami, Shlomo. *Scars of War, Wounds of Peace: The Israeli-Arab Tragedy*. Oxford: Oxford University Press, 2006.

Ben-Arieh, Yehoshua. *The Rediscovery of the Holy Land in the Nineteenth Century*. 2nd ed. Jerusalem: Magnes Press, Hebrew University/Israel Exploration Society, 1983.

Ben-Arieh, Yehoshua. *Jerusalem in the 19th Century, the Old City*. Jerusalem: Yad Izhak Ben-Zvi Institute, 1984.

Berlin, Andrea M. "Jewish Life before the Revolt: The Archaeological Evidence." *Journal for the Study of Judaism in the Persian, Hellenistic, and Roman Period* 36.4 (2005): 417–470.

Berthelot, Katell, Joseph E. David, and Marc Hirshman, eds. *The Gift of the Land and the Fate of the Canaanites in Jewish Thought*. Oxford: Oxford University Press, 2014.

Bickerman, E. J. *Der Gott der Makkabäer. Untersuchungen über Sinn und Ursprung der makkabäischen Erhebung* [The God of the Maccabees: Studies on the Meaning and Origin of the Maccabean Revolt]. Berlin: Schocken Verlag, 1937.

Bloch, René. "Di Neglecti. La Politique Augustéenne d'Hérode Le Grand" [Di Neglecti: The Augustan Politics of Herod the Great]. *Revue de l'histoire des religions (RHR)* (2006): 123–147.

Blum, Erhard. *Die Komposition der Vätergeschichte* [The Composition of the Patriarchal Narrative]. Neukirchen-Vluyn, Germany: Neukirchener Verlag, 1984.

Boas, Adrian J. *Crusader Archaeology: The Material Culture of the Latin East*. London: Routledge, 1999.

Boas, Adrian J. *Jerusalem in the Time of the Crusades: Society, Landscape, and Art in the Holy City under Frankish Rule*. London: Routledge, 2001.

Boehm, Barbara Drake, and Melanie Holcomb, eds. *Jerusalem 1000–1400. Every People under Heaven*. New York: The Metropolitan Museum of Art, 2016.

Boogert, Maurits H. van den. *The Capitulations and the Ottoman Legal System: Qadis, Consuls, and Beraths in the 18th Century*. Leiden: Brill, 2005.

Boustan, Ra'anan S., Martha Himmelfarb, and Peter Schäfer. *Hekhalot Literature in Context: Between Byzantium and Babylonia*. Tübingen, Germany: Mohr Siebeck, 2013.

Bowden, William, Adam Gutteridge, and Carlos Machado. *Social and Political Life in Late Antiquity*. Leiden: Brill, 2006.

Bowersock, G. W., John Leonard Clive, and Stephen Richards Graubard. *Edward Gibbon and the Decline and Fall of the Roman Empire*. Cambridge, Massachusetts: Harvard University Press, 1977.

Brecher, F. W. "Charles R. Crane's Crusade for the Arabs, 1919–39." *Middle Eastern Studies* 24.1 (1988): 42–55.

Bringmann, Klaus. *Hellenistische Reform und Religionsverfolgung in Judäa: Eine Untersuchung zur jüdisch-hellenistischen Geschichte (175–163 v. Chr.)* [*Hellenistic Reform and Religious Persecution in Judea: A Study on Jewish-Hellenistic History (175–163 BC)*]. Abhandlungen der Akademie der Wissenschaften in Göttingen. Philologisch-Historische Klasse. Göttingen, Germany: Vandenhoeck & Ruprecht, 1983.

Brown, Peter. *The Rise of Western Christendom: Triumph and Diversity, A.D. 200–1000.* The Making of Europe. 2nd ed. Oxford: Blackwell, 2003.

Brown, Peter. *The Rise of Western Christendom Triumph and Diversity, A.D. 200–1000.* 10th anniversary rev. ed. Chichester, England: Wiley-Blackwell, 2013.

Brueggemann, Walter. "Old Testament Covenant: A Survey of Current Opinions (Book Review)." *Journal of the American Academy of Religion* 42 (1974): 553–554.

Burgoyne, Michael Hamilton. *Mamluk Jerusalem: An Architectural Study.* Published on behalf of the British School of Archaeology in Jerusalem by World of Islam Festival Trust, 1987.

Busine, Aude. "From Stones to Myth: Temple Destruction and Civic Identity in the Late Antique Roman East." *Journal of Late Antiquity* 6.2 (2013): 325–346.

Busse, Heribert. "Zur Geschichte und Deutung der frühislamischen Harambauten in Jerusalem" [On the History and Interpretation of the Early Islamic Haram Buildings in Jerusalem]. *Zeitschrift des Deutschen Palästina-Vereins* 107 (1991): 144–154.

Busse, Heribert, and Georg Kretschmar. *Jerusalemer Heiligtumstraditionen in alt-kirchlicher und frühislamischer Zeit* [Jerusalem Holiness Traditions in Early Christian and Early Muslim Times]. Wiesbaden, Germany: Otto Harrassowitz, 1987.

Büssow, Johann. *Hamidian Palestine: Politics and Society in the District of Jerusalem 1872–1908.* Leiden: Brill, 2011.

Cameron, Averil. *Christianity and the Rhetoric of Empire: The Development of Christian Discourse.* Sather Classical Lectures. Berkeley: University of California Press, 1991.

Cameron, Averil. "Byzantines and Jews: Some Recent Work on Early Byzantium." *Byzantine and Modern Greek Studies* 20 (1996): 249–274.

Cameron, Averil. "Blaming the Jews: The Seventh-Century Invasions of Palestine in Context." *Travaux et Mémoires* 14 (2002): 57–78.

Cameron, Averil, and Stuart George Hall, (eds.). *Eusebius Pamphilii. Life of Constantine.* Oxford: Clarendon Press, 1999.

Campos, Michelle U. *Ottoman Brothers: Muslims, Christians, and Jews in Early Twentieth-Century Palestine.* Stanford, California: Stanford University Press, 2011.

Carmel, Alex. *Palästina-Chronik: 1883 bis 1914: Deutsche Zeitungsberichte von der ersten jüdischen Einwanderungswelle bis zum Ersten Weltkrieg* [Palestine

Chronicle: 1883 to 1914: German News Reports on the First Wave of Jewish Immigration to the First World War]. 2 vols. Ulm, Germany: Vaas, 1978–1983.

Carroll, James. *Jerusalem, Jerusalem: How the Ancient City Ignited the Modern World*. Boston, Massachusetts: Houghton Mifflin Harcourt, 2011.

Christian, William A. *Local Religion in Sixteenth-Century Spain*. Princeton, New Jersey: Princeton University Press, 1981.

Cohen, Amnon. "On the Realities of the *Millet* System: Jerusalem in the Sixteenth Century." In Benjamin Braude and Bernard Lewis (eds.), *Christians and Jews in the Ottoman Empire. The Functioning of a Plural Society. Vol. 2: The Arabic-Speaking Lands*. New York: Holmes & Meier, 1982, 7–18.

Cohen, Hillel. *The Rise and Fall of Arab Jerusalem: Politics and the City since 1967*. Routledge Studies on the Arab-Israeli Conflict. Abingdon, England: Routledge, 2011.

Cohen, Hillel. *Year Zero of the Arab-Israeli Conflict 1929*. The Schusterman Series in Israel Studies. Ed. Watzman, Haim. Waltham, Massachusetts: Brandeis University Press, 2015.

Cohen, Shaye J.D. *The Beginnings of Jewishness: Boundaries, Varieties, Uncertainties*. Berkeley: University of California Press, 1999.

Collins, John J. *The Oxford Handbook of Apocalyptic Literature*. New York: Oxford University Press, 2014.

Congar, Yves. *After Nine Hundred Years: The Background of the Schism between the Eastern and Western Churches*. New York: Fordham University Press, 1959.

Constable, Giles. *Crusaders and Crusading in the Twelfth Century*. Farnham, England: Ashgate, 2008.

Conybeare, Frederick C. "Antiochus Strategos' Account of the Sack of Jerusalem in A.D. 614." *The English Historical Review* 25.99 (1910): 502–517.

Cook, David. *Studies in Muslim Apocalyptic*. Princeton, New Jersey: Darwin Press, 2002.

Dauphin, Claudine. *La Palestine Byzantine: Peuplement et populations* [Byzantine Palestine: Settlement and Populations] *Oxford: Archaeopress*, 1998.

Davies, Philip R. *In Search of "Ancient Israel."* Journal for the Study of the Old Testament Supplement Series. Sheffield, England: JSOT Press, 1992.

Delegation, Palestine Arab. *The Holy Land: The Moslem-Christian Case Against Zionist Aggression: Official Statement*. [The Delegation], 1922.

Dellapergola, Sergio. "Jerusalem's Population, 1995–2020: Demography, Multiculturalism and Urban Policies." *European Journal of Population* 17.2 (2001): 165–199.

Demandt, Alexander. *Die Spätantike: Römische Geschichte von Diocletian bis Justinian, 284-565 n. Chr.* [Late Antiquity: Roman History from Diocletian to Justinian, 284–565 CE]. Munich: C.H. Beck, 1989.

Dever, William G. *Who Were the Early Israelites, and Where Did They Come From?* Grand Rapids, Michigan: William B. Eerdmans, 2003.

Devji, Faisal. *Landscapes of the Jihad: Militancy, Morality, Modernity.* London: Hearst & Co., 2017.

Donner, Fred M. *The Early Islamic Conquests.* Ed. American Council of Learned Societies. Princeton, New Jersey: Princeton University Press, 1981.

Donner, Fred M. *The Expansion of the Early Islamic State.* Farnham, England: Ashgate/Variorum, 2008.

Donner, Fred M. "The Formation of the Islamic State." *Journal of the American Oriental Society* 106.2 (1986): 283–296.

Donner, Herbert. *Pilgerfahrt ins Heilige Land: Die ältesten Berichte christl. Palästinapilger (4.-7. Jh.).* Stuttgart: Verlag Katholisches Bibelwerk, 1979.

Donner, Herbert. *The Mosaic Map of Madaba: An Introductory Guide.* Kampen, Netherlands: Kok Pharos, 1992.

Drijvers, Jan Willem. *Helena Augusta: The Mother of Constantine the Great and the Legend of Her Finding of the True Cross.* Leiden: Brill, 1992.

Dumper, Michael. *The Politics of Jerusalem Since 1967.* New York: Columbia University Press, 1997.

Eckhardt, Benedikt. *Jewish Identity and Politics between the Maccabees and Bar Kokhba: Groups, Normativity, and Rituals.* Leiden: Brill, 2012.

Eddé, Anne-Marie. *Saladin.* Ed. Todd, Jane Marie. Cambridge, Massachusetts: Belknap Press of Harvard University Press, 2011.

Efrat, Elisha. *Geography and Politics in Israel since 1967.* London: Frank Cass, 1988.

Ehrenkreutz, Andrew S. *Saladin.* 1st ed. Albany: State University of New York Press, 1972.

Eisler, Jacob. "Das Syrische Waisenhaus in Jerusalem," online at Württembergische Kirchengeschichte, https://www.wkgo.de/institutionen/syrisches-waisenhaus-jerusalem. Last updated December 17, 2014 (accessed December 5, 2017).

Elsner, Jaś. "The Itinerarium Burdigalense: Politics and Salvation in the Geography of Constantine's Empire." *Journal of Roman Studies* 90 (2000): 181–195.

Ephron, Dan. *Killing a King: The Assassination of Yitzhak Rabin and the Remaking of Israel.* New York: W. W. Norton, 2016.

Eynikel, Erik. *The Reform of King Josiah and the Composition of the Deuteronomistic History.* Leiden: Brill, 1996.

Fabri, Felix, and Aubrey Stewart. *Felix Fabri (circa 1480–1483 A.D.).* London: Palestine Pilgrims' Text Society, 1892.

Fenn, Richard K. *Key Thinkers in the Sociology of Religion.* London: Continuum, 2009.

Fetvacı, Emine. *Picturing History at the Ottoman Court.* Bloomington: Indiana University Press, 2013.

Fine, Steven. *Art and Judaism in the Greco-Roman World: Toward a New Jewish Archaeology.* Cambridge: Cambridge University Press, 2010.

Finkel, Irving L. *The Cyrus Cylinder: The King of Persia's Proclamation from Ancient Babylon.* London: I.B. Tauris, 2013.

Finkelstein, Israel, and Amihay Mazar. *The Quest for the Historical Israel: Debating Archaeology and the History of Early Israel: Invited Lectures Delivered at the Sixth Biennial Colloquium of the International Institute for Secular Humanistic Judaism, Detroit, October 2005.* Eds. Mazar, Amihay, Brian B. Schmidt, and Colloquium International Institute for Secular Humanistic Judaism. Atlanta, Georgia: Society of Biblical Literature, 2007.

Finkelstein, Israel, and Neil Asher Silberman. *David and Solomon: In Search of the Bible's Sacred Kings and the Roots of the Western Tradition.* New York: Free Press, 2006.

Finn, Elizabeth Anne. *Home in the Holy Land: A Tale Illustrating Customs and Incidents in Modern Jerusalem.* London: James Nisbet, 1866.

Finn, James. *A View from Jerusalem, 1849–1858: The Consular Diary of James and Elizabeth Anne Finn.* Eds. Finn, Elizabeth Anne McCaul, and Arnold Blumberg. Plainsboro, New Jersey: Associated University Presses, 1980.

Fischbach, Michael R. *Records of Dispossession: Palestinian Refugee Property and the Arab–Israeli Conflict.* New York: Columbia University Press, 2003.

Fowden, Garth. *Empire to Commonwealth: Consequences of Monotheism in Late Antiquity.* Princeton, New Jersey: Princeton University Press, 1993.

Frakes, Robert M., Elizabeth DePalma Digeser, and Justin Stephens. *The Rhetoric of Power in Late Antiquity: Religion and Politics in Byzantium, Europe and the Early Islamic World.* New York: Palgrave Macmillan, 2010.

Frankfurter, David. *Pilgrimage and Holy Space in Late Antique Egypt.* Leiden: Brill, 1998.

Frankfurter, David. "Syncretism and the Holy Man in Late Antique Egypt." *Journal of Early Christian Studies* 11.3 (2003): 339–385.

Fredriksen, Paula. *Augustine and the Jews: A Christian Defense of Jews and Judaism.* 1st ed. New York: Doubleday, 2008.

Freud, Sigmund. *The Future of an Illusion.* Ed. Strachey, James. New York: W. W. Norton, 1975 [1927].

Friedland, Roger, and Richard Hecht. *To Rule Jerusalem.* Berkeley: University of California Press, 2000.

Friedman, Thomas L. "Baker, in a Middle East Blueprint, Asks Israel to Reach Out to Arabs." *New York Times,* May 23, 1989. Online at http://www.nytimes.com/1989/05/23/world/baker-in-a-middle-east-blueprint-asks-israel-to-reach-out-to-arabs.html (accessed December 5, 2017).

Fromherz, Allen James. *The Almohads: The Rise of an Islamic Empire.* New York: Palgrave Macmillan, 2010.

Furseth, Inger. *An Introduction to the Sociology of Religion: Classical and Contemporary Perspectives.* Ed. Repstad, Pål. Farnham, England: Ashgate, 2006.

Fustel de Coulanges, Numa Denis. *The Ancient City: A Study on the Religion, Laws, and Institutions of Greece and Rome.* Baltimore, Maryland: Johns Hopkins University Press, 1980 [1864].

Gardner, Gregg. "Jewish Leadership and Hellenistic Civic Benefaction in the Second Century B.C.E." *Journal of Biblical Literature* 126.2 (2007): 327–343.

Gardner, Gregg, and Kevin Lee Osterloh. *Antiquity in Antiquity: Jewish and Christian Pasts in the Greco-Roman World*. Tübingen, Germany: Mohr Siebeck, 2008.

Geary, Patrick J. *Furta Sacra: Thefts of Relics in the Central Middle Ages*. Ed. American Council of Learned Societies. Rev. ed. Princeton, New Jersey: Princeton University Press, 1990.

Gerber, Haim. *Ottoman Rule in Jerusalem, 1890–1914*. Berlin: K. Schwarz, 1985.

Gibbon, Edward. *The History of the Decline and Fall of the Roman Empire*. London: George Bell & Son, 1877.

Gil, Moshe. *A History of Palestine, 634–1099*. Cambridge: Cambridge University Press, 1992.

Goldschmidt, Arthur. "*A Concise History of the Middle East*." 6th ed. Boulder, Colorado: Westview Press, 1999.

Goodman, Martin. *Rome and Jerusalem: The Clash of Ancient Civilizations*. New York: Alfred A. Knopf, 2007.

Gorenberg, Gershom. *The End of Days*. New York, NY: Free Press, 2000.

Grabar, Oleg, Mohammad al-Asad, Abeer Audeh, and Saïd Nuseibeh. *The Shape of the Holy: Early Islamic Jerusalem*. Princeton, New Jersey: Princeton University Press, 1996.

Grayson, Albert Kirk, and Jamie R. Novotny. *The Royal Inscriptions of Sennacherib, King of Assyria (704–681 BC) Part 1*. Winona Lake, Indiana: Eisenbrauns, 2012.

Greenberg, Joel. "Israeli Police Question 2 Rabbis in Rabin Assassination." *New York Times*, November 27, 1995. Online at http://www.nytimes.com/1995/11/27/world/israeli-police-question-2-rabbis-in-rabin-assassination.html (accessed December 5, 2017).

Grossi, Ken, Maren Milligan, and Ted Maddelow. "Restoring Lost Voices of Self-Determination" (2011). Online at Oberlin College, King-Crane Commission Digital Collection, http://www2.oberlin.edu/library/digital/king-crane/intro.html (accessed December 5, 2017).

Gruen, Erich S. *Cultural Identity in the Ancient Mediterranean*. Los Angeles: Getty Research Institute, 2011.

Günther, Linda-Marie. *Herodes und Rom* [Herod and Rome]. Stuttgart: Steiner, 2007.

Haverkamp, Alfred. *Juden und Christen zur Zeit der Kreuzzüge* [Jews and Christians during the Crusades]. Sigmaringen, Germany: J. Thorbecke, 1999.

Hengel, Martin. *Judaism and Hellenism: Studies in Their Encounter in Palestine During the Early Hellenistic Period*. Philadelphia: Fortress Press, 1981.

Heszer, Catherine. "Torah als 'Gesetz'? Überlegungen zum Torahverständnis im antiken Judentum" [Torah as 'Law.' Considerations on the Conception of Torah in Ancient Judaism.] In Rüterswörden, Udo, Jan Dochhorn, and

Catherine Hezser (eds.), *Ist Die Tora Gesetz?: Zum Gesetzesverständnis im Alten Testament, Frühjudentum Und Neuen Testament*. Göttingen, Germany: Vandenhoeck & Ruprecht, 2017, 119–140.

Hillenbrand, Carole. *The Crusades: Islamic Perspectives*. Chicago, Illinois: Fitzroy Dearborn, 1999.

Hinds, Kathryn. *The City*. New York: Benchmark Books, 2004.

Hirsch, Moshe, Deborah Housen-Couriel, and Ruth Eschelbacher Lapidoth. *Whither Jerusalem? Proposals and Positions Concerning the Future of Jerusalem*. Eds. Housen-Couriel, Deborah, Ruth Eschelbacher Lapidoth, and Mekhon Yerushalayim le-hekker Yisra'el. The Hague: M. Nijhoff, 1995.

Hoffmann, Christhard, Werner Bergmann, and Helmut Walser Smith. *Exclusionary Violence: Antisemitic Riots in Modern German History*. Ann Arbor: University of Michigan Press, 2002.

Holum, Kenneth G. *Theodosian Empresses: Women and Imperial Dominion in Late Antiquity*. Berkeley: University of California Press, 1982.

Hourani, Albert Habib. *Arabic Thought in the Liberal Age, 1798–1939. Issued under the Auspices of the Royal Institute of International Affairs*. London: Oxford University Press, 1962.

Housley, Norman. *Contesting the Crusades*. Oxford: Blackwell, 2006.

Hoyland, Robert G. *Seeing Islam as Others Saw It: A Survey and Evaluation of Christian, Jewish, and Zoroastrian Writings on Early Islam*. Princeton, New Jersey: Darwin Press, 1997.

Hughes, Aaron W. *Abrahamic Religions: On the Uses and Abuses of History*. Oxford: Oxford University Press, 2012.

Hull, John M. *Hellenistic Magic and the Synoptic Tradition*. London: SCM Press, 1974.

Hunt, E. D. *Holy Land Pilgrimage in the Later Roman Empire, AD 312–460*. Oxford: Oxford University Press, 1982.

Inbari, Motti. *Jewish Fundamentalism and the Temple Mount: Who Will Build the Third Temple?* Albany, New York: State University of New York Press, 2009.

Inbari, Motti. *Jewish Radical Ultra-Orthodoxy Confronts Modernity, Zionism and Women's Equality*. Cambridge: Cambridge University Press, 2016.

Jacobs, Andrew S. *Remains of the Jews: The Holy Land and Christian Empire in Late Antiquity*. Stanford, California: Stanford University Press, 2004.

Jacobson, Abigail. *From Empire to Empire: Jerusalem between Ottoman and British Rule*. Space, Place, and Society. 1st ed. Syracuse, New York: Syracuse University Press, 2011.

James, Liz. *Empresses and Power in Early Byzantium*. London: Leicester University Press, 2001.

Jawhariyah, Wasif. *The Storyteller of Jerusalem: The Life and Times of Wasif Jawhariyyeh, 1904–1948*. Eds. Tamari, Salim, Issam Nassar, and Nada Elzeer. Northampton, Massachusetts: Olive Branch Press, 2014.

Jones, A. H. M. *The Later Roman Empire, 284–602: A Social, Economic and Administrative Survey*. Ed. Rogers, D. Spotswood Collection: Baltimore, Maryland: Johns Hopkins University Press, 1986.

Juergensmeyer, Mark. *Terror in the Mind of God: The Global Rise of Religious Violence*. Berkeley: University of California Press, 2000.

Kaegi, Walter Emil. *Heraclius, Emperor of Byzantium*. Cambridge: Cambridge University Press, 2003.

Kaplony, Andreas. *The Ḥaram of Jerusalem, 324–1099: Temple, Friday Mosque, Area of Spiritual Power*. Freiburger Islamstudien. Stuttgart: Franz Steiner Verlag, 2002.

Kark, Ruth, and Michal Oren-Nordheim. *Jerusalem and Its Environs: Quarter, Neighborhoods, Villages, 1800–1948*. Israel Studies in Historical Geography. Detroit, Michigan: Wayne State University Press, 2001.

Karlinsky, Nahum. "Jaffa and Tel Aviv before 1948 – The Underground Story." In Maoz Azaryahu and S. Ilan Troen (eds.), *Tel-Aviv at 100: Myths, Memories and Realities*. Bloomington: Indiana University Press, 2012, 138–164.

Kasher, Aryeh, and Eliezer Witztum. *King Herod: A Persecuted Persecutor: A Case Study in Psychohistory and Psychobiography*. Studia Judaica. Berlin: De Gruyter, 2007.

Kasinitz, Philip. *Metropolis: Center and Symbol of Our Times*. New York: New York University Press, 1995.

Katz, Kimberly. *Jordanian Jerusalem: Holy Places and National Spaces*. Gainesville: University of Press of Florida, 2005.

Kelner, Shaul. *Tours That Bind: Diaspora, Pilgrimage, and Israeli Birthright Tourism*. New York: New York University Press, 2010.

Kern, Karen M. *Imperial Citizen: Marriage and Citizenship in the Ottoman Frontier Provinces of Iraq*. 1st ed. Syracuse, New York: Syracuse University Press, 2011.

Khalaf, Issa. *Politics in Palestine: Arab Factionalism and Social Disintegration, 1939–1948*. Albany: State University of New York Press, 1991.

Khalidi, Rashid. *The Iron Cage: The Story of the Palestinian Struggle for Statehood*. Boston, Massachusetts: Beacon Press, 2006.

Kister, M. J. "Sanctity Joint and Divided: On Holy Places in the Islamic Tradition." *Jerusalem Studies in Arabic and Islam* 20 (1996): 18–65.

Klawans, Jonathan. *Josephus and the Theologies of Ancient Judaism*. Oxford: Oxford University Press, 2013.

Klein, Menachem. *Jerusalem: The Contested City*. New York: New York University Press, 2001.

Klein, Menachem. *The Jerusalem Problem: The Struggle for Permanent Status*. Gainesville: University Press of Florida, 2003.

Klein, Menachem. "Jerusalem as an Israeli Problem – a Review of Forty Years of Israeli Rule over Arab Jerusalem." *Israel Studies* 13.2 (2008): 54–72.

Klein, Menachem. "From the Margins to the Mainstream: Impact of Extreme Religious Discourse in Israel." *Palestine – Israel Journal of Politics, Economics, and Culture* 16.3 (2010): 125–128.

Krämer, Gudrun. *A History of Palestine: From the Ottoman Conquest to the Founding of the State of Israel.* Princeton, New Jersey: Princeton University Press, 2008.

Kretzenbacher, Leopold. *Kreuzholzlegenden zwischen Byzanz und dem Abendlande: Byzantinisch-Griechische Kreuzholzlegenden vor und um Basileios Herakleios und ihr Fortleben im lateinischen Westen bis zum Zweiten Vaticanum* [Legends of the Holy Wood between Byzantium and the Occident: Byzantine-Greek Legends of the Holy Wood before and around Emperor Heraclius and their Reception in the Latin West down to the Second Vatican Council] Sitzungsberichte, Bayerische Akademie der Wissenschaften, Philosophisch-Historische Klasse. Munich: Verlag der Bayerischen Akademie der Wissenschaften: C.H. Beck, 1995.

Krey, August C. *The First Crusade: The Accounts of Eye-Witnesses and Participants.* Gloucester, Massachusetts: P. Smith, 1958 [1921].

Kronish, Ron. "The Future of Interreligious Dialogue in Israel." *Huffington Post*, August 12, 2015, https://www.huffingtonpost.com/ron-kronish/the-future-of-interreligi_b_8737076.html (accessed December 14, 2017).

Langer, Ruth, and Steven Fine. *Liturgy in the Life of the Synagogue: Studies in the History of Jewish Prayer.* Winona Lake, Indiana: Eisenbrauns, 2005.

Lapidoth, Ruth Eschelbacher, and Moshe Hirsch. *The Jerusalem Question and Its Resolution: Selected Documents.* Dordrecht, Netherlands: Kluwer Academic, 1994.

Lask Abrahams, Beth-Zion. "James Finn: Her Britannic Majesty's Consul at Jerusalem between 1846 and 1863." *Transactions & Miscellanies* (Jewish Historical Society of England) 27 (1978): 40–50.

Leder, Stefan. *Story-Telling in the Framework of Non-Fictional Arabic Literature.* Wiesbaden, Germany: Harrassowitz, 1998.

Lenski, Noel Emmanuel. *The Cambridge Companion to the Age of Constantine.* Cambridge: Cambridge University Press, 2006.

Leoni, Giacomo. "Inheritance and Legacy: A Phenomenological Exploration." PhD Dissertation, Boston University, 2016.

Le Strange, Guy. *Diary of a Journey through Syria and Palestine: By Nasir-I-Khusrau, in 1047 A.D.* Translated by Guy Le Strange. London: Palestine Pilgrims' Text Society, 1888.

Levenson, Jon Douglas. *Creation and the Persistence of Evil: The Jewish Drama of Divine Omnipotence.* Princeton, New Jersey: Princeton University Press, 1994.

Levine, Lee I. *The Synagogue in Late Antiquity.* Philadelphia, Pennsylvania: American Schools of Oriental Research, 1987.

Levine, Lee I. *Visual Judaism in Late Antiquity: Historical Contexts of Jewish Art.* New Haven, Connecticut: Yale University Press, 2012.

Levy-Rubin, Milka. *Non-Muslims in the Early Islamic Empire: From Surrender to Coexistence*. Cambridge: Cambridge University Press, 2011.

Liebeschuetz, J. H. W. G. *The Decline and Fall of the Roman City*. Oxford: Oxford University Press, 2001.

Lion, Siegfried G. "Über die Einweihung der Erlöserkirche in Jerusalem 1898" [On the Dedication of the Church of the Redeemer in Jerusalem in 1898] (2011). Online at Deutsches Historisches Museum, Lebendiges Museum Online, https://www.dhm.de/lemo/zeitzeugen/dr-siegfried-g-lion-ueber-die-einweihung-der-erloeserkirche-in-jerusalem-1898.html (accessed December 5, 2017).

Lippold, Adolf. *Theodosius der Grosse und seine Zeit* [Theodosius the Great and his Time]. Stuttgart: W. Kohlhammer, 1968.

Little, Donald P. "The Significance of the *Haram* Documents for the Study of Medieval Islamic History." *Der Islam* 57 (1980): 189–217.

Little, Donald P. "Mujīr Al-Dīn Al-'ulaymī's Vision of Jerusalem in the Ninth/ Fifteenth Century." *Journal of the American Oriental Society* 115.2 (1995): 237–247.

Littmann, Enno. *Semitic Inscriptions*. New York: The Century Co., 1904.

Liverani, Mario. *Israel's History and the History of Israel*. London: Equinox, 2005.

Lufti, Huda. *Al-Quds al-Mamlukiyya: A History of Mamluk Jerusalem Based on the Haram Documents*. Berlin: K. Schwarz, 1985.

Lundquist, John M. *The Temple of Jerusalem: Past, Present, and Future*. Westport, Connecticut: Praeger, 2007.

Maalouf, Amin. *The Crusades through Arab Eyes*. New York: Schocken Books, 1984.

Margry, P. J. *Shrines and Pilgrimage in the Modern World: New Itineraries into the Sacred*. Amsterdam: Amsterdam University Press, 2008.

McBride, S. Dean, John T. Strong, and Steven Shawn Tuell. *Constituting the Community: Studies on the Polity of Ancient Israel in Honor of S. Dean Mcbride, Jr*. Winona Lake, Indiana: Eisenbrauns, 2005.

McCane, Byron R. "Simply Irresistible: Augustus, Herod, and the Empire." *Journal of Biblical Literature* 127.4 (2008): 725–735.

McCarthy, Dennis J. *Old Testament Covenant: A Survey of Current Opinions*. Richmond, Virginia: John Knox Press, 1972.

Mendenhall, George E. *Law and Covenant in Israel and the Ancient Near East*. Pittsburgh, Pennsylvania: Biblical Colloquium, 1955.

Meyer, Marvin W., and Paul Allan Mirecki. *Ancient Magic and Ritual Power*. Boston, Massachusetts: Brill, 2001.

Mieg, Harald A., Astrid O. Sundsboe, and Majken Bieniok. *Georg Simmel und die aktuelle Stadtforschung* [Georg Simmel and Current Urban Studies]. Wiesbaden, Germany: VS Verlag, 2011.

Mirsky, Yehudah. *Rav Kook: Mystic in a Time of Revolution*. New Haven, Connecticut: Yale University Press, 2014.

Misselwitz, Philipp, and Tim Rieniets. *City of Collision: Jerusalem and the Principles of Conflict Urbanism.* Basel: Birkhäuser, 2006.

Molinaro, Enrico. *The Holy Places of Jerusalem in Middle East Peace Agreements: The Conflict between Global and State Identities.* Brighton, England: Sussex Academic Press, 2009.

Mommsen, Theodor. *The History of Rome.* Ed. Dickson, William P. A. New York: Scribner's, 1900.

Montefiore, Simon Sebag. *Jerusalem: The Biography.* London: Phoenix, 2011.

Moran, William L. *The Amarna Letters.* Baltimore, Maryland: Johns Hopkins University Press, 1992.

Morris, Benny. *1948: A History of the First Arab–Israeli War.* New Haven, Connecticut: Yale University Press, 2008.

Morris, Colin. *The Sepulchre of Christ and the Medieval West: From the Beginning to 1600.* Oxford: Oxford University Press, 2005.

Müller, Christian. "A Legal Instrument in the Service of People and Institutions: Endowments in Mamluk Jerusalem as Mirrored in the Haram Documents." *Mamluk Studies Review* 12.1 (2008): 173–191.

Mumford, Lewis. *The City in History: Its Origins, Its Transformations, and Its Prospects.* New York: Harcourt, 1961.

Munro, Dana C. "Urban and the Crusaders." *Translations and Reprints from the Original Sources of European History.* Vol. 1:2. Philadelphia: University of Pennsylvania, 1895, 5–8. Online at Fordham University, "Medieval Sourcebook: Urban II (1088–1099): Speech at Council of Clermont, 1095, Five versions of the Speech." http://sourcebooks.fordham.edu/Halsall/source/urban2-5vers.asp (accessed December 5, 2017).

Murdoch, Brian. *The Apocryphal Adam and Eve in Medieval Europe: Vernacular Translations and Adaptations of the* Vita Adae Et Evae. Oxford: Oxford University Press, 2009.

Murphy-O'Connor, J. *The Holy Land: An Oxford Archaeological Guide from Earliest Times to 1700.* Oxford Archaeological Guides. 5th ed. Oxford: Oxford University Press, 2008.

Musallam, Sami. *The Struggle for Jerusalem: A Programme of Action for Peace.* Jerusalem: PASSIA, 1996.

Na'aman, Nadav. "When and How Did Jerusalem Become a Great City? The Rise of Jerusalem as Judah's Premier City in the Eighth-Seventh Centuries B.C.E." *Bulletin of the American Schools of Oriental Research* 347 (2007): 21–56.

Nagy, Maria von. *Die Legenda Aurea und ihr Verfasser Jacobus De Voragine* [The Golden Legend and Its Author Jacobus de Voragine] Bern: Francke, 1971.

Neff, Donald. "Jerusalem in U.S. Policy." *Journal of Palestine Studies* 23.1 (1993): 20–45.

Netzer, Ehud, with Rachel Laureys-Chachy. *The Architecture of Herod, the Great Builder.* Grand Rapids, Michigan: Baker Academic, 2008.

Neusner, Jacob, and Bruce Chilton. *In Quest of the Historical Pharisees*. Waco, Texas: Baylor University Press, 2007.

Nicholson, Helen J. *The Knights Templar: A New History*. Stroud, England: Sutton, 2001.

Noth, Martin. *The Deuteronomistic History*. Sheffield, England: University of Sheffield, 1981a.

Noth, Martin. *A History of Pentateuchal Traditions*. Translated by Bernhard Ward Anderson. Chico, California: Scholars Press, 1981b [1948].

Obenzinger, Hilton. *American Palestine: Melville, Twain, and the Holy Land Mania*. Princeton, New Jersey: Princeton University Press, 1999.

Obenzinger, Hilton. "Herman Melville Returns to Jerusalem." *Jerusalem Quarterly* 43 (2010): 31–39.

Oswald, Wolfgang. *Staatstheorie im Alten Israel: Der Politische Diskurs im Pentateuch und in den Geschichtsbüchern des Alten Testaments* [Theories of State in Ancient Israel: Political Discourse in the Pentateuch and in the Historiographical Books of the Old Testament]. Stuttgart: Kohlhammer, 2009.

Otto, Rudolf. *The Idea of the Holy [Das Heilige: Über das Irrationale in der Idee des Göttlichen und sein Verhältnis zum Rationalen]*. Translated by John W. Harvey. London: Humphrey Milford, 1923 [1917].

Ousterhout, Robert. "The Temple, the Sepulchre, and the Martyrion of the Savior." *Gesta* 29.1 (1990): 44–53.

Palmer, Andrew, Sebastian P. Brock, and Robert G. Hoyland. *The Seventh Century in the West-Syrian Chronicles*. Translated Texts for Historians. Liverpool, England: Liverpool University Press, 1993.

Pappe, Ilan. Atzulat Ha'aretz: Mishpakhat al-Husseini, Biografia Politit [Aristocracy of the Land: The Husayni Family: Political Biography]. Jerusalem: Bialik Institute, 2002.

Parolin, Gianluca Paolo. *Citizenship in the Arab World: Kin, Religion and Nation-State*. Amsterdam: Amsterdam University Press, 2009.

Parsons, Jotham. *The Church in the Republic: Gallicanism and Political Ideology in Renaissance France*. 1st ed. Washington, DC: Catholic University of America Press, 2004.

Pedahzur, Ami, and Arie Perliger. *Jewish Terrorism in Israel*. New York: Columbia University Press, 2009.

Pentz, Peter. *The Invisible Conquest: The Ontogenesis of Sixth and Seventh Century Syria*. Copenhagen: National Museum of Denmark, Collection of Near Eastern and Classical Antiquities, 1992.

Perlitt, Lothar. *Bundestheologie im Alten Testament* [Covenant Theology in the Old Testament]. Neukirchen Vluyn, Germany: Neukirchener Verlag, 1969.

Peters, F. E. *Jerusalem: The Holy City in the Eyes of Chroniclers, Visitors, Pilgrims, and Prophets*. Princeton, New Jersey: Princeton University Press, 1985.

Prawer, Joshua, and Haggai Ben-Shammai. *The History of Jerusalem: The Early Muslim Period, 638–1099*. Jerusalem: Yad Izhak Ben-Zvi, 1996.

Pullan, Wendy, Maximilian Sternberg, Lefkos Kyriacou, Craig Larkin, and Michael Dumper. *The Struggle for Jerusalem's Holy Places*. Abingdon, England: Routledge, 2013.

Qafisheh, Mutaz M. *The International Law Foundations of Palestinian Nationality: A Legal Examination of Nationality in Palestine under Britain's Rule*. Leiden: M. Nijhoff, 2008.

Quinn, Esther Casier. *The Quest of Seth for the Oil of Life*. Chicago, Illinois: Chicago University of Chicago Press, 1962.

Qumsiyeh, Mazin B. *Popular Resistance in Palestine: A History of Hope and Empowerment*. London: Pluto Press, 2011.

Rabbat, Nasser. "The Dome of the Rock Revisited: Some Remarks on Al-Wasiti's Accounts." *Muqarnas* 10 (1993): 67–75.

Rabbat, Nasser. *Mamluk History through Architecture: Monuments, Culture and Politics in Medieval Egypt and Syria*. London: I.B. Tauris, 2010.

Rabinowitz, Dan, and Daniel Monterescu. "Reconfiguring The 'Mixed Town': Urban Transformations of Ethnonational Relations in Palestine and Israel." *International Journal of Middle East Studies* 40.2 (2008): 195–226.

Raheb, Mitri. *Faith in the Face of Empire: The Bible through Palestinian Eyes*. Maryknoll, New York: Orbis Books, 2014.

Reinink, G. J., and Bernard H. Stolte. *The Reign of Heraclius (610–641): Crisis and Confrontation*. Leuven, Belgium: Peeters, 2002.

Ricca, Simone. *Reinventing Jerusalem: Israel's Reconstruction of the Jewish Quarter after 1967*. London: I.B. Tauris, 2007.

Richardson, Peter. *Herod: King of the Jews and Friend of the Romans. Studies on Personalities of the New Testament*. Columbia: University of South Carolina Press, 1996.

Riley-Smith, Jonathan. *The Oxford Illustrated History of the Crusades*. Oxford: Oxford University Press, 1995.

Ryan, G., and H. Ripperger. *The Golden Legend of Jacobus De Voragine*. New York: Arno Press, 1969 [1941].

Safrai, Shemuel. '*Aliyah le-Regel bi-Yeme ha-Bayit ha-Sheni: Monografyah Historit* [Pilgrimage at the Time of the Second Temple]. Tel-Aviv: 'Pi ha-Sefer, 1965.

Sakr, Yasir. *The Subversive Utopia: Louis Kahn and the Question of the National Jewish Style in Jerusalem*. Hollister, Massachusetts: MSI Press, 2015.

Sardis, Melito of. *On Pascha: With the Fragments of Melito and Other Material Related to the Quartodecimans*. Crestwood, New York: St. Vladimir's Seminary Press, 2001.

Schalit, Abraham. *König Herodes: Der Mann und sein Werk* [King Herod: The Man and His Work]. Berlin: De Gruyter, 2001.

Schleiermacher, Friedrich. *On Religion: Speeches to Its Cultured Despisers*. Cambridge: Cambridge University Press, 1996 [1799].

Schmelz, Usiel O. *Modern Jerusalem's Demographic Evolution.* Eds. Institute of Contemporary Jewry, Hebrew University of Jerusalem: Jerusalem Institute for Israel Studies, 1987.

Schniedewind, William M. *How the Bible Became a Book: The Textualization of Ancient Israel.* Cambridge: Cambridge University Press, 2004.

Schäfer, Peter. *Hekhalot-Studien* [Hekhalot Studies]. Tübingen, Germany: Mohr Siebeck, 1988.

Schäfer, Peter. *Judeophobia: Attitudes toward Jews in the Ancient World.* Cambridge, Massachusetts: Harvard University Press, 1997.

Schölch, Alexander. *Palästina im Umbruch, 1856–1882: Untersuchungen zur Wirtschaftlichen und sozio-politischen Entwicklung* [Palestine in Transformation, 1865–1882: Studies in Economic and Social-Political Development]. Stuttgart: F. Steiner, 1986.

Schölch, Alexander. *Palestine in Transformation, 1856–1882: Studies in Social, Economic, and Political Development.* Washington, DC: Institute for Palestine Studies, 1993.

Schölch, Alexander. "An Ottoman Bismarck from Jerusalem: Yusuf Diya' al-Khalidi (1842–1906)." *Jerusalem Quarterly* 24 (2005), 65–76.

Sivan, Emanuel. "The Beginnings of the Fada'il Al-Quds Literature." *Israel Oriental Studies* 1 (1971): 263–271.

Sloterdijk, Peter. *God's Zeal: The Battle of the Three Monotheisms.* Cambridge, Massachusetts: Polity, 2009.

Spiegel, Shalom. *The Last Trial: On the Legends and Lore of the Command to Abraham to Offer Isaac as a Sacrifice: The Akedah.* New York: Pantheon Books, 1967.

Sprinzak, Ehud. *The Ascendance of Israel's Radical Right.* New York: Oxford University Press, 1991.

Sprinzak, Ehud. *Brother against Brother: Violence and Extremism in Israeli Politics from Altalena to the Rabin Assassination.* New York: Free Press, 1999.

Stanger, Cary David. "A Haunting Legacy: The Assassination of Count Bernadotte." *Middle East Journal* 42.2 (1988): 260–272.

Steinsapir, Ann. "Rural Sanctuaries in Roman Syria: The Dynamics of Architecture in the Sacred Landscape." PhD Dissertation, University of California, Los Angeles, 1998.

Tamari, Salim. *Jerusalem 1948: The Arab Neighbourhoods and Their Fate in the War.* Jerusalem: Institute of Jerusalem Studies; Bethlehem: Badil Resource Center for Palestinian Residency and Refugee Rights, 1999.

Tamari, Salim. *Mountain against the Sea: Essays on Palestinian Society and Culture.* Berkeley: University of California Press, 2008.

Tamari, Salim. *Year of the Locust: A Soldier's Diary and the Erasure of Palestine's Ottoman Past.* Berkeley: University of California Press, 2011.

Tannous, Izzat. *The Palestinians: A Detailed Documented Eyewitness History of Palestine under British Mandate*. New York: IGT Co., 1988.

Tarnopolsky, Noga. "Christians, Muslims, and Jews to Build Joint House of Worship in Jerusalem." *Jerusalem Post*, June 27, 2016. Online at http://www.jpost.com/ Israel-News/Christians-Muslims-and-Jews-to-build-joint-house-of-worship-in-Jerusalem-457837.

Thompson, John B. *Studies in the Theory of Ideology*. Berkeley: University of California Press, 1984.

Tohe, Achmad. "Muqātil Ibn Sulaymān: A Neglected Figure in the Early History of Qur'ānic Commentary." PhD Dissertation, Boston University, 2015.

Tottoli, Roberto. "Origin and Use of the Term Isrā'īliyyāt in Muslim Literature." *Arabica: Journal of Arabic and Islamic Studies* 46.2 (1999): 193–210.

Trémouille, Marie-Claude. *D'hebat: Une Divinité Syro-Anatolienne* [Hebat. A Syro-Anatolian Deity]. Bivigliano, Italy: LoGisma, 1997.

Tsafrir, Yoram, and Gideon Foerster. "The Dating of the 'Earthquake of the Sabbatical Year' of 749 C.E. in Palestine." *Bulletin of the School of Oriental and African Studies, University of London* 55.2 (1992): 231–235.

Turner, Victor W., and Edith L. B. Turner. *On the Edge of the Bush: Anthropology as Experience*. Tucson: University of Arizona Press, 1985.

Twakkal, Abd. "Ka'b Al-Ahbār and the Isrā'īliyyāt in the Tafsīr Literature." Masters Thesis, McGill University, 2008.

Tyerman, Christopher. *The Crusades: A Very Short Introduction*. Oxford: Oxford University Press, 2005.

Vajda, Georges. "Isrā'īliyyāt." In Bearman, P., et al. (eds.), *Encyclopaedia of Islam, Second Edition*. Online edition: First published 2012. Leiden: Brill, 2012, iv:221a.

Walker, P. W. L. *Holy City, Holy Places: Christian Attitudes to Jerusalem and the Holy Land in the Fourth Century*. Oxford Early Christian Studies. Oxford: Clarendon Press, 1990.

Wasserstein, Bernard. *Divided Jerusalem: The Struggle for the Holy City*. 3rd ed. New Haven, Connecticut: Yale University Press, 2008.

Weber, Florian. *Herodes – König von Roms Gnaden? Herodes als Modell eines Römischen Klientelkönigs in Spätrepublikanischer und Augusteischer Zeit* [Herod, King by the Grace of Rome? Herod as Model of a Roman Client King in the Late Republican and Augustan Age]. Berlin: Logos, 2003.

Weippert, Manfred, Ulrich Hübner, and Ernst Axel Knauf. *Kein Land für sich allein: Studien zum Kulturkontakt in Kanaan, Israel/Palästina und Ebirnari. Für Manfred Weippert zum 65. Geburtstag* [No Land by Itself: Studies in Cultural Contact in Canaan, Israel/Palestine, and Ebernari. For Manfred Weippert on the Occasion of His 65th Birthday]. Fribourg, Switzerland: Universitätsverlag, 2002.

Weisman, Steven R. "Reagan Affirms His Mideast Plan." *New York Times*, August 28, 1983. Online at http://www.nytimes.com/1983/08/28/world/reagan-reaffirms-his-mideast-plan.html (accessed December 5, 2017).

Weiss, Daniel H., and Lisa Mahoney. *France and the Holy Land: Frankish Culture at the End of the Crusades*. Baltimore, Maryland: Johns Hopkins University Press, 2004.

Weitzman, Steven. "Plotting Antiochus's Persecution." *Journal of Biblical Literature* 123.2 (2004): 219–234.

Wharton, Annabel Jane. *Selling Jerusalem: Relics, Replicas, Theme Parks*. Chicago, Illinois: University of Chicago Press, 2006.

Wilken, Robert Louis. *The Land Called Holy: Palestine in Christian History and Thought*. New Haven, Connecticut: Yale University Press, 1992.

Wilkinson, John. *Jerusalem Pilgrims: Before the Crusades*. Aris & Phillips, 2002.

Woods, David. "Arculf's Luggage: The Sources for Adomnán's *De Locis Sanctis*." *Ériu* 52 (2002): 25–52.

Zank, Michael. "Holy City: Jerusalem in Time, Space, and the Imagination." In *Transformations: The Journal of Inclusive Scholarship and Pedagogy*, 19.1 (2008): 40–67.

Zank, Michael. "Jaspers' Achsenzeit Hypothesis: A Critical Reappraisal." In Wautischer, Helmut, Alan Olson and Gregory J. Walters (eds.), *Philosophical Faith and the Future of Humanity*. Dordrecht, Netherlands: Springer Verlag, 2012, 189–202.

Zank, Michael. "Jerusalem in Religious Studies: The City and Scripture." In Elman, Miriam and Madeleine Adelman (eds.), *Jerusalem: Conflict and Cooperation in a Contested City*. Syracuse, New York: Syracuse University Press, 2014, 114–142.

Zank, Michael. "The Grinch Who Stole the Bible: Teaching Scripture through Distance, Proximity, & Engagement." *Religion & Literature* 47.1 (2015): 175–182.

Zank, Michael. "The Holy between the Imaginary and the Real. *Jerusalem 1000–1400* at the Metropolitan Museum of Art." *Mizan* (2016a), http://www.mizanproject.org/the-holy-between-the-imaginary-and-the-real/(accessed December 17, 2017).

Zank, Michael. "The Jerusalem Basic Law (1980) and the Jerusalem Embassy Act (1995): A Comparative Investigation of Israeli and US Legislation on the Status of Jerusalem." *Israel Studies* 21.3 (2016b): 20–35.

Zerubavel, Yael. *Recovered Roots: Collective Memory and the Making of Israeli National Tradition*. Chicago, Illinois: University of Chicago Press, 1995.

Index

Jerusalem: A Brief History, First Edition. Michael Zank.
© 2018 Michael Zank. Published 2018 by John Wiley & Sons Ltd.